Umberto Eco, *The Da Vinci Code*,
and the Intellectual in the Age of
Popular Culture

Douglass Merrell

Umberto Eco, *The Da Vinci Code*, and the Intellectual in the Age of Popular Culture

Douglass Merrell
Seattle, Washington, USA

ISBN 978-3-319-85482-3   ISBN 978-3-319-54789-3 (eBook)
DOI 10.1007/978-3-319-54789-3

© The Editor(s) (if applicable) and The Author(s) 2017
Softcover reprint of the hardcover 1st edition 2017
This work is subject to copyright. All rights are solely and exclusively licensed by the Publisher, whether the whole or part of the material is concerned, specifically the rights of translation, reprinting, reuse of illustrations, recitation, broadcasting, reproduction on microfilms or in any other physical way, and transmission or information storage and retrieval, electronic adaptation, computer software, or by similar or dissimilar methodology now known or hereafter developed.
The use of general descriptive names, registered names, trademarks, service marks, etc. in this publication does not imply, even in the absence of a specific statement, that such names are exempt from the relevant protective laws and regulations and therefore free for general use.
The publisher, the authors and the editors are safe to assume that the advice and information in this book are believed to be true and accurate at the date of publication. Neither the publisher nor the authors or the editors give a warranty, express or implied, with respect to the material contained herein or for any errors or omissions that may have been made. The publisher remains neutral with regard to jurisdictional claims in published maps and institutional affiliations.

Cover illustration: © Alan Wylie / Alamy Stock Photo

Printed on acid-free paper

This Palgrave Macmillan imprint is published by Springer Nature
The registered company is Springer International Publishing AG
The registered company address is: Gewerbestrasse 11, 6330 Cham, Switzerland

Contents

1	The Intermediate Thinker	1
2	The Intellectual Species	25
3	A Medievalist in Hibernation	51
4	The Exiled Heretic	79
5	The Art of Adventure: Eco, Joyce, and the Open Work	103
6	The Gruppo 63 and the Italian Neo-avant-garde	131
7	The Aesthetics of Superman and Charlie Brown	149
8	The Semiotic Species: A Grand Unified Theory of Culture	169
9	The Reader in the Story	201
10	The Literary Provocateur	235

Bibliography 281

Index 287

CHAPTER 1

The Intermediate Thinker

INDEXES OF POPULARITY

The internet is a great potential democratizer of knowledge. As a medium of communication, it offers a vast array of information readily accessible to a mass popular audience. Through the internet, one can instantly obtain a variety of facts such as the list compiled by Wikipedia of books that have become international bestsellers.[1] The bestseller list, while including a disclaimer concerning its accuracy and completeness, and obviously subject to constant revision, provides at least a general indicator of the ranking of the most popular readings over time based on available sales figures. In an age increasingly dominated by visual culture, the bestseller list provides an index of the taste of a broad popular audience for books, which are otherwise the privileged medium of intellectuals. In this way, the list can serve as a window into the relation between intellectuals and popular culture.

Although the international bestseller list cites the *Bible*, the *Qur'an*, and Chairman Mao's *The Little Red Book* with sales in the billions, they are not ranked among the bestsellers because of the lack of reliable sales data. With those exceptions accounted for, what the international bestseller list reveals in part is the enduring popular taste for fantasy fiction and children's literature. *The Little Prince* (1943) by Antoine de Saint-Exupery, is ranked fourth on the list with 140 million sold, *The Hobbit* (1937) by J.R.R. Tolkien is ranked sixth with over 100 million sold, and *Alice in Wonderland* (1865) is ranked ninth with 100 million sold. They are closely followed by numerous other works from the same genre with 50

© The Author(s) 2017
D. Merrell, *Umberto Eco, The Da Vinci Code, and the Intellectual in the Age of Popular Culture*, DOI 10.1007/978-3-319-54789-3_1

to 100 million sold such as *The Lion, the Witch, and the Wardrobe* (1950) by C.S. Lewis, *Heidi* (1880) by Johanna Spyri, *Anne of Green Gables* (1908) by Lucy Montgomery, *Black Beauty* (1877) by Anna Sewell, and *Charlotte's Web* (1952) by E.B. White. Of the 37 readings listed with 50 million or more sold, 15, or almost one half, are works of fantasy fiction or children's literature.

The prominence of fantasy fiction and children's literature may be attributed to a reverence for the imaginative innocence of youth that is perpetuated through sentimental attachment to readings shared between parent and child. Fantasy and children's literature also tops the list of more recent bestsellers including, as one would expect, the Harry Potter series by J.K. Rowling, with the first in the series, *Harry Potter and the Philosopher's Stone* (1997) selling over 107 million. The phenomenal popularity of these recent youthful fantasies can also be attributed to the fact that they are written with a simplified vocabulary and style that is highly accessible to young readers as well as a broad popular audience. Their popularity can thus be the result of their introductory appeal for the young, not yet taken over by contemporary visual media, for developing a taste and proficiency for reading.

The Harry Potter series, in particular, has been credited with fostering a new generation of readers who were drawn to its mix of fantasy and mystery. As a generational index of popularity, the Harry Potter series set new records for pre-order sales as well as overall sales volume for a series with over 500 million sold worldwide. However, according to a *New York Times* article, there is some doubt about the lasting impact of the Harry Potter phenomenon on the so-called millennial generation that has been characterized as "post-literate" by prominent writers such as the Nobel Prize winning novelist John Coetzee.[2] As the *New York Times* article points out, "federal statistics show that the percentage of youngsters who read for fun continues to drop significantly as children get older, at almost exactly the same rate as before Harry Potter came along."[3] In any case, the broad appeal of children's fantasies to a mass audience is otherwise reflected in the recent film adaptations of the *Lord of the Rings*, and the *Chronicles of Narnia*. The *Harry Potter* novels, in particular, have now been adapted as the highest grossing film series of all time by drawing on the desire of a young audience to see the characters they read about in private become visualized for the cinema and publicly shared with a new generation of readers as a cult-like experience.

Apart from the longstanding popularity of youthful fantasies, what does the list tell us about adult-themed bestsellers? Oddly enough, the preponderance of wholesome stories of youthful idealism is somewhat offset by a classic tale of youthful alienation, J.D. Salinger's *Catcher in the Rye* (1951) with more than 65 million sold; and an adult's sexual obsession for a provocative adolescent in Vladimir Nabokov's *Lolita* (1955) with more than 50 million sold. Interspersed in the bestseller ranks, with more than 50 million sold, are adult works of non-fiction including practical guides to material fulfillment in Napoleon Hill's *Think and Grow Rich* (1937), Benjamin Spock's longstanding guide to childrearing, the *Book of Baby and Child Care* (1946), and Shere Hite's analysis of human sexuality, *The Hite Report* (1976). A recent entry to the upper ranks of adult-themed bestsellers is the *Fifty Shades of Grey* (2011) series by E.L. James with 125 million sold. While the new generation of readers fostered by the Harry Potter series may be losing their taste for reading as they get older, the high ranking of the *Fifty Shades of Grey* series would suggest that they can be lured back by adult-themed sexual fantasies.

Besides the works of fiction and non-fiction indicated earlier, one would expect that the list would include the full pantheon of literary classics. The list does include classics such as Homer's *Odyssey* (8th c. B.C.) with 45 million sold, Leo Tolstoy's *War and Peace* (1869) with 36 million sold, and Jane Austen's *Pride and Prejudice* (1813), with 20 million sold. But, as the bestseller site acknowledges, cumulative sales figures from the date of publication are not available for most of the major literary classics. Cervantes' *Don Quixote* (1612) is listed at the top of the ranks with 500 million sold but the source of this ranking seems questionable, and Dante's *Divine Comedy* (1304) is credited with 12 million sold but only from sales originating from the twentieth century.

While most of the major literary classics are not included in the top ranks of the bestseller list, it should be noted that Agatha Christie's *And Then There Were None* (1939) which is the most widely read murder mystery of all time with more than 100 million sold, is ranked seventh on the list. In a separate Wikipedia list that ranks the bestselling cumulative works of major authors of fiction, Agatha Christie is tied at the top of the list with William Shakespeare. Her 66 mystery novels have generated sales estimated between two billion and four billion.[4] In the same genre, Sir Arthur Conan Doyle's *The Adventures of Sherlock Holmes* (1887) is highly ranked with more than 60 million sold. The high ranking of Agatha Christie's and Sir Arthur Conan Doyle's mysteries indicates that detective fiction is one of the most prominent categories on the bestseller list.

THE DA VINCI CODE CONTROVERSY

Since the ranking on the bestseller list is based on consumer demand, it reflects the varied taste of a broad public readership over the past century and a half based on the availability of reliable sales figures. For this reason, as noted before, literary classics such as Hawthorne's *The House of the Seven Gables* (1851), for example, are not included. But since reliable sales figures from independent sources are now readily obtainable, the list can currently serve more accurately as a profile of the contemporary popular taste for reading. Unsurprisingly, apart from the Harry Potter series by J. K. Rowling, the most popular recent bestseller (on its own and not as a series such as the *Fifty Shades of Grey* novels) is Dan Brown's *The Da Vinci Code* (2003) which is the second highest-ranking mystery novel to date. With over 80 million sold, more than three years on the bestseller list, and 59 weeks at number one, *The Da Vinci Code* is considered the bestselling English language novel of the twenty-first century, and the second biggest selling novel in any language.[5,6] The enormous readership of *The Da Vinci Code* spawned a movie version starring Tom Hanks that, despite generally negative critical reviews and especially harsh condemnation by the Catholic Church, was the second highest grossing movie in 2006.

The Da Vinci Code, as an index of popular culture, indicates the powerful appeal of the mystery novel, but also for historical fiction, along with art, religion, and the occult which is the secret, privileged knowledge of an elite group of initiates. In *The Da Vinci Code*, the exploration of occult history, which is ordinarily the domain of the intellectual elite, is made accessible to a popular audience through the mediation of a fictional detective hero, Robert Langdon, who is portrayed as a Harvard professor of symbology. The huge popularity of *The Da Vinci Code* drew readers to a previous novel by Dan Brown, *Angels and Demons* (2000) that featured the same protagonist and a similar synthesis of murder mystery with historical explorations of secret knowledge that sold over 39 million copies and was also adapted for the cinema. A third installment, *The Lost Symbol* (2009), that has sold more than 30 million, had an initial printing of 6.5 million copies, the largest in the history of the publisher, Doubleday. With first-day sales of over one million, it became the fastest selling adult novel in history.[7,8] A fourth installment, *Inferno* (2013) has also entered the bestseller ranks with the same narrative formula and has similarly been adapted for the cinema.

The phenomenal popularity of *The Da Vinci Code* and the other novels in the Robert Langdon series by Dan Brown can be attributed to the fact that they combine the detective or mystery novel, one of the most popular genres on the bestseller list in terms of total sales (as reflected in the Agatha Christie and Sherlock Holmes novels, as well as the Harry Potter series which combines fantasy and mystery), with an exploration of "high culture" and secret knowledge from the past. The combination of these two genres, called an "historical whodunit," can thus serve as a useful point of reference for considering the interface between intellectuals and popular culture. The huge following for the Dan Brown series suggests that a popular readership is drawn to intellectual explorations into art, religion, philosophy, history, etc., which are ordinarily pursued by the intellectual elite, when these ideas are made broadly accessible as literary entertainment.

An Unread Bestseller?

To explore this relationship further, we can consider a comparison between Dan Brown's *The Da Vinci Code* and Umberto Eco's *The Name of the Rose*. As a number of reviewers have pointed out, *The Da Vinci Code* bears a strong resemblance to *The Name of the Rose*. They are both historical whodunits that explore secret knowledge about religious mysteries from the past featuring a protagonist who is an expert at deciphering signs and symbols. They are also both highly ranked on the bestseller list with *The Name of the Rose* selling over 50 million copies. But *The Name of the Rose* (1980) preceded *The Da Vinci Code* by more than 20 years. The phenomenal popularity of Eco's first novel also aroused the puzzlement and skepticism of some reviewers who questioned whether it was actually read by a popular audience. Howard Kaminsky, then president of Warner Books, suggested that *The Name of the Rose* should be considered in a special category: "Every year there is one great unread best-seller. A lot of people who will buy the book will never read it."[9] According to Kaminsky, there is supposedly a broad popular readership that would be attracted to a particular book for status reasons. They would display the book on their coffee table but not actually read it, presumably because of its overly challenging intellectual content. The same skepticism was reflected in the introduction to a scholarly analysis of the novel entitled *Naming the Rose*, published in 1988. The author, Theresa Coletti, an Associate Professor of English at the University of Maryland, noted that the phenomenal success of *The Name of the Rose* "has also puzzled observers of the literary scene, who have wondered how many copies of the novel purchased have actually been read."[10]

Eco's *The Name of the Rose* could be considered an especially appropriate candidate for an "unread bestseller" due to its dense historical references to ancient and medieval philosophy, and obscure issues of Church doctrine from the late Middle Ages, as well as numerous passages of untranslated Latin, French, and German. According to the English author and literary critic David Lodge in the introduction to the 2006 edition of *The Name of the Rose*:

> It is an example of that rare publishing phenomenon, the literary megabestseller which transcends linguistic boundaries. By 'mega' I denote sales calculated in millions not thousands and by 'literary,' I mean a novel with the kind of artistic ambition and stylistic individuality that usually deters a mass audience: a category that includes, say, *Midnight's Children* [by Salman Rushdie] but not *The Da Vinci Code*.[11]

After *The Name of the Rose* became an international bestseller, even Eco was initially puzzled, as he put it, about "why the book was being read by people who surely could not like such 'cultivated' books."[12] But despite these imposing challenges, or, as Eco has since suggested, because of them, a popular audience did, in fact, read the novel and became so enthralled that the number of personal inquiries to the author prompted Eco to publish a separate book of responses to his readers in 1983 entitled *Reflections on the Name of the Rose*. His response to his readers' questions is now included as the "Postscript" to *The Name of the Rose* in the numerous subsequent editions, most recently in 2014, that indicate its enduring popularity since its original publication more than three decades ago. As Eco suggested in an interview: "It's only publishers and some journalists who believe that people want simple things. People are tired of simple things. They want to be challenged."[13] But his first novel's broad popularity did not diminish its value for intellectuals in academia. According to David H. Richter, Professor of English at Queens College: "On the other side of the cultural divide, *The Name of the Rose* became a textual icon, subjected to scrutiny at literary conferences and in special issues of critical journals. In the dozen years since its publication, the academic community produced nearly two hundred books and articles on *The Name of the Rose*..."[14]

Like *The Da Vinci Code*, the huge popularity of *The Name of the Rose* generated a film adaptation released in 1986 by the French director, Jean-Jacques Annaud, and starring Sean Connery, F. Murray Abraham, and Christian Slater. The huge audience for the book has also generated a number of published spinoffs. Besides the analytical perspectives by Theresa Coletti, *The Name of the Rose* inspired another scholarly analysis entitled *Eco's Chaosmos* in 2003 by Cristina Farronato, an assistant professor in the Department of Romance Languages and Literatures at Colgate University, as well as a collection of scholarly essays about the novel in 1988, also entitled *Naming the Rose*, edited by Thomas Inge with a forward by Eco.[15] And persistent questions about particular historical aspects of the novel, as well as persistent requests for translations of the numerous passages in Latin and other languages, prompted the creation of a companion guide, *The Key to "The Name of the Rose"* that was published independently of Eco in 1999.[16] The authors of *The Key to "The Name of the Rose"* indicate that they were initially motivated by finding themselves "constantly besieged by overwrought friends who – convinced that Eco had, with malice aforethought, concealed in Latin some of the juicier clues to the murders set in his Benedictine Abbey – requested 'free translations'..."[17] Eco's second novel, *Foucault's Pendulum* (1988), became an international bestseller as well by exploring similar themes with even more dense historical references to esoteric knowledge and occult practices. It should be noted, however, that neither Eco nor his publisher anticipated the phenomenal popularity of Eco's first novel. According to an article in the *Guardian*, "Eco thought the initial print-run of 30,000 excessive, but the book sold 2m copies in Italy."[18] Apart from some instances when books specifically target a broad popular audience, such as the *Fifty Shades of Grey* series, it can thus be a mystery in itself why a particular work of fiction happens to connect so broadly with a popular audience at a particular time. However, as mentioned previously, the thematic and narrative formula of the historical whodunit has a particular appeal for a mass audience which will be explored in Chapter 10.

THE "THINKING PERSON'S" BESTSELLER?

Besides their phenomenal popularity as historical whodunits, other comparisons have been drawn between Dan Brown's *The Da Vinci Code* and Umberto Eco's *The Name of the Rose*. While the voluminous inquiries into the historical mysteries of *The Name of the Rose* produced a postscript by Eco as well as an independent guide, *The Da Vinci Code* generated a special illustrated version as well as nearly two-dozen companion books by other writers exploring its religious controversies linked to the decoding of Da Vinci's painting of *The Last Supper*. But, besides noting similarities between the two novels, as indicated previously, some reviewers characterized Eco's first ventures as a novelist as "the thinking person's *Da Vinci Code*"[19] presumably based on Eco's background as an internationally renowned scholar noted for his encyclopedic knowledge. Some reviewers also criticized *The Da Vinci Code* for being historically unreliable due to faulty interpretations based on dubious sources. For example, the *New York Times* writer Laura Miller disparaged *The Da Vinci Code* as being "based on a notorious hoax" that, according to Miller, was drawn from fabricated documents that "were planted in the Bibliotheque Nationale in Paris by a man named Pierre Plantard" who was known as "an inveterate rascal with a criminal record for fraud and affiliations with wartime anti-Semitic and right-wing groups."[20] Dan Brown's citing of this questionable source constitutes another curious link between the two authors because of Eco's exploration in some of his novels of the impact of historical fabrications, for example, *The Protocols of the Elders of Zion*, an infamous anti-Semitic text appropriated by Hitler that Eco explores in his sixth novel *The Prague Cemetery* (2011).

Eco even suggested a personal link to *The Da Vinci Code* author by asserting that: "Dan Brown is one of the characters in my novel *Foucault's Pendulum* which is about people who start believing in occult stuff.... In *Foucault's Pendulum*, I wrote the grotesque representation of these kind of people. So Dan Brown is one of my creatures."[21] In an interview for *Time Magazine* in 2005, Eco also offered his own critical assessment of *The Da Vinci Code*: "The whole conspiracy of that plot... is contained in *Foucault's Pendulum* [Eco's second novel published in 1988]. It's all old material that's been covered a thousand times before. Brown was very good at taking trash lying around and turning it into a page turner. But it makes me laugh that people take it seriously."[22] In fact, a brief excerpt from *Foucault's Pendulum*, written 15 years before *The Da Vinci Code*, contains the core premise of Dan Brown's novel. Without including the connection to *The Last Supper* of Leonardo Da Vinci, one of Eco's characters in *Foucault's Pendulum*, while trying to make up the most outlandish historical fictions as a lure for lunatic conspiracy theorists, comes up with the following scenario:

> In the Gospels why aren't we told who was married at Cana? It was the wedding of Jesus, and it was a wedding that could not be discussed because the bride was a public sinner, Mary Magdalene. That's why, ever since, all

the Illuminati from Simon Magus to Postel seek the principle of the eternal feminine in a brothel. And Jesus, meanwhile, was the founder of the royal line of France.[23]

The epigraph to chapter 66 of *Foucault's Pendulum*, that follows the previous quote, also includes this reference:

If our hypothesis is correct, the Holy Grail... was the breed and descendent of Jesus, the "Sang real" of which the Templars were the guardians... At the same time, the Holy Grail must have been, literally, the vessel that had received and contained the blood of Jesus. In other words it must have been the womb of the Magdalene.
M. Baigent, R. Leigh, H. Lincoln, *The Holy Blood and the Holy Grail*, 1982, London, Cape, xiv[24]

BECOMING A POPULAR NOVELIST

Because of the strong associations drawn between these two authors, a comparison between their motives for becoming a novelist and their particular strategy for appealing to a popular audience is useful to consider. Dan Brown, the leading contemporary author in generating a popular adult readership, arose, as did Eco, from an elite academic background. But their paths and objectives in becoming a novelist are much different. Dan Brown, unlike Eco, was actually born into academia. His father was the mathematics teacher at Phillips Exeter Academy, a prestigious private school in Exeter, New Hampshire, that is one of the oldest secondary schools in the USA. As an elite educational institution, Phillips Exeter is distinguished for its tutorial form of close interaction between student and teacher based on the Socratic form of teaching through dialogue. From Phillips Exeter, Dan Brown went on to complete a bachelor's degree in English in 1986 from Amherst College, one of the highest ranked liberal arts colleges in the USA. At Amherst, his activities as a member of a fraternity, Psi Upsilon, and as a singer in the Glee Club suggest that he was a typical preppy. Thus, concerning his educational roots, Dan Brown was born into and bred by the elite intellectual culture of American academia.

Dan Brown completed his college degree in 1986. But, instead of pursuing graduate studies, he turned his attention toward composing and self-publishing music CDs intended for both children and adults which unfortunately generated disappointing sales of only a few hundred. Undeterred, however, Dan Brown went to Hollywood in 1991 with the intention of becoming a popular singer/songwriter. The aspiration for a musical career can be traced to his family upbringing. Both his father and mother were singers and musicians who served as choirmasters at the local Episcopal Church where his mother was also the Church organist. But Dan Brown's experience in pursuing a musical career in L.A. also turned out to be a disappointment. After the release of five CDs that, once again, generated minimal sales, he abandoned the pursuit of a musical career and returned to New Hampshire to teach English at his alma mater, Phillips Exeter. He was accompanied by Blythe Newlon, his future wife, whom he met during his stay in Hollywood where she worked at the National Academy of Songwriters in charge of mentoring aspiring singers/composers. In 1996, Dan Brown decided to devote himself fulltime to the writing of novels for a popular audience. He and Blythe Newlon married in 1997, and she collaborated with him in researching and promoting his writings. His wife's skills as an art historian and painter, for example, were later applied to the research and development of *The Da Vinci Code*, and her skills from the National Academy of Songwriters in supporting young artists would have been useful in promoting his writings among publishers.

Dan Brown engaged in research for his novels on secret codes and conspiracy plots based on his interest since childhood in intellectual games and puzzles. He was also fascinated by the intersection between science and religion,[25] a theme that is also featured in Eco's *The Name of the Rose* from a medieval perspective. Although he did not pursue a career as an academic theorist like Eco, Dan Brown was raised in an intellectual environment, and he was motivated to write as a way of exploring intellectual questions. His way of pursuing this goal was to become a successful author by appealing to the taste of a broad popular audience. He has acknowledged that he was inspired by the "simplicity of the prose and efficiency of the storyline" of a popular bestseller, Sidney Sheldon's *The Doomsday Conspiracy*, 1991.[26] Sheldon is ranked by the Wikipedia list as the seventh most popular writer of fiction with sales estimated at 300 to 600 million copies of his 21 books.[27] Concerning the relation between elite and popular culture, it's interesting to note that Sheldon was originally a playwright on Broadway, and then the creator of several highly popular television series such as "I Dream of Jeanie." Much later in his career he began to write novels that have been categorized as mystery thrillers. The effectiveness of his writing style and narrative focus attracted the attention of Dan Brown as a kind of template for appealing to a mass popular audience. According to one account, while Dan Brown was inspired by Sheldon, he also believed that he was capable of writing stronger and more substantive plots.[28] Consequently Dan Brown's motive in becoming a writer was to explore intellectual puzzles through a narrative formula that would appeal to the broadest possible popular audience by using the model of an already established bestselling novelist.

With their huge popular following, Dan Brown's novels are especially useful for considering the relation between intellectuals and popular culture because they engage the curiosity of a broad popular readership into occult religious and historical mysteries. Aside from being motivated by his early fascination with intellectual puzzles, Dan Brown's novels are vehicles for exploring particular historical and cultural themes. He has indicated, for example, that *The Da Vinci Code* was based on his interest in the "sacred feminine."[29] He also noted that: "I never imagined so many people would be enjoying it this much. I wrote this book essentially as a group of fictional characters exploring ideas that I found personally intriguing." He indicated in a BBC interview that *The Da Vinci Code* was also inspired by a college program in art history that he took in Spain at the University of Seville that aroused his interest in "the mysteries of Da Vinci's paintings."[30]

As historical whodunits, Brown's novels consequently involve research into the historical circumstances of the mysteries he explores, although his use and interpretation of these sources, as indicated previously, have been called into question. It would be unfair, however, to say that Dan Brown's novels are popular solely because their narrative formula is pitched to a popular audience. They are novels of ideas that arouse the interest of a popular audience because they evidently appeal to a curiosity about historical and intellectual mysteries, a theme that is similar to what Eco explores in his novels although from an entirely different intellectual background.

THE CRITICAL BACKLASH

Because Dan Brown set out to become a popular novelist through a narrative structure and writing style that was proven to appeal to a mass audience, his accomplishment as a writer who has engaged a huge popular audience in intellectual explorations of art, religion, gender, political conspiracies, etc. has been questioned. In response to the enormous popularity of Dan Brown's novels, it is curious, in particular, that some fellow authors of popular fiction have responded in such a harshly critical manner. Eco has also become a popular novelist by pursuing similar intellectual questions while being much more favorably regarded by the critical elite. This, as indicated previously, is presumably because of his stature as a prominent international scholar that is reflected in the writing style and content of his novels. The strongly negative critical response to Dan Brown's novels by comparison is useful to consider as another index of the relation between the elite arbiters of cultural value and the reading taste of a mass audience. For example, Salman Rushdie, an internationally acclaimed author of the previously mentioned *Midnight's Children*, who was knighted for his contributions to English literature, described *The Da Vinci Code* as "A novel so bad that it gives bad novels a bad name."[31] It should be noted, however, that Rushdie also wrote a scathing review in The *London Observer* of Eco's 1988 novel, *Foucault's Pendulum*, as "humorless, devoid of character, entirely free of anything resembling a credible spoken word, and mind-numbingly full of gobbledygook of all sorts." In response, Eco, as a featured participant on a literary panel in New York in 2008, that included Rushdie, made a point of reading from *Foucault's Pendulum*.[32]

A number of other authors and reviewers have offered similarly negative assessments of *The Da Vinci Code*. British reviewer Mark Lawson described it as "irritatingly gripping tosh."[33] Stephen Fry, a highly regarded English novelist and actor, attacked Dan Brown's writings in a particularly vicious manner as "complete loose stool-water" and "arse gravy of the worst kind." Fry also disparaged the popular readership of *The Da Vinci Code* by suggesting that it "plays to the worst and laziest in humanity."[34] Even Stephen King, one of the most prolific contemporary writers of pulp fiction, the author of more than 50 novels with sales topping 350 million and ranked nineteenth on the list of bestselling fiction authors, dismissed *The Da Vinci Code* as "Jokes for the John" and "the intellectual equivalent of Kraft Macaroni and Cheese."[35] Besides denouncing the content of the book, some critics wrote scathing reviews of Brown's writing style. A *New York Times* review characterized it as "Dan Brown's best-selling primer on how not to write an English sentence."[36] Academic scholars such as the linguist Geoffrey Pullum decried Dan Brown as one of the "worst prose stylists in the history of literature."

Pullum characterized Dan Brown's writing as "not just bad; it is staggeringly, clumsily, thoughtlessly, almost ingeniously bad."[37] The critical attack on *The Da Vinci Code* extended as well to the movie version. *Rotten Tomatoes*, the online rating site, gave the film version a "rotten" approval rating of just 25 percent. The rotten rating was, however, completely ignored by filmgoers who made it the second highest grossing film worldwide in 2006.[38]

The disproportionally negative and oddly petulant character of these responses by fellow writers of fiction, as well as academic scholars, is in sharp contrast to the highly favorable response by the *New York Times* reviewer Janet Maslin who used the word "wow" as the response that "concisely conveys the kind of extreme enthusiasm with which this riddle-filled, code-breaking, exhilaratingly brainy thriller can be recommended.... The author is Dan Brown (a name you will want to remember). In this gleefully erudite suspense novel, Mr. Brown takes the format he has been developing through three earlier novels and fine-tunes it to blockbuster perfection."[39] She also praised Dan Brown for turning "profound wisdom into a pretext for escapist fun."[40] Thus while he was being viciously criticized as a hack writer of novels with superficial intellectual content based on dubious sources, he was being strongly praised specifically for making intellectual topics accessible and enjoyable as engaging entertainment for a mass popular audience. It should be noted as well that, despite the negative dismissals of his contributions as a writer and intellectual, he was acknowledged in 2005 by Michelle Orecklin as one of Time Magazine's 100 Most Influential People in the World by crediting him with "renewed interest in Leonardo da Vinci, Gnostic texts and early Christian history."[41]

The caustic backlash by fellow writers of fiction to Dan Brown's debut as an immensely popular novelist who dabbles in occult history raises questions about the critical criteria for evaluating popular culture entertainment products that take up themes that would otherwise be the province of the intellectual elite. Is it an offense against the intellectual class to write about these themes in a simplified writing style and plot structure that makes them accessible to a popular audience? Or is the popularity of a cultural product with intellectual themes in itself a mark of its inauthentic character for intellectuals? The cultural reference most often used in this context is from the gospel of Matthew, Chapter 7, verse 6: "Give not that which is holy unto the dogs, neither cast ye pearls before swine, lest they trample them under their feet, and turn again and rend you." Should intellectual content be reserved for an elite audience because they are the only ones qualified to appreciate it? These questions can be pursued further through a comparison between the work of Dan Brown and Umberto Eco.

In relation to Dan Brown, Eco's emergence as a novelist occurred much later in his career and through a much different approach to a popular audience. His origins as an Italian who grew up under the Fascist regime of Benito Mussolini, and his rise as a scholar of the Middle Ages will be considered in Chapter 3. But, in comparison to Dan Brown, we can initially consider that, although Eco became a novelist much later in his career at age 46, he had already been writing for a mass popular audience since his early years as an academic. Eco's debut as a bestselling novelist occurred long after he had established himself as an academic theorist who also wrote about everyday life in newspapers and magazines for an Italian public audience. Eco's first novel was published 26 years after his foundational work in medieval philosophy entitled *The Aesthetics of Thomas Aquinas* (1954) at the University of Turin. And it came 18 years after his highly acclaimed turn to contemporary theory in *The Open Work* (1962) that eventually led to his status as a leading theorist in the field of semiotics (which will be considered in Chapter 8). Many years before his first novel became an international publishing phenomenon, Eco was recognized as one of Italy's most famous intellectuals by engaging in academic theory while also exploring ideas for a public audience through numerous essays on contemporary culture for Italian newspapers and magazines. Eco's writings as an intellectual are thus distinguished by a longstanding practice of bridging between "academic" and "popular" culture as an "intermediate thinker" or "public intellectual."

TRAVELS IN HYPERREALITY

As previously indicated, we will consider more fully Eco's origins as a medieval scholar and academic theorist in Chapter 3, but first we can sample the flavor of Eco's singular mode of applying academic theory to an analysis of popular culture, and his communication of these ideas in an accessible manner to a public audience, by looking back at his account of his travels to the USA in 1975. At that point in his academic career, Eco was just establishing himself as a pioneering theorist through his inauguration at the University of Bologna in 1971 of the first university program in semiotics. But he had already become a celebrated "public intellectual" in Italy through his writings on contemporary culture for Italian newspapers and magazines.[42]

On his journey to the USA in 1975, that he later characterized as travels in "hyperreality," one of the many tourist sites he visited was San Francisco's Fisherman's Wharf. As an historical site, Fisherman's Wharf commemorates the maritime history of California that arose out of the Gold Rush of 1848. It features a display of vintage ships as well as a focus on sea-life with an aquarium. Beginning in the seventies, Fisherman's Wharf gradually morphed into a popular tourist attraction, like many historical sites in the USA, with a proliferation of non-site-specific attractions such as *Ripley's Believe It or Not*, arcade amusements, and major shopping outlets catering to tourists with souvenir t-shirts and trinkets. A curious footnote to the impact of popular tourism on Fisherman's Wharf is that it became known as the site of the "World Famous Bushman." The "Bushman" was an otherwise unemployed local who would hide behind a bush and startle unsuspecting tourists. The spectacle of frightened passersby was apparently so amusing to fellow tourists that they gave money to the Bushman as a kind of demented street performer. Popular tourist sites can thus become a magnet for a variety of street performers because they generate an aura of expectation for diversions of various kinds from everyday life.

As a traveler to the USA from Italy, Eco might have been attracted to Fisherman's Wharf through his identification with the Italian immigrant fishermen who were its founders during the California Gold Rush. Their legacy is still reflected in places like Ghirardelli Square, famous for its chocolate, and third generation Italian eateries such as Alioto's, the inventors of the fish stew "*cioppino.*" But what Eco found especially noteworthy here and at similar sites in the USA in the early seventies were spectacles of popular culture found at museums, theme parks, and other tourist destinations where historical preservation, high art, and tourist consumption intersected.

Focusing on the consumer aspect of Fisherman's Wharf, Eco described it as an "Eldorado of restaurants, shops selling tourist trinkets...[and] Italian stands where you can have a crab cooked to order." What intrigued him in particular, however, was that "At Fisherman's Wharf you find, one after another, four waxwork museums" in a country that is "spangled with wax museums advertised in every hotel" and promoted as "attractions of considerable importance."[43] By comparison, according to Eco, "The contents of a European wax museum are well-known: 'live' speaking images, from Julius Caesar to Pope John XXIII, in various settings" where "the environment is squalid, always subdued, diffident." As Eco indicated, wax museums in Europe are not highly regarded as tourist attractions and certainly not promoted as prominent cultural destinations. In contrast, Eco found that "Their American counterparts are loud and aggressive, they assail you with big billboards on the freeway miles in advance. They announce themselves from the distance with glowing signs, shafts of light in the dark sky." According to Eco, upon arrival at these sites, the traveler experiences the aura of "hyperreality":

> The moment you enter you are alerted that you are about to have one of the most thrilling experiences of your life; they comment on the various scenes with long captions in sensational tones; they combine historical reconstruction with religious celebration, glorification of movie celebrities, and themes of famous fairytales and adventure stories; they dwell on the horrible, the bloody; their concern with authenticity reaches the point of reconstructive neurosis.

Eco's travels to this and similar tourist destinations in the USA were the inspiration for an essay that was initially published in the weekly Italian magazine l'Espresso under the title "Nell Cuore Dell'Impero: Viaggio Nell Iperrealita" (In the Heart of the Empire: Travels in Hyperreality) and subsequently included in a collection of essays entitled "Dalla Periferia Dell'Impero" (From the Periphery of the Empire) in 1977. In 1986, following the international success of his first novel, *The Name of the Rose*, these essays were first published in English as *Faith in Fakes* and later as *Travels in Hyperreality*.

What Eco characterized as "hyperreal" were tourist sites "where the American imagination demands the real thing and, to attain it, must fabricate the absolute fake."[44] But why would Eco, at that point already a high-profile intellectual in Italy, find these popular tourist attractions in the USA especially worthy of his attention and suitable for commentary from an academic perspective? Why not simply dismiss the wax museum representations of Da Vinci's *The Last Supper*, for example, as cheap imitations of an internationally famous work of art for the "unsophisticated" masses? Why would Eco give even passing attention to these sites other than to entirely dismiss them for degrading the experience of an iconic work of Italy's artistic heritage?

Eco does, in fact, distinguish these sites from American "Pop art" that he suggests would legitimately draw the attention of the European and American intellectual. But he directs his journey in the USA, as he puts it, to "another, more secret America (or rather, just as public, but snubbed by the European visitor and also by the American intellectual) [that] creates somehow a network of references and influences that finally spread also to the products of high culture and the entertainment industry..."[45] Eco was interested in sites that attempted to mix popular and elite culture where they were commercially promoted to appeal to a mass popular audience. To locate these sites, according to Eco, "You have only to go beyond the Museum of Modern Art and the art galleries [where] you enter another universe, the preserve of the average family, the tourist, the politician."[46] In contemporary society, according to Eco, "high" and "low" culture are intermingled in both the art museum, for example, in Andy Warhol's pop art paintings of Campbell soup cans, and the tourist site, through wax replicas of Da Vinci's *The Last Supper*. Eco, as an elite intellectual, who would ordinarily be drawn to the museum and art gallery, took it upon himself to become a tourist in the domain of the "popular" in order to explore the intersection of elite and popular culture as a kind of anthropologist among the "natives."

The title of the Italian language collection of these essays, "The Periphery of the Empire" is a reference to an attitude by prominent Italian intellectuals, such as Eco, who were associated with the Italian Neo-avant-garde of the sixties. They joined together in resistance to what they perceived as the "imperialist" proliferation of American popular culture in Italy after WWII. Italians are justifiably proud of their historical heritage as the center of the vast Roman Empire that ruled over the ancient world for more than a thousand years. But, for Eco's generation of intellectuals, the USA became the center of world domination after WWII, with Italy at the periphery. Although Italians rejoiced at their liberation from Germany by American military forces, one of the consequences of the liberation was the exportation of American consumer culture throughout Europe but especially in Italy. The impact of this cultural "invasion" led prominent Italian intellectuals such as Eco to describe themselves ironically as occupying a cultural periphery in relation to the USA. In this way, they expressed a disdainful attitude toward what they perceived as the American commercialization of culture while also acknowledging the need to analyze the products of popular culture because of their impact on society. Consequently, as an Italian intellectual,

Eco was especially interested in the ways in which cultural attractions in the USA were organized and marketed for mass consumption, and, in particular, through references to the world of art or elite culture. As we will consider in Chapter 6, Italian intellectuals of Eco's post–WWII generation were attempting to analyze the impact of popular culture and what they perceived to be its potential corruption and degradation of the arts.

The intersection of history, high art, and popular culture that Eco found particularly characteristic of tourist sites of American popular culture can perhaps be best appreciated in his commentary on the numerous wax museum reproductions of *The Last Supper*, the painting at the center of Dan Brown's *The Da Vinci Code*. Eco noted that, through wax replicas of such famous paintings, "this industry of absolute iconism has to deal with the problem of art."

> As a rule the Last Supper is displayed in the final room, with symphonic background music and a *son et lumiere* atmosphere. Not infrequently you are admitted to a room where the waxwork Supper is behind a curtain that slowly parts, as the taped voice, in deep and emotional tones, simultaneously informs you that you are having the most extraordinary spiritual experience of your life, and that you must tell your friends and acquaintances about it. Then comes some information about the redeeming mission of Christ and the exceptional character of the great event portrayed, summarized in evangelical phrases. Finally, information about Leonardo, all permeated with the intense emotion inspired by the mystery of art.[47]

Eco suggests ironically that, at these encounters with waxwork copies of *The Last Supper*, "you have been touched by the thrill of artistic greatness, you have had the most stirring spiritual emotion of your life and seen the most artistic work of art in the world." According to Eco, the taped voice informs you that the experience of the wax replica is much more powerful than the "original fresco" located in the Convent of Santa Maria delle Grazie in Milan, Italy, which, you are told, "is by now ruined, almost invisible, unable to give you the emotion you received from the three-dimensional wax, which is more real, and there is more of it."[48] The waxwork replica, Eco asserts, is promoted as being more effective and powerful in evoking the artistic and religious experience of the artwork. It is more "real" than the original, and thus "hyperreal."

THE PUBLIC INTELLECTUAL

Eco's account of his travels in the USA focused on sites of popular tourism that appropriated the symbols of "high" culture, and these accounts were in turn written in an accessible manner for a "popular" Italian audience by a celebrated representative of the elite world of academia. This practice of mediating between cultural domains in terms of both the topics discussed, the target audience, and the mode of expression is what makes Umberto Eco one of the exemplary "public intellectuals" of our time, and, according to some sources, "the most famous intellectual in the world."[49] In the introduction to *Travels in Hyperreality*, Eco acknowledges this parallel practice of mediating between elite and popular culture:

> I don't believe there is any gap between what I write in my 'academic' books and what I write in the papers. I cannot say precisely whether, for the papers, I try to translate into language accessible to all and apply to the events under consideration the ideas I later develop in my academic books, or whether it is the opposite that happens. Probably many of the theories expounded in my academic books grew gradually, on the basis of the observations I wrote down as I followed current events.[50]

Eco's later turn as a novelist beginning with *The Name of the Rose* in 1980, which we will explore more fully in Chapter 10, can be seen as a similar extension of his unique practice as a public intellectual.

Three decades before Dan Brown's *The Da Vinci Code* became an international publishing phenomenon by intriguing a vast public audience with scandalous speculations about the secret foundations of Christianity concealed in Da Vinci's Renaissance masterpiece, Eco was inquiring into the popular fascination with the religious aura of Da Vinci's *The Last Supper* as a wax museum replica for popular tourist consumption. Eco focused on wax museum replicas of Da Vinci's *The Last Supper* as an instance of highbrow art made accessible to a lowbrow audience while Dan Brown appropriated *The Last Supper* as a way of exploring the occult knowledge of an elite secret society linked to the artist Da Vinci and a purported female descendent of Christ, as intellectual stimulation for a popular audience. Both Eco and Dan Brown were dealing with the intersection of elite and popular culture but with different approaches and motives. Dan Brown was attempting to arouse the interest of a mass popular audience in exploring the mysteries of art and occult knowledge through the medium of an established, commercially successful genre, the historical whodunit, while Eco was attempting to analyze the corruption of elite aesthetics by popular culture consumerism through the medium of an essay written for a mass circulation Italian magazine.

As a result, Eco's work spans the divide between elite and popular culture in an especially useful way. In *Naming the Rose*, the scholar Theresa Coletti notes that Eco "is no stranger to mass culture. His works have repeatedly bridged the gap between high-brow and low-brow–witness his interest in Woody Allen, 'Peanuts,' James Bond, Sherlock Holmes, comic books, and, more recently, his use of Superman, Bo Derek, and Disneyland as illustrations of contemporary cultural semiotics."[51] Eco's practice as an intellectual not only reaches out to a public audience through his essays in popular newspapers and magazines and bestselling novels, he has also written three books for children in collaboration with the illustrator Eugenio Carmi. His first children's book, *The Bomb and the General* (1988), recounts the conflict between a general and atomic particles who refuse to be made into a bomb. *The Three Astronauts* (1989) explores cultural differences through the encounter between an American, Chinese, and Russian astronaut and an astronaut from Mars. *The Gnomes of Gnu* (1992) focuses on environmental preservation. Like his writings for adult readers, Eco's books for children are extensions of his theoretical practice as a semiotician by engaging young readers in considering the relation between things and the symbols or signs we use to make them meaningful.

Travels in Ecotopia

As the original Italian title of Eco's collection of essays, *Dalla Periferia Dell'Impero*, (From the Periphery of the Empire), indicates, his particular perspective on the relationship between elite and popular culture comes from his experience as an Italian intellectual whose native culture was "invaded" by the products of the American Empire of popular culture, beginning in 1929, and expanding greatly after WWII. But there is a longer historical background that should be considered in order to adequately understand these issues in contemporary society. For that purpose, our Travels in Ecotopia will explore Eco's origins as an intellectual, and then consider the impact of "popular" culture in Italy and the relation between intellectuals and a popular audience today. In pursuing this exploration of the relation between the intellectual and popular culture, another brief quote from Eco's introduction to *Travels in Hyperreality* can serve as a guide:

> I believe that it is my job as a scholar and a citizen to show how we are surrounded by 'messages,' products of political power, of economic power, of the entertainment industry and the revolution industry, and to say that we must know how to analyze and criticize them.[52]

Previous explorations of Eco's work have focused on his foundations as a medieval scholar in relation to his first novel, *The Name of the Rose*. His contributions to aesthetic theory through his concept of "the open work" have been explored through an earlier study, and his pioneering role as a leading theorist in the field of semiotics has been the subject of numerous publications. His place among postmodern theorists through his writings on the methods and limits of literary interpretation has been taken up in earlier studies as well. While touching on these aspects of his work, my intention is to explore Eco's unique practice as an intellectual who attempts to write for both an academic and a popular audience by analyzing the products of culture that span the cultural spectrum. The purpose of this study of Eco's work is to consider the potential, as Eco suggests, for analyzing and criticizing the "messages" that surround us all as inhabitants of cultural processes intersecting elite and popular culture. In relation to the project of raising a critical awareness, the focus on Eco's practice as an intellectual will also consider the problem and potential for communicating these ideas to a broad popular audience. If the tools of critical analysis are typically the product of elite educational institutions, what is the potential for a popular audience in contemporary democratic societies dominated by the mass media, to develop an awareness of the forces that determine us culturally and constrain or divert us from realizing our potential as humans?

But before we explore Eco's background as an Italian scholar of the Middle Ages who adapted these foundations to the analysis of art and beauty in the age of popular culture, it will be useful to first consider a broader background. In order to fully engage in an inquiry into the relation between the intellectual elite and popular culture, we can begin by considering what we mean by an intellectual and the specific social role of the intellectual in relation to our distinguishing character as a species. What sets humans apart from other species, and how did the specialized role of the intellectual develop historically? This focus will help us to explore our contemporary situation, as Eco puts it, of being surrounded by powerful "messages" and how we can "analyze and criticize them" to pursue our potential for a higher consciousness of our potential as members of human society.

Notes

1. https://en.wikipedia.org/wiki/List_of_best-selling_books.
2. From "Like a Dog" a review of Coetzee's *Disgrace* in the London Review of Books, Vol. 21, No. 20, October 1999.
3. Motoko Rich, "Potter Has Limited Impact on Reading Habits," The *New York Times*, July 11, 2007.
4. http://en.wikipedia.org/wiki/List_of_best-selling_fiction_authors.
5. https://en.wikipedia.org/wiki/Lists_of_The_New_York_Times_Fiction_Best_Sellers.
6. http://en.wikipedia.org/wiki/List_of_best-selling_books.
7. https://en.wikipedia.org/wiki/List_of_best-selling_books.
8. Motoko Rich, "Dan Brown's 'Lost Symbol' Sells 1 Million Copies in the First Day," The *New York Times*, September16, 2009.
9. As quoted from *Contemporary Authors, New Revision Series, Volume 12* p. 152.
10. Theresa Coletti, *Naming the Rose: Eco, Medieval Signs, and Modern Theory*, (Ithaca: Cornell University Press, 1988), p. 1.
11. From the introduction to the 2006 edition by David Lodge of *The Name of the Rose*, (New York: Everyman's Library, 2006), p. vii.
12. Eco, from the *Postscript to the Name of the Rose* which is now included in subsequent editions of the novel, (Orlando, Harcourt Brace & Company, 1983), p. 519.
13. http://www.theguardian.com/books/2011/nov/27/umberto-eco-people-tired-simple-things.
14. David H. Richter, "The Mirrored World: Form and Ideology in Umberto Eco's *The Name of the Rose*," from *Reading Eco*, p. 256.
15. Thomas Inge, editor, *Naming the Rose*, (Jackson: University Press of Mississippi, 1988).
16. Adele J. Haft, Jane G. White, and Robert J. White, *The Key to "The Name of the Rose" Including Translations of All Non-English Passages*, (Ann Arbor: The University of Michigan Press), 1999. The guide touts itself as "Demystifying Umberto Eco's Novel, *The Name of Rose*.".
17. Adele J, Haft, Jane G. White, Robert J. White, *The Key to "The Name of the Rose*," p. 17.

18. http://www.theguardian.com/books/2002/oct/12/fiction.academicexperts.
19. "Questions for Umberto Eco," Interview by Deborah Solomon, published November 25, 2007.
20. Laura Miller, "The Last Word: The Da Vinci Con," The *New York Times*, February 22, 2004.
21. Sullivan, Jane (2004-12-24). "Religious conspiracy? Do me a fervour," http://www.theage.com.au/articles/2004/12/23/1103391886435.html.
22. Jeff Israely, @Time, Milan, Sunday, June 5, 2005.
23. Eco, *Foucault's Pendulum*, translated by William Weaver, (New York: Ballantine Books, 1990), p. 313.
24. Eco, *Foucault's Pendulum*, p. 313.
25. https://www.isnare.com/encyclopedia/Dan_Brown.
26. https://www.isnare.com/encyclopedia/Dan_Brown.
27. http://en.wikipedia.org/wiki/List_of_best-selling_fiction_authors.
28. BBC News, "Decoding the Da Vinci Code Author," April 7, 2006.
29. Dan Brown, Official Website, www.danbrown.com/meet_dan/index.html.
30. BBC News, "Decoding the Da Vinci Code Author," April 7, 2006.
31. *"Famed author takes on Kansas"*. *LJWorld. October 7, 2005. Retrieved 2011-01-04.*
32. http://www.nytimes.com/2016/02/20/arts/international/umberto-eco-italian-semiotician-and-best-selling-author-dies-at-84.html?_r=0.
33. BBC News, "Decoding the Da Vinci Code Author," April 7, 2006.
34. "3x12," *QI* (episode transcript).
35. *"Stephen King address, University of Maine." Archive. Archived from the original on 2007-10-13. Retrieved 2011-01-04.*
36. *Sorkin, Aaron (December 30, 2010). "Movie Review: The Da Vinci Code (2006)." The New York Times. Retrieved 2011-01-04.*
37. *"The Dan Brown code," Language Log, University of Pennsylvania.*
38. Cited from Box Office Mojo. Retrieved December 16, 2006.
39. Maslin, Janet (March 17, 2003). "Spinning a Thriller from a Gallery at the Louvre.".
40. Janet Maslin,http://www.nytimes.com/2009/09/14/books/14maslin.html?_r=0.
41. http://content.time.com/time/specials/packages/article/0,28804,1972656_1972696_1973088,00.html.
42. Eco's *Trattato di semiotica generale* was published in 1975, and translated into English in 1976.
43. Eco, *Travels in Hyperreality*, (New York: Harcourt, Brace, Jovanovich, 1986), p. 12.
44. Eco, *Travels in Hyperreality*, p. 8.

45. Eco, *Travels in Hyperreality*, p. 7.
46. Eco, *Travels in Hyperreality*, p. 6.
47. Eco, *Travels in Hyperreality*, p. 17.
48. Eco, *Travels in Hyperreality*, p. 18.
49. http://www.chronicle.com/article/The-Irrepressible-Lightness-of/235525.
50. Eco, *Travels in Hyperreality*, p. x.
51. Theresa Coletti, *Naming the Rose*, p. 200.
52. Eco, *Travels in Hyperreality*, p. xi.

CHAPTER 2

The Intellectual Species

For determining the distinguishing character of the human species, a comparative approach can offer an insightful perspective. In *The Dynamic Human*, coauthors Dr. Arthur Saniotis, and Dr. Maciej Henneberg, professors at the School of Medical Sciences at the University of Adelaide in Australia, cast some doubt on the superior status of humans:

> For millennia, all kinds of authorities – from religion to eminent scholars – have been repeating the same idea ad nauseam, that humans are exceptional by virtue that they are the smartest in the animal kingdom. Even Aristotle, probably the most influential of all thinkers, argued that humans were superior to other animals due to our exclusive ability to reason.

But reasoning, according to the authors, is just one form of intelligence.[1]

WHAT IS AN INTELLECTUAL?

Since Eco has established a reputation as an elite academic who attempts to communicate his ideas across the social spectrum as a "public intellectual," it's helpful to consider, at this point, what an "intellectual" is and what is the role of the intellectual in contemporary society. We can begin by looking at how the intellectual capacity distinguishes humans as a species and how it became associated with a specialized social class over the course of human development.

The story, according to the Bible, is that we are the species created in God's image that ate the apple from the tree of knowledge and were cast out of the natural paradise of Eden. As exiles from the "natural world," humans then became the species that constantly modifies its environment, which, in turn, modifies its own "nature" as a species over time. But how did this come about in relation to the other species?

The Tool-Making Species

Our "nature" as humans is derived from a couple of fundamental differences from other species that have given rise to immense and very complex consequences. Firstly, we are the species that can modify our environment through the use of tools. We are the only four-limbed, bipedal species that evolved to stand and move in an erect posture which enhances our field of view and frees our other two limbs, through the advantage of an opposable thumb and dexterous fingers, to grasp objects, make tools, and modify the environment. Although the archeological record indicates that erect stance preceded the advent of tool making by as much as 2 to 4 million years, it is initially the transition to tool making that greatly expanded our capacity as humans and differentiated us from other species. In academia, this capacity is referred to as *Homo Faber*, the Latin expression for "Man the Maker."

Other species, of course, have been observed to use rudimentary tools. Our forebears the chimpanzees, who gave us the opposable thumb, have great dexterity in grasping rocks to open nuts and to fashion natural materials into basic tools such as chisels. But humans have the distinction of being able to alter natural materials to make a broad variety of tools with elaborate uses. And humans developed the social capacity for large-scale organized labor enabling us to use our tool-making capacity to greatly alter the environment. Thus we are the species that alters nature to adapt it to our needs.

The Linguistic Species

Secondly, as the linguist Derek Bickerton puts it, we are the species that can think "offline."[2] This distinguishing capacity should be somewhat qualified because there are continuing questions concerning the relative cognitive and linguistic capacity of other species. But humans are generally acknowledged as the species with the capacity to think through symbols that are detached, or offline, from the physical environment. These symbols, or "signs" as semiotic theorists call them, are linked through the internal structural relations of human language in a way that is beyond or at least vastly different from what other species can do with sounds and gestures. Human's ability to think offline is referred to as the symbolic or linguistic capacity, and in Latin as *Homo Sapiens*, "Man the Thinker."

However, as Derek Bickerton points out, all species "think." All species engage in conscious interaction with the world in response to sensory stimuli through instinct and learned behaviors to satisfy their basic needs for survival, social organization, reproduction, etc. In other words, all species mentally process a constant stream of information that is decoded and interpreted, based on their relation to the physical world, to respond in various ways to particular circumstances. But the "thinking" of other species is primarily "online," instinctual, or "hard-wired" to the sensory world.

Humans, like other species, also experience the physical world through "online" sensory receptors of taste, touch, hearing, smelling, and, seeing. In relation to other species, humans developed a greater emphasis on seeing and a lesser reliance on hearing and smelling. It's common for us to use dogs, for example, to make up for our relative deficiency in smelling to help us find missing persons and detect dangerous and illegal substances. In relation to other species, however, humans have an additional, parallel capacity to think offline. Although other species, such as primates and dolphins, can refer to things not physically present, so far as we know they can do so only through simple reference. Humans can think through symbols linked together by the complex structural relations of language that constitute an elaborate, internal model of the world.

Through offline thinking, we have the ability to refer to things completely separate from our immediate relation with the physical environment, and we can refer to things that exist only in our imagination. We can bring to mind, for example, the image of a human with wings. This mental image is associated with a sound and a graphic set of symbols in the English language as the word "angel." By thinking offline, we can bring this image into our consciousness and associate it with the conception of a spiritual messenger of God. Other species can actively "think" of things only drawn from their direct sensory experience of nature. Humans can deliberately bring to mind symbols of things not physically present and even outside their sensory experience of nature, and they can communicate these ideas to other humans through sounds and graphic symbols.

The capacity to refer to things not physically present through signs effectively makes us the species that can lie, and, as we will consider in Chapter 8, Eco asserts that semiotics constitutes, in fact, a theory of the lie. Not because we are a species that is naturally dishonest, but because of our strange capacity to refer to things separate from their physical presence or factual existence.

The offline thinking capacity of humans obviously has made us a highly adaptive species in overcoming the limitations of our instincts and the natural environment which we can modify at will. As we will consider in the next chapter, the offline thinking capacity through language also became the central problem in the development of Western philosophy. The problem of language as a medium for understanding our world has thus persisted into our own time, and it became the primary focus of Eco's intellectual practice as a pioneering theorist in the field of semiotics which studies how humans create meaning and order in the world through the language capacity. As we will consider in Chapter 8, semiotics was first developed in the late nineteenth and early twentieth centuries in response to the persistent problem of understanding how language determines our relation to the world.

THE PLAYFUL SPECIES

A third characteristic has also been proposed for differentiating us from other species: the human propensity for play. According to the scholar Johan Huizinga (1872–1945), we are the species that engages in playful expression of our possibilities. Huizinga conceived of *Homo Ludens*, or "Man the Player," as the basis for human culture. While other creatures also engage in play, humans can do so with the symbolic capacity to express the diversity of human experience through our modes of dress, cuisine, habitat, the arts, architecture, etc. Other characteristics could be considered as well such as human's use of fire to adapt to the earth's variable climate and seasons and to take advantage of diverse food sources that we are otherwise not naturally adapted to chew and digest. Humans are also the species that buries and commemorates its dead through monuments and cultural ceremonies although some other species such as crows exhibit behaviors that seem to be similar to human mourning.[3] In addition, although other species engage in predatory violence, humans are the most violent species, especially since the advent of agriculture and the advances in weapons technology, such that we pose a real threat to earthly existence. And, humans are the species that laughs which is a central theme of Eco's first novel *The Name of the Rose*. But, for the purposes of understanding our essential character as a species, the capacity to alter the environment along with our ability to think offline are the two fundamental factors for understanding what it means to be human.

THE CULTURAL SPECIES

What, then, are the immense and complex consequences of humans having the capacity as both *Homo Faber* and *Homo Sapiens*? Because of the ability to stand erect and use our hands to fashion and use tools, we are the species that constantly modifies the environment. *Whereas all other species adapt themselves to the environment, humans adapt the environment to themselves.* Other species, such as ants and beavers, for example, are able to modify their natural habitat, but only in a very limited way in relation to the environment and through instinctual behaviors that don't change over extended periods of time. In contrast, humans, as *Homo Faber*, have the ability to constantly modify the environment on an increasingly massive scale in ways that change dramatically over time. Humans are not only more adept than other species at fashioning and using tools to modify the environment as *Homo Faber*, we also possess the singular capacity as *Homo Sapiens* to think offline that allows us to imagine possible worlds outside our experience of nature and to alter the world accordingly. Humans are consequently the "cultural" species that creates its own world over time apart from the natural world. While other species leave fossil traces of their existence, humans leave relics of their struggles, imagination, and ingenuity such as Stonehenge, the Pyramids, the Great Wall of China, the Colosseum, and the 2,722 foot Burj Kalifa in Dubai.

The ability of humans to "think offline" has other consequences as well for us as a species and for our impact on the world. Since we are the species with a dual capacity for thinking through direct sensory stimuli as well as through language, we can oscillate between these modes. One theory concerning the rise of the language capacity or offline thinking is that it allowed humans to free themselves from the constraints and potential negative consequences of instinctual behavior. This would suggest that the intellect came to function as a way of allowing humans to reprogram their own behavior through rational reflection when instinctive behaviors became limiting or maladaptive. In effect, the ability to think offline allowed humans to free themselves from the constraints of instinct to adapt themselves through human culture. "In other words," as the famous paleoanthropologist Richard Leakey suggests in *Origins Reconsidered,* "culture became an active component of natural selection, enhancing it still more. My father used to say that, through culture, humans effectively domesticated themselves."[4]

According to Richard Leakey, the cultural factor is what radically differentiates us from the other species: "*Homo Sapiens* is a cultural creature, to an extent and in a manner unmatched by any other species. This extra dimension of behavior essentially creates another world, one that may be constantly reshaped."[5] As the species that is constantly modifying the environment and ourselves over time, we can say that humans are the "cultural species" without a fixed "nature." Besides the immense technological changes that have radically altered human society, humans have developed distinctly different languages, social structures, architecture, cuisine, clothing, sports, entertainment, literature, the arts, etc., and these aspects of human culture change dramatically over time, and not always in ways that we might think of as progressive. The social role of women in European society, for example, was greatly altered during the Enlightenment and the industrial revolution, but rather than fostering the emancipation of women, it initially had the opposite effect by restricting women's sphere of activity primarily to the home supposedly to maintain the moral sanctity of society.

Our character as the "cultural" species is another core aspect for understanding Eco's practice as an intellectual. Eco became a pioneer in the development of the relatively recent field of semiotics which he described more broadly as a theory of culture: "...my first hypothesis makes a general theory of culture out of semiotics and in the final analysis makes semiotics a substitute for cultural anthropology."[6] The intensified focus on how language generates meaning provided a model that the early founders of semiotics believed could be applied more generally to the analysis of culture as a whole.

The Aesthetic Species

Another way to consider the cultural aspect of our species is that our constant modification of the world and ourselves over time makes us the "artistic" or "aesthetic" species. We are the artisans of our world which differentiates us radically from the other species. Every human activity can be seen as a form of art that fashions us and our environment. This is important in relation to Eco's intellectual practice as well because his original focus as an academic was on aesthetic theory which explores how art and beauty can provoke a higher consciousness in our sensory experience of the world. Eco's particular role as a public intellectual also developed out of the rise of "popular" culture in the twentieth century. The advent of popular culture had an especially powerful impact on Eco and his fellow postwar Italian intellectuals who were trying to respond to what they perceived as the degrading impact of mass consumerism on the traditional role of the arts which is taken up in Chapter 6. Their concern was that a passive response to culture was being fostered by mass media consumerism which would distract from our ability to actively determine ourselves in relation to the world.

The Historical Species

Because of the language capacity, humans are also the species with a sense of time, which, unfortunately, means that we are confronted with the consciousness of our inevitable mortality. As Richard Leakey points out: "Self-awareness and death-awareness flow together."[7] The awareness of our finite lifespan is the principal motivation for human religion that provides us with an aspiration for an afterlife. Our sense of time, however, also means that we can distinguish a present from a past, which allows us to reflect on our changing character over time, and to project a future of possible worlds beyond anything presently in existence. Because of the capacity to constantly modify the environment and ourselves in our relation between past, present, and future, humans are distinguished from the rest of nature as the "historical" species. History, from this perspective, is not just the record of our past modifications of the world, but more significantly as the dynamic engine of change that makes us so radically different from all other species. Ask other species about their history, and they won't have much to tell except for gradual, biological changes and adaptations to nature over an extended period of time. Humans, in contrast, are constantly changing the world on an increasingly vast scale. And these changes cause us as a species to change, in turn, by having to adapt ourselves to our own constant modifications of the world. Richard Leakey, again, citing Kenneth Oakley from *Man the Tool-Maker*, notes that our own adaptations cause us to change physiologically: "not only did man make tools, but effectively, tools made man."[8] According to Oakley, our tool-making capacity contributed to the exponential growth in human brain size. In this sense, we could say that: *While all other species adapt themselves to the environment, humans adapt the environment to themselves, and adapt themselves, in turn, to their own adaptations.*

Through our unique capacities as a species, we are responsible for history as an engine of change that has come to dominate the world in marvelously imaginative ways, but also to the point of threatening the world's existence through global warfare and environmental destruction. Other species evolve in adaptation to the environment over extended periods of time. Humans constantly adapt the environment to themselves through technological innovations at a constantly accelerating pace that, in turn, constantly alter us over time as a species. In considering what distinguishes humans from other species, we can say that we are the "historical species" without a fixed "nature" apart from the infinite capacity for change as *Homo Faber* and *Homo Sapiens.* The agricultural revolution from about 10,000 years ago, for example, caused a massive reorganization of human society resulting in a hierarchy of social classes, specialized labor, the rise of urban environments, large-scale warfare, etc. The industrial revolution beginning in the eighteenth century completely altered the environment and the social order, and the impact of the rapidly accelerating technological transformation arising from it has become difficult for us to be fully aware of, for example, through the advent of computer technology that has completely altered virtually every aspect of contemporary life.

The Italian Humanist-Historicist Tradition

Our character as the cultural and historical species constitutes another core aspect for understanding Eco's practice as an intellectual. Italian intellectuals such as Eco have been greatly influenced by the seventeenth-century Italian scholar Giambattista Vico (1668–1744) who asserted that the way in which humans practically and creatively alter the world over time is the proper focus of human knowledge rather than abstract timeless truths. Vico's prominent influence over Italian intellectuals established what came to be called the Italian "humanist-historicist" tradition. "Humanism" is the emphasis on the human-centered aspiration for meaning and order expressed through philosophy, literature, the arts, etc., from the ancients that was greatly expanded through the legacy of the Renaissance. "Historicism" emphasizes how ideas and cultural practices are not the product of the inevitable march of progress over time, but instead are determined in relation to the particular historical circumstances from which they arise. In other words, rather than thinking of our knowledge of the world as timeless truths or the inevitable progression toward the truth in our own age, an historicist perspective asserts that our understanding must always take into consideration how ideas are rooted in the historical and cultural circumstances of the period from which they were generated. For example, the rise of the modern secular state and the principle of the separation of Church and state arose in response to the horrors of the religious wars between Catholics and Protestants during the sixteenth and seventeenth centuries as well as the scientific revolution that called into question the authority of the Church in determining the truth about the world. As beings in time, our temporal horizon allows for, but also limits, what and how we can think. Because of this tradition, Eco was wary of any theoretical perspectives that were asserted as timeless truths outside the forces of human culture and history.

The Existentialist Species

Because of the capacity for offline thinking, humans developed over time an interior consciousness and the ability to modify our sense of self in relation to the world which makes us the "existentialist" species. Existentialism is a philosophical perspective that arose in the nineteenth century in response to the rapid transformation of contemporary society by science and technology that undermined the traditional role of religion and motivated philosophers to move beyond abstract concepts to focus on the actual lived experience of the individual in modern industrial society. Existentialism seeks to understand how our character as humans is determined through our being born into a world that has been created before us through the forces of history and culture that we must confront to fashion ourselves as individuals. In this sense, "existence" means our interactive relationship with other people and the products of our culture such as the modern impact of digital technology and the products of mass consumerism. Because of our constant modification of the world and ourselves over time, we could say that there is an inherent existentialist character to our being as humans.

The existentialist aspect of our species is another especially important point of reference for understanding Eco's practice as an intellectual. As we will explore in the next chapter, Eco's foundations as an intellectual arose from his university studies on the medieval philosopher Thomas

Aquinas (1225–1274). Aquinas conceived of aesthetics as the interaction of humans with the art and beauty of the sensory world that would lead to the higher consciousness of God which was seen as an existentialist perspective. Eco later adapted that religious perspective to the modern world in which high culture is confronted with the impact of mass media consumerism. From Eco's existentialist perspective, our interaction with the products of elite and popular culture is what determines us as individuals which calls for a conscious awareness of our potential for self-determination rather than being passively determined by the forces of history and culture.

The Educational Species

Since we are constantly altering ourselves over time as the "historical" and "cultural" species, another consequence of our unique capacities is that we are the "educational" species. We are the species that is dependent upon and determined by the need for extensive schooling over progressively longer periods of time for adaptation to our increasingly complex world. According to Richard Leakey, "Humans become humans through intense learning – not just of survival in the practical world, but of customs and social mores, kinship and social laws. In other words: culture. Culture can be said to be *the* human adaptation."[9] Our character as the historical and cultural species determined by education is genetically encoded in our "life history" as a species. Life history involves the amount of time allotted for each stage of a species' growth from infancy to maturity, age of reproductive capacity, etc. While other species experience a fairly brief period of "immaturity" before reaching reproductive capacity, humans are distinguished by a prolonged period of childhood, until age 13 to 15, that is necessary for absorbing the increasing complexity of our changing culture. This extended childhood is followed by a rapid growth spurt into adolescence. Richard Leakey, citing Barry Bogin, indicates that:

> The extremely extended childhood in humans is the result of a much reduced rate of growth during that period. The brain, however, is an exception during this period. It achieves virtually adult size when body growth is only 40 percent complete. These growth patterns help establish teacher-student roles that remain stable for a decade or more, allowing a great deal of learning, practice, and modification of survival skills to occur.[10]

While other species adapt very quickly to their environment, humans, as the species that constantly modifies the world, require increasingly longer periods for adapting to the complexities of our culture, technology, society, etc. The family dog might need to go to obedience school to learn how to adapt to humans, but it won't need to go through extensive schooling to learn how to be a dog. Humans, however, are the species dependent upon and determined by at least 13 years of basic schooling from kindergarten through high school. Since the advent of the digital age, another four years of college has become the norm. In addition, because of the greatly accelerating pace of technological change, humans are increasingly called upon to be lifelong learners continuing well beyond childhood in order to constantly adapt to our rapidly changing world. In the relation between intellectuals and popular culture, the focus and extent of one's education is thus a major factor. Elite Intellectuals, such as Eco, pursue a specialized, advanced education in the humanities required by our increasingly complex society and culture which can make their knowledge increasingly inaccessible to a popular audience.

The Intellectual Species

We became the cultural and historical species because we could separate ourselves from nature by thinking offline and by modifying the environment. Because of these inherited capacities that determine all of us as humans, it is important to emphasize a point first proposed by the Italian political theorist Antonio Gramsci (1891–1937) who was a highly influential figure for Eco and his fellow Italian postwar intellectuals. Gramsci was one of the founders of the Italian Communist Party who developed his ideas while imprisoned by the Fascist regime of Benito Mussolini (1883–1945) for 11 years until his death. Gramsci was trying to understand why a worldwide revolution of the working class had not occurred as anticipated in Marx's theory of class struggle. Instead, the Russian Revolution and others that followed were instigated and dominated by an elite intellectual class. As a result, Gramsci became a major contributor to the understanding of the relation between intellectuals – as a specialized social class – and the society as a whole which had a powerful impact on how Eco and his generation of university students thought about the social role and responsibility of the intellectual.

It should be emphasized, however, that Gramsci asserted that ***ALL HUMANS ARE INTELLECTUALS***:

> There is no human activity from which every form of intellectual participation can be excluded: *homo faber* cannot be separated from *homo sapiens*.

Each man, finally, outside his professional activity, carries on some form of intellectual activity, that is, he is a "philosopher", an artist, a man of taste, he participates in a particular conception of the world, has a conscious line of moral conduct, and therefore contributes to sustain a conception of the world or to modify it, that is, to bring into being new modes of thought.[11]

According to Gramsci, regardless of one's social class, all humans determine for their own purposes what is real, what has value, what is right and wrong, and what is beautiful in ways that can change dramatically over the course of one's lifetime. Consequently, due to the human capacity to think offline, all of us, as members of the human species, possess the intellectual capacity, which, as Gramsci asserted, gives all of us the potential to creatively determine our own being as humans. But, due to the broad range in human adaptability to cultural complexity especially in contemporary society, the variability in intellectual capacity may seem to be entirely based on genetic inheritance. However the scientist Stephen Jay Gould (1941–2002) in *The Mismeasure of Man*[12] called into question the idea of genetic determination. Adaptability can be affected by gender, culture, and socioeconomic differences that have evolved over the course of human history.

To be fully human, then, in relation to our species' potential, means engaging the intellect to determine and fashion our own being because that's what distinguishes us as a species. But, as Gramsci acknowledged: "All men are intellectuals… but not all men have in society the function of intellectuals."[13] Although all humans have the intellectual capacity, not all humans are actively aware of their intellectual capacity as a means of determining themselves, and not all humans function in a social role as the leader and organizer of a social class. Why that is the case is a major focus of this exploration of Eco as an intellectual in the age of popular culture. Since not all humans function in a social role as an intellectual, Gramsci differentiated between "traditional" and "organic" intellectuals: "The traditional and vulgarized type of the intellectual is given by the man of letters, the philosopher, the artist" to which he adds the "journalists" who, according to Gramsci, "regard themselves as the 'true' intellectuals." He notes that they are being joined in "the modern world" by those with a "technical education" which he characterizes as "the new type of intellectual."[14] "Organic" intellectuals are those who arise as the leaders of a new social consciousness, for example, the entrepreneurial class that rose up against the traditional aristocracy in the French Revolution. Concerning the role of "traditional" intellectuals in arousing the consciousness of the human potential for self-determination, Gramsci asserted that:

> The mode of being of the new intellectual can no longer consist in eloquence, which is an exterior and momentary mover of feelings and passions, but in active participation in practical life, as constructor, organizer, "permanent persuader" and not just a simple orator ... [15]

For Gramsci, this involved the critical role of education:

> School is the instrument through which intellectuals of various levels are elaborated. The complexity of the intellectual function in different states can be measured objectively by the number and gradation of specialized schools: the more extensive the "area" covered by education and the more numerous the "vertical" "levels" of schooling, the more complex is the cultural world, the civilisation, of a particular state.[16]

THE RISE OF THE INTELLECTUAL AS A SPECIALIZED SOCIAL CLASS

Since, according to Gramsci, all humans are intellectuals, why did a specialized class of "thinkers" develop over time when all humans have the capacity for intellectual reflection? What has been the role of these specialized thinkers in human development, and what is their potential for communicating their ideas to a public audience today? These questions are especially useful to consider because the central focus of the long historical legacy of intellectual inquiry has been the development of an emancipatory consciousness which is central to Eco's practice as an intellectual. How can we engage our capacities as humans to free ourselves from the constraints of social custom in order to fully pursue our individual potential? How can we become the artists of our own self-creation? In our contemporary world dominated by technological innovation, what is the "technology" of the self? Exploring the development of the specialized role of the intellectual will allow us to consider Eco's chosen path of intellectual practice in relation, for example, to Gramsci's idea of "permanent persuader."

THE INTELLECTUAL HUNTER-GATHERER

To consider why, as Gramsci suggested, not all humans actively engage their intellect to reflect on their circumstances and pursue their full potential, we can begin with an inquiry into the organization of the earliest human societies, the hunter-gatherers, and how human society evolved over time. Since humans have a dual capacity to think both online through instinctual response to physical stimuli, as well as offline through reflection on our relation to the world, why did the capacity for offline thinking result in a specialized class of thinkers?

Hunter-gatherer societies consist of families joined in extended clans who sustain themselves by foraging for natural edibles and hunting for wild animals. Our hunter-gatherer forebears were essentially egalitarian without a complex social hierarchy and specialized labor except for a differentiation of social roles based on gender. Women, for the most part, because of their child-raising role, engaged as foragers and men as hunters. Although there are numerous theories, with no consensus among scholars, about how the language capacity came about in the earliest human societies, it is generally acknowledged that hunter-gatherer societies were and still are socially egalitarian. Consequently they share equally in the use of the language capacity or offline thinking for communicating and organizing their social functions. In other words, there is no differentiation among members of hunter-gatherer societies in their use of the "intellectual" capacity.

Some paleoanthropologists have proposed, in fact, that the origin of the language capacity was linked specifically to the egalitarian organization of early human societies. This speculation is based on the stark difference between hunter-gatherer societies and some of our closest evolutionary forebears, for example, the chimpanzees, who are not at all egalitarian. Chimpanzees are organized into highly stratified social groups that are dominated by an alpha male.[17] In the evolution of human society from our ancestors such as the chimpanzee, the language capacity would have served to coordinate the acquiring and distributing of food, finding or constructing shelter, caring for the young, burying the dead, and, according to one theory, maintaining social cohesion through gossip.[18] The language capacity would have thus made possible the transition from stratified primate social organization to the egalitarian relations of hunter-gatherer societies.

The egalitarian character of hunter-gatherer societies would have been facilitated through the equitable sharing of their labor and resources. Richard Leakey, again, points this out citing another paleoanthropologist Glynn Isaac: "If you could interview a chimpanzee about the differences between humans and apes, including the way we walk, the way we communicate, and our subsistence, I think it might say: 'You humans are very odd, when you get food, instead of eating it promptly like any sensible ape, you haul it off and share it with others."[19] Glynn Isaac also suggests that: "The physical selection pressures that promoted an increase in the size of the brain, thereby surely enhancing the hominid capacity for communication, are a consequence of the shift from individual foraging to food sharing some two million years ago."[20] What characterized early hunter-gatherer societies was the development of social bonds of cooperation as an adaptive mode of survival. According to Nick Humphrey, an associate of Richard Leakey: "Studies on hunter-gatherer societies show that the demands of their daily lives are not great. Hunting techniques do not greatly outstrip those of other social carnivores. And gathering strategies are of the same order as you might find in, say, chimpanzees or baboons."[21] What makes humans, and our primate forebears, so different as a species is our complex social life which, in humans, became even more complex through the interdependent bonds of cooperation. Hunter-gatherer societies evolved, as Richard Leakey puts it, through "the social skill of cooperation" which "became a set of rules of conduct, of morals, an understanding of right and wrong in a complex social system." He cites the biologist Conrad Waddington in concluding that: "Through evolution humans have become the ethical animal."[22]

The Shaman and the Oral Historian

But despite the egalitarian character of the earliest human societies, there arose from those origins the first specialized "thinker." As indicated previously, humans are distinguished from other species by having a consciousness of their own mortality. The uncertainty and dread aroused by the specter of mortality have confronted human society from the beginning of human consciousness through language. Although the consciousness of time and mortality arose from the ability to think offline, it also allowed humans to conceive of a spiritual life and an afterworld. The specialized role of mediating the spirit world and afterlife goes back thousands of years before the advent of agriculture to the shaman, who, according to archeological evidence, could have been either man or woman.

The shaman provided guidance concerning the mysteries of life and death and treated illnesses by mediating with the spirit world. He or she was the one person who possessed a specialized knowledge that was not directly held by the others except for the role of designated elders who kept a memory of their oral history and myths. According to some anthropologists, the shaman came about through a traumatic illness that "initiated" them into contact with the otherworldly spirits through a trance state. The altered state precipitated by illness would have allowed the shaman to conceive of things "beyond" what other humans experienced through the offline capacity. According to the historian of religion, Mircea Eliade, the shaman had a specialized capacity for "religious ecstasy."[23]

The Agricultural Revolution

The specialized knowledge and practice of the shaman as mediator of the spirit world evolved into the priestly class that attained a prominent role in society following the transition from small-scale, egalitarian, hunter-gatherer societies into large-scale, hierarchical, agricultural societies around 10,000 years ago. Why the agricultural revolution occurred is also subject to numerous theories without a scholarly consensus, and it is a curious one to resolve in relation to the theory by some paleoanthropologists that the language capacity arose in support of egalitarianism. In any case, the advent of agriculture would have allowed for the great expansion of human societies in their relation to the land which may have been precipitated by population growth and competition for resources.

The agricultural revolution brought about the rise of the warrior as the dominant class that evolved from the skill of hunting. According to Richard Leakey: "The archeology of warfare fades fast in human history, rapidly disappearing beyond the Neolithic, ten thousand years ago, when agriculture and permanent settlements began to develop." He concludes that: "warfare is rooted in the need for territorial possession once populations became agricultural and necessarily sedentary" but "I do not believe that violence is an innate characteristic of humankind, merely an unfortunate adaptation to certain circumstances."[24]

Intellectual Specialization

The social hierarchy of agricultural societies that persisted over thousands of years consisted primarily of three social classes: the warrior/ruler class; the priestly class, who were the descendants of the shaman and were typically integrated with the ruling class; and the laborer or peasant class. But the transition to the complex social organization of agricultural societies also brought about writing from about 5,000 years ago. As William Bernstein points out in *Master of the Word*, "the first writing arose not from the desire to record history or produce literature, but rather to measure grain, count livestock, and organize and control the labor of the human animal."[25] Writing and reading became the specialized labor of the scribe who kept records in support of agricultural production, taxation, and trade carried out through large-scale human labor. The scribe also facilitated long distance communication between members of the ruling class, and the written language would have allowed for the commitment to writing of what had been oral history. In addition to the scribe, agricultural society fostered the specialized labor of mathematicians for calculating trade transactions, taxes, and construction projects, as well as astronomy for determining the cycle of the seasons, the religious calendar, etc. As a result, individuals who specialized in a form of mental labor involving language and technical skills gradually evolved from the origins of human society and became one of the pillars of human civilization.

Humanistic Intellectuals and the Technical Intelligentsia

The intellectual as a specialized social function can be seen to arise, then, from the priestly class, beginning with the shaman, and through the specialized labor of the scribe, the mathematician, the astronomer, etc. who possessed technical expertise and maintained the cultural order. But the relation between the specialists in interpreting the will of the gods and maintaining the cultural order, and those involved in technical expertise, although often closely aligned, became separated in contemporary society between what are sometimes referred to as the "humanistic intellectuals" and the "technical intelligentsia" who are both intellectual specialists but with a focus and practice that eventually developed into much different social roles. Contemporary scholars focusing on the social role of the intellectual have suggested that today's humanistic intellectuals such as Eco are the heirs of the priestly/scribal specialists. According to the sociologist Lewis Coser, intellectuals are "descendants of the priestly upholders of sacred tradition." A fellow sociologist, Edward Shils, has asserted that intellectuals are distinguished by their "unusual sensitivity to the sacred."[26] Talcott Parsons, in his explorations of the social role of intellectuals, suggested that: "the establishment of a contact for the laity with the sacred values of their society"[27] is "the most important of all the traditions of the intellectuals."[28]

The Philosopher

Apart from the priestly function, today's humanistic intellectuals can be traced to the origins of philosophical rationalism in the fourth century BC from the Greek philosophers Socrates, Plato, and Aristotle (with similar intellectual traditions arising in other cultures such as China and India). Instead of interpreting the signs of the gods, the Greek philosophers began to focus on human affairs through a dialogue of questions and answers about practical aspects of politics, society, truth, beauty, etc. The advent of philosophical rationalism by the Greeks signaled a departure from the rituals of the priestly class toward an analysis of worldly concerns, but with a similar sense of the sacred. The priestly class and the rational philosophers later merged in the role of the Christian monk in Medieval Scholasticism which was the tradition that Eco inherited through his study of the medieval philosopher Thomas Aquinas.

The Artist

Besides the role of religion and philosophical rationalism, it should be emphasized that the intellectual specialist also arose from practitioners of the arts through literature, such as Homer's *Iliad* and *Odyssey*; through architecture and sculpture, as seen in the Greek temples and statues of the gods; and through music, dance, and the theater where Greek dramatists explored the horrors and follies of human society. The artists expressed the sacred values of society in ways that encouraged a broadly shared reflection that was different but equally powerful in relation to the role of the priestly class and the rational philosophers. The humanistic intellectual thus developed in three areas of social life: religion, philosophy, and the arts. Philosophy for the ancients would have included mathematics and what we call natural science today, and the arts would have included practical applications of mathematics and engineering through architecture. As mentioned previously, these practices later merged in the role of the medieval monk.

The Expanding Encyclopedia

After becoming established in particular domains of specialization, the role of the intellectual expanded greatly because the ever-increasing complexity of human society and its constant transformation over time generated an enormous storehouse of recorded knowledge since the advent of writing about 5,000 years ago. As indicated previously, the oldest human societies, the hunter-gatherers, were essentially egalitarian with no specialization of labor and no specialized knowledge apart from the role of designated elders in maintaining their oral history and the shaman. Whatever hunter-gatherer societies needed to know about the world, they would learn through direct experience that could be shared equally among its members. This is in stark contrast to the later development of human society and our situation today. As Eco points out in *Six Walks in the Fictional Woods*, citing Hilary Putnam, "there is a 'linguistic division of labor' which corresponds to a social division of knowledge: I delegate to others the knowledge of nine-tenths of the real world, keeping for myself the knowledge of the other tenth."[29] Although all humans have the intellectual capacity, vast changes in social and cultural complexity generated by the engine of historical development have caused the rise of intellectual specialists in a variety of domains to organize and maintain what Eco calls the "Encyclopedia" of world knowledge. As humans continuously modify the environment and themselves over time, the progressive complexity of human society and culture makes us increasingly dependent on others for orienting ourselves in the world. This dependency raises a practical question concerning the relation of the general public to the intellectual specialists who organize and maintain the great profusion of human knowledge. How much of the nine-tenths of world knowledge maintained by intellectual specialists do we need as individuals to guide us in relation to the one-tenth that we know directly? How the intellectual specialists maintain and make available their specialized areas of knowledge is at the heart of the relation between intellectuals and the public.

Literacy

A related factor in the rise of the social role of the intellectual is that the access to and production of human knowledge required the highly specialized skill of literacy in specialized languages. Although the social role of the intellectual expanded greatly from the time of Plato up to the European Enlightenment, it remained for most of this period a highly restricted activity practiced by a very small proportion of the population. Access to the knowledge of the world required the ability to read and write in the ancient languages in which it had been generated and preserved. The foundational works of Greek philosophy, for example, were recorded by hand and translated with commentaries by Roman and Muslim scholars into Latin and Arabic. The Bible was translated into Latin from the Greek and Aramaic. After the fall of the Roman Empire and the gradual evolution of colloquial Latin into the European Romance Languages for the common people, Latin became the specialized language of the Christian monk who maintained the historical inheritance of knowledge in monastery libraries with highly restricted access.

For the ancient and medieval world, the specialized language of the learned was thus Latin, along with Greek and Arabic which was the tradition, again, that Eco inherited. The ability to read and write in these specialized languages was held by a very small minority of the population, probably less than 10 percent. Literacy would not have been common even among the ruling class of kings until the later Middle Ages. Consequently, the keepers of the inheritance of human knowledge restricted intellectual practice to a tiny minority who served to legitimize the ruling elite while excluding the majority of the population as illiterate. As noted previously, Eco confronted contemporary readers with the problem of specialized access to world knowledge, characteristic of the Middle Ages, by including numerous passages of un-translated Latin in his first novel, *The Name of the Rose*.

The restricted access to the human inheritance of knowledge that prevailed since the ancient world was dramatically altered through the invention of the printing press by Johannes Gutenberg in 1439. The large-scale, mechanical reproduction, and increasingly broad distribution, of the written repositories of knowledge ended the monopoly of the monks and the rigid intellectual methods of medieval scholasticism. The expanded access to written knowledge was also facilitated through the translation of major works from Latin and Greek into the common language of each country. The expansion of literacy from the fifteenth century was one of the most powerful factors in the transition to the Renaissance. It also facilitated the gradual "democratization" of Christianity by Martin Luther by making the Bible available in the languages of the common people.

THE ENLIGHTENMENT INTELLECTUAL

The increasing access to knowledge through the printing press subsequently fostered the rise of the Enlightenment, the Age of Reason, and the industrial revolution that spawned the transition to our contemporary age and the greatly expanded role of the intellectual. Although specialists in analysis and interpretation arose from the earliest human societies, the term "intellectual" to designate a specific social role only arose in the early nineteenth century. Because of the broad expansion of education and what the German sociologist Max Weber (1864–1920) called the "rationalization" of contemporary life from the Enlightenment, the ancient inheritance of knowledge was taken up by a new wave of "humanistic" scholars, as well as a separate breed of scientific and technological thinkers who established themselves as the new class of specialized intellectuals. As a consequence, the term "intellectual" is now so broadly applied in contemporary society that it's difficult to identify it as a distinct vocation or social type. As Weber noted, "The more complicated and specialized modern culture becomes, the more its external supporting apparatus demands the personally detached and strictly 'objective' expert."[30] According to Weber, the Enlightenment brought about "the ever-increasing importance of expert and specialized knowledge."[31] A more recent analysis of contemporary society by Carl Boggs suggests that:

> With the rise of mass education and popular culture in the twentieth century, modern society blurs the distinction between intellectual and non-intellectual realms to an unprecedented degree. The crisis of modernity means that there are fewer established points of reference than ever: social and intellectual identities, never uniform or secure, are today shaped more and more by a fragmented, dissonant, and ever-shifting universe of experiences and needs.[32]

HUMANIST INTELLECTUALS AND THE TECHNICAL INTELLIGENTSIA

To clarify the meaning and practice of the contemporary intellectual, some theorists have suggested a distinction between those engaged in the study of the realm of the ideal and the general, in contrast to the practical and particular. Weber, for example, defined intellectuals as "exponents of theoretical rationalism in contrast to civic strata [which he referred to as 'intelligentsia'] geared to everyday practical needs."[33] In relation to the everyday, practical engagement of the "intelligentsia," Weber suggested that "Intellectuals ideal interests lie in the constant rationalization of the sphere of ideas and in a relentless attempt to transcend the immediate world in search of its meaning, its essence or its beauty."[34] According to Lewis Coser, the practice of the intellectual "presumes a capacity for detachment from immediate experience, a moving beyond the pragmatic tasks of the moment, a commitment to comprehensive values transcending professional or occupational involvement."[35] Edward Shils distinguishes intellectuals from the "ordinary run of their fellow-men" because they transcend "the immediate concrete situations of everyday life." Shils suggests that the "self-regard" of the intellectual that results from "preoccupation and contact with the most vital facts of human and cosmic existence," is also associated with an "implied attitude of derogation towards those who act in more mundane or more routine capacities."[36] The specialized sense of detachment from everyday concerns of the intellectual is one reason for the perception of a broad gulf between intellectuals and popular culture. In contemporary society, specialized thinkers are engaged in a variety of fields both purely practical in character as well as engaged in detached theoretical analysis.

The social role of the intellectual that arose from the religious impulse that attempts to determine the ultimate meaning and essence of our existence as humans later merged with the traditional focus of philosophy. But the Enlightenment emphasis on rational analysis separated philosophy from religion because of the constraints of religious dogma and superstition. As a result, the contemporary intellectual's focus on the "sacred" essence of our humanity is detached from the rituals and practices of religion toward the rational contemplation of the ultimate truth of the human condition.

Because modern society is so heavily dependent on specialized, technical knowledge, the sociologist Alvin Gouldner (1920–1980) suggests that the intellectual has emerged as a powerful, new social class. In terms of contemporary class struggle, Gouldner characterizes the new specialists in technical knowledge as a third class, apart from the corporate elite and the laboring class, who are changing the power relations of economic life. Like Weber and others, he distinguishes between the "intelligentsia" whose interests are fundamentally technical such as scientists, engineers, and especially in today's economy, the information technology specialists, on one side, and "humanistic intellectuals" whose interests are "primarily critical, emancipatory, hermeneutic and hence often political."[37] His distinction between them is useful to consider in relation to Eco's role as an intellectual:

> While intellectuals often contribute to revolutionary leadership, they also serve to accommodate the future to the past and they reproduce the past in the future. That's what comes of the love of books. While the technical intelligentsia often wish nothing more than to be allowed to enjoy their opiate obsessions with technical puzzles, it is their social mission to revolutionize technology continually and hence disrupt established social solidarities and cultural values by never contenting themselves with the status quo.

Revolutionary intellectuals are the medium of an ancient morality; accommodative intelligentsia are the medium of a new amorality. Which is more revolutionary?[38]

Using Gouldner's distinction between the technological "intelligentsia" and the humanistic "intellectual," we can get a better sense of how Eco has taken up the ancient tradition of the humanistic intellectual while attempting to adapt that role to the impact of science and technology as well as the mass media consumerism of popular culture. What Gouldner calls the "humanistic intellectuals" traditionally engage in serving society by fostering an understanding of the present in relation to the past in order to fully explore our possibilities for the future. Eco is an especially prominent representative of contemporary humanistic intellectuals who, as Gouldner suggests, are involved in navigating a course toward the future guided by the past. As a scholar of our cultural inheritance, Eco has also distinguished himself for his encyclopedic knowledge, and as an exemplary bibliophile whose "love of books" has generated a personal library of more than 50,000 volumes.[39]

As a public intellectual, Eco also attempts to share his ideas across the cultural spectrum that is heavily dominated by visual media. Through these efforts, he has engaged in reasserting the value of humanistic studies in response to their displacement in contemporary society by the technical intelligentsia. The emphasis in higher education today is clearly on the advancement of the technical intelligentsia engaged in the privileged STEM fields – science, technology, engineering, and math – in the service of technological management and innovation, and corporate globalism. The humanistic intellectuals, as Gouldner indicates, are focused on the world of books in order to make sense of the relation between past and future. But they also threaten the status quo by constantly raising questions about its legitimacy. Exploring Eco's role as an exemplary humanistic intellectual can allow us to consider the continuing relevance of this specialized knowledge and how it can be made available to a broad popular audience for arousing an awareness of each individual's potential for "intellectual" reflection and self-determination. As recent critics have asserted, the humanistic focus should be reclaimed as the core function of education in any society that purports to be a democracy.[40]

Notes

1. http://primalnaturenetwork.org/human-intelligence-isnt-superior-animals-researchers-say/.

2. Derek Bickerton, *Language and Species*, (Chicago: The University of Chicago Press, 1990).
3. http://www.mnn.com/earth-matters/animals/stories/do-animals-mourn-their-dead.
4. Leakey, Richard, *Origins Reconsidered*, (New York: Anchor Books, 1992), p. 212.
5. Leakey, Richard, *Origins Reconsidered*, p. 351.
6. Eco, *A Theory of Semiotics*, (Bloomington: Indiana University Press, 1979), p. 26.
7. Eco, *A Theory of Semiotics*, p. 270.
8. Eco, *A Theory of Semiotics*, p. 249.
9. Eco, *A Theory of Semiotics*, p.145.
10. Eco, *A Theory of Semiotics*, p. 145.
11. Antonio Gramsci, "The Intellectuals," from *Selections From The Prison Notebooks*, edited and translated by Quinton Hoare and Geoffrey Nowell Smith (New York: International Publishers, 1971), p. 9.
12. Stephen Jay Gould, *The Mismeasure of Man*, (New York: W. W. Norton and Company, 1996).
13. Gramsci, *The Prison Notebooks*, p. 9.
14. Gramsci, *The Prison Notebooks*, p. 9.
15. Gramsci, *The Prison Notebooks*, p. 10.
16. Gramsci, *The Prison Notebooks*, p. 11.
17. Erdal, D. and Whiten, A. (1994). "On human egalitarianism: an evolutionary product of Machiavellian status escalation?". *Current Anthropology* **35** (2): 175–183. doi:10.1086/204255.
    Erdal, D. and A. Whiten. Egalitarianism and Machiavellian intelligence in human evolution. In P. Mellars and K. Gibson (eds), *Modelling the early human mind*. (Cambridge: McDonald Institute Monographs, 1996).
    Christopher Boehm, Hierarchy in the Forest: The Evolution of Egalitarian Behavior, (Cambridge MA: Harvard University Press, 2001).
18. Dunbar, Robin, *Grooming, Gossip, and the Evolution of Language* (London: Faber and Faber, 1996).
19. Leakey, Richard, *Origins Reconsidered*, p. 181.
20. Leakey, *Origins Reconsidered*, p. 185.
21. Leakey, *Origins Reconsidered*, p. 285.
22. Leakey, *Origins Reconsidered*, p. 305.
23. Eliade, Mircea, *Shamanism, Archaic Techniques of Ecstasy*, (Bollingen Series, LXXVI, Princeton University Press, 1972), pp. 3–7.
24. Leakey, Richard, *Origins Reconsidered*, pp. 233–234.
25. Bernstein, William, *Masters of the Word*, (New York, Grove Press, 2013).

26. Coser, Lewis A., *Men of Ideas, A Sociologist's View*, (New York: The Free Press, 1970), p. viii; and Edward Shils, *The Intellectuals and the Powers*, (Chicago: University of Chicago Press, 1972), p. 16.
27. Coser, Lewis A., *Men of Ideas, A Sociologist's View*, p. 31.
28. Shils, *The Intellectuals and the Powers*, p. 16.
29. Eco, Umberto, *Six Walks in the Fictional Woods* (Harvard University Press, 1995), p. 89.
30. Weber, Max, from a collection of his texts entitled *From Max Weber*, edited by H.H. Gerth and C. Wright Mills, (New York: Oxford University Press, 1958), p. 216.
31. Weber, Max, from a collection of his texts entitled *From Max Weber*, edited by H.H. Gerth and C. Wright Mills, p. 243.
32. Boggs, Carl, *Intellectuals and the Crisis of Modernity*, (Albany: State University of New York, 1993), p. 181.
33. Sadri, Ahmed, *Max Weber's Sociology of Intellectuals*, (New York: Oxford University Press, 1992), p. 59.
34. Sadri, Ahmed, *Max Weber's Sociology of Intellectuals*, p. 118.
35. Coser, Lewis A., *Men of Ideas, A Sociologist's View*, p. viii.
36. Rieff, Phillip, editor, *On Intellectuals*, (New York: Doubleday and Co., 1969), p. 42.
37. Gouldner, Alvin W., *The Future of Intellectuals and the Rise of the New Class*, p. 48.
38. Gouldner, Alvin W., *The Future of Intellectuals and the Rise of the New Class*.
39. "The Open Book: This Is Not the End of the Book" by Philip Marchand, from http://arts.nationalpost.com/2011/07/15/open-book-this-is-not-the-end-of-the-book/.
40. Deresiewicz, William, "How College Sold Its Soul," Harper's Magazine, September 2015, pp. 25–32.

CHAPTER 3

A Medievalist in Hibernation

In Eco's breakthrough first novel, a pair of medieval monks, a highly learned Franciscan, and his novice Benedictine protégé, investigate a series of mysterious deaths at a monastery in 1327. In Dan Brown's *The Da Vinci Code* a contemporary professor of symbology investigates historical mysteries about ancient religious conspiracies and secret plots linked to the artist Leonardo Da Vinci from the Renaissance. Both novels are historical whodunits that became phenomenal bestsellers, but what fundamentally differentiates them is the way in which they reflect their author's personal background and motives for becoming a novelist because Eco's entry into the bestseller list came after almost 30 years as a prominent international scholar rooted in the Middle Ages.

In the "Postscript" to *The Name of the Rose*, Eco described himself as a "medievalist in hibernation": "At a certain point, I said to myself that, since the Middle Ages were my day-to-day fantasy, I might as well write a novel actually set in that period. As I have said in interviews, I know the present only through the television screen, whereas I have a direct knowledge of the Middle Ages."[1] Although the brief preface to *The Name of the Rose*, by the unnamed discoverer of the medieval manuscript, describes the novel in escapist terms as "a tale of books" that is "immeasurably remote in time...gloriously lacking in any relevance for our day, atemporally alien to our hopes and our certainties,"[2] Eco asserts just the opposite in the previously mentioned collection of essays entitled *Travels in Hyperreality*. Rather than being totally "alien" and "lacking in

© The Author(s) 2017
D. Merrell, *Umberto Eco, The Da Vinci Code, and the Intellectual in the Age of Popular Culture*, DOI 10.1007/978-3-319-54789-3_3

any relevance" to our contemporary concerns, Eco asserts in "The Return of the Middle Ages" that: "all the problems of the Western world emerged in the Middle Ages: Modern languages, merchant cities, capitalistic economy (along with banks, checks, and prime rate) are inventions of medieval society." He goes on to cite the "rise of modern armies," "the modern concept of the national state," "the struggle between the poor and the rich," "our contemporary notion of love," "the conflict between church and state," and "the technological transformation of labor." For Eco, "looking at the Middle Ages thus means looking at our infancy." But the Middle Ages, according to Eco, can also be viewed "as a sort of escapism a la Tolkien"[3] which is evidenced by the enduring popularity of the *Lord of the Rings* saga. This indicates, for Eco, that there is a strong attraction to the Middle Ages by a popular readership: "Indeed, it seems that people like the Middle Ages. A few minutes in an American bookstore allows you to discover many interesting specimens of this neo-medieval wave."[4]

Concerning his motive for becoming a novelist, Eco indicated that: "I wrote a novel because I had a yen to do it. I believe this is sufficient reason to set out to tell a story. Man is a storytelling animal by nature."[5] Let's explore briefly then the story of what led Eco to become a scholar of the Middle Ages, and how his medieval studies became a foundation for his practice as a contemporary public intellectual who mediates between the somewhat cloistered domain of academia and the consumerist, mass media marketplace of popular culture.

Eco's first published works as a medieval scholar were highly acclaimed studies of *The Aesthetics of Thomas Aquinas* (1956), and *Art and Beauty in the Middle Ages* (1959) which grew out of his doctoral dissertation at the University of Turin in 1954. He explains in the preface to the English version of *The Aesthetics of Thomas Aquinas* (1988) that he was drawn to the study of Aquinas for "his method, his exemplary rigor and clarity... [that] were for me the great lessons of medieval philosophy. I still accept its clean style of argument, and I suspect that I am still under its influence..."[6] In the "Postscript" to *The Name of the Rose*, Eco indicates how the Middle Ages have served him as a way of understanding contemporary society:

> I arrived at scholarship by crossing symbolic forests inhabited by unicorns and gryphons... under the surveillance of a plump and rationalistic Aquinas... This taste and this passion have never abandoned me, even if later, for moral reasons... I have pursued other things. And so the Middle

Ages have remained, if not my profession, my hobby – and a constant temptation: I see the period everywhere, transparently overlaying my daily concerns, which do not look medieval, though they are.[7]

Eco also notes in the preface to *The Aesthetics of Thomas Aquinas* that he "began [his dissertation] in 1952 [at age 20] in a spirit of adherence to the religious world of Thomas Aquinas."[8] Apart from being drawn to the intellectual method of inquiry and argumentation of the Middle Ages and its usefulness for understanding contemporary society, the focus of Eco's medieval studies arose out of his early upbringing as a Catholic youth in Italy. As one would expect, based on its long history as the capital of the worldwide Catholic Church, Italy has one of the highest percentages of Catholics of any major country in the world, up to 81 percent according to some sources.[9] But, while the overwhelming majority of Italians are Catholic by virtue of their cultural heritage, they are not all devoted adherents to the faith. Eco, however, by his own account and according to other sources, was not only a pious Catholic, but, in fact, became a devout Catholic lay activist. As we will consider further, while Eco pursued his intellectual development by focusing on the synthesis of religion and philosophy in the study of Thomas Aquinas, he was a prominent student leader in the national Catholic youth organization, the *Gioventu Italiana di Azione Cattolica* (GIAC, or Young Italians for Catholic Action) as a self-described "militant Catholic intellectual."[10]

Ex Caelis Oblatus

Eco's development as a devout Catholic activist can be traced to the circumstances of his early childhood and the special significance of his family name derived from his grandfather who was abandoned at birth and given the surname "Eco" by "an inventive civil servant" as an acronym for "*ex caelis oblatus*" which means "offered by the heavens."[11] Whether this instilled in Eco a fervent religious devotion from an early age he doesn't say. But, according to his own acknowledgment about his religious affiliations, his later focus of study would be understandable as a direct consequence of his Italian cultural heritage dominated by the Catholic Church and Aquinas as its exemplary intellectual. Aquinas was given the title of "Common Doctor" because of his great breadth of knowledge which Eco reflected through his encyclopedic scope as a contemporary scholar.

Eco was born in 1932 in the small northern Italian town of Alessandria and thus outside of the major urban cultural centers of northern Italy. According to a review in *The Chronicle of Higher Education* by Carlo Romano, "Umberto grew up seeing Turin and Milan as promised lands for a child born to lower-middle-class parents yet hungry for a cultural life."[12] Eco's father was an accountant and an ardent patriot who served as a soldier in the Italian military in three wars. As Eco recalled in an interview, when his father was called to military duty during WWII, Eco "was relocated with his mother and sister to live in the countryside, up in Monferrato, a Piedmontese village that was at the epicenter of the resistance"[13] to seek refuge from the Allied bombing of Alessandria. From these early formative years Eco's identity as a devout Catholic was instilled in him in a potent way through his schooling by priests from the Salesian order. During WWII (1939–1945), when Eco was between seven and 13 years of age, he came under the tutelage of Salesian priests whom he credits in his writings and interviews as being a powerful influence in his early development.[14]

Giovanni Bosco and the Salesian Order

The Salesian Order was founded in 1845 by Giovanni Bosco (1815–1888) to provide assistance to young children displaced from impoverished rural areas to the emerging industrial centers of northern Italy centered in Turin. Giovanni Bosco adopted the name of the order from St. Francis de Sales (1567–1622), a monk who was inspired to pursue a more benevolent approach to the underprivileged after a crisis of faith. As a remedy for his crisis, De Sales had sought the guidance of St. Philip Neri who changed his conception of God as a figure of nurturing love rather than stern moral judgment. That inspiration motivated De Sales to found an innovative religious community without formal vows called the Oratory of St. Phillip Neri dedicated to the common people. Although De Sales was born to a noble family and distinguished himself as an intellectual, he was noted for his *Introduction to the Devout Life*, a religious guidebook written especially to be accessible to laypeople with a limited education.

In the wake of the industrial revolution that rapidly transformed Italian society in the nineteenth century, especially in northern Italy, Giovanni Bosco followed in the tradition of St. Phillip Neri and St. Frances de Sales to establish the Salesian Order. Due to his upbringing in a family of farm laborers in a rural village in the northern province of Piedmont, Giovanni

Bosco had firsthand experience of the deprivations of the Italian rural poor which inspired his dedication to the impoverished Italian youth who fled the countryside in great numbers seeking work in the industrialized urban centers of northern Italy. His oratorium involved a synthesis of reason, religion, and empathy instead of the previous emphasis on rigid discipline in adapting rural youth to the industrial workforce.

Eco recalled in an interview how San Giovanni Bosco provided him with a strong sense of the value of community:

> I always like to tell the story of Bosco. San Giovanni Bosco. This Salesian priest in the middle of the 19th century who got the idea that there was a whole new generation of young people who were working from a very young age in factories, and so were dispersed and separated from the family. He invented the oratorium, which was a community, to which those who worked could go to play and discuss. And for those who couldn't work, he established typographies, activities in which they could take part. So, he was matching the problem of despair and isolation in the industrial society with the possibility of people meeting each other, and obviously also having a religious purpose. It was a great social invention.

Although Eco's family was not among the working poor of northern Italy, his displacement during WWII to a rural village exposed him to the approach of the Salesian Order who adapted the elitist institution of the Catholic Church to the needs of the uneducated and socially disadvantaged, for example, through St. Francis de Sales' treatise on devotion that was unusual for its time in attempting to communicate religious doctrine to a broad lay audience with a rudimentary education. The legacy of Don Bosco would have given Eco a sense of the need for elite institutions such as the Church and academia to be critically aware of the impact of modern social transformation on the masses and to engage in educational practices accessible to those outside of these institutions.

Fascists, Partisans, and Liberators

Eco also grew up under the Fascist regime of Benito Mussolini (1883–1945) who became Italy's Prime Minister in 1922, ten years before Eco was born. Mussolini was initially very popular in Italy for reasserting social order after a long period of political strife and disruptive labor strikes. Like Hitler, Mussolini promoted himself through the Fascist cult of personality, and he established a similar Fascist youth movement that glorified heroic ideals and athleticism. In a lecture at Columbia University in 1995 commemorating the fiftieth anniversary of the liberation of Europe entitled "Ur-Fascism," Eco recalled his youthful experience of growing up under Mussolini:

> In 1942 when I was ten, I won the first prize at the *Ludi Juveniles*, a compulsory open competition for all young Italian Fascists – that is to say, for all young Italians. I had written a virtuoso piece of rhetoric in response to the essay title "Should We Die for the Glory of Mussolini and the Immortal Destiny of Italy?" My answer was in the affirmative. I was a smart kid.

After the fall of Mussolini in 1943 and the German occupation of northern Italy when Eco was just 11 years old, he found himself in the middle of the resistance movement because Nizza Monferrato, where he spent the war years, became the capital of what was called the Partisan Republic of Monferrato which was one of the most hotly contested areas during the occupation:

> I spent two of my earliest years surrounded by SS, Fascists, and Resistance fighters all busily shooting at one another, and I learned how to dodge bullets. It wasn't bad training.[15]

Despite his family's attempt to protect him from the effects of the war, Eco thus had direct experience of regular skirmishes between Fascist forces and resistance fighters that he discussed in an interview in *The Paris Review*:

> I remember watching shoot-outs between Fascists and Partisans, and almost wishing I could join the brawl. At one point I even remember dodging a bullet myself, and jumping to the ground from a perch.... During this period, living in the countryside, a young man was forced to learn how to survive.[16]

After living during these skirmishes, Eco recalled the celebration at the end of the war:

> In April 1945 the partisans took Milan. Two days later they arrived in the little town where I lived. It was a joyous moment. The main square was crowded with people singing and waving flags, calling loudly for Mimo, the leader of the local Resistance movement... [who] appeared on the balcony

of the town hall, pale; with one hand, he tried to calm the crowd. I was waiting for him to begin his speech, given that my entire childhood had been marked by Mussolini's great historic speeches, the most important parts of which we used to memorize at school. Silence. Mimo's voice was hoarse, you could hardly hear him. He said: "Citizens, friends. After so many painful sacrifices... here we are. Glory to those who fell for freedom." That was it. He went back inside. The crowd gave a shout, the partisans raised their weapons and fired into the air in festive mood. We kids rushed to collect the shell cases, precious collector's items, but I had also learned that freedom of speech means freedom from rhetoric.[17]

Eco also recalled his first meeting with the American liberators:

Some days later I saw the first American soldiers. They were African-Americans. The first Yankee I met was a black man, Joseph, who introduced me to the wonders of Dick Tracy and L'il Abner.... One of the officers... was a well educated man and knew a little French. So my first image of the American liberators, after all those pale faces in black shirts, was of a cultivated black man in a yellow green uniform... who gave me my first chewing gum and I chewed it all day. At night I would put the gum in a glass of water, to keep it fresh for the next day.

Eco's experience of growing up during the violence and deprivations of WWII, and the euphoria of liberation by the American soldiers, was so powerful for him that it became the source of an episode recounted in his second novel *Foucault's Pendulum* which prompted the town of Nizza Monferrato to make Eco an honorary citizen in 2010. The home of his uncle where Eco lived during the war and the oratorium of Don Bosco are also memorials to his time there although the oratorium has since been converted into a sports complex.

THE *LICEO CLASSICO*

After WWII, Eco returned to Alessandria to pursue his middle school education at a *liceo classico*. This institution, particular to the Italian educational system and more generally to the European classical inheritance, is also a key factor for understanding Eco's intellectual foundations. The *liceo classico* fosters the ancient tradition of humanist learning emphasizing literature, history, and philosophy with an intensive grounding in both Latin and Greek. It is the privileged track for

Italians aspiring to the professional elite in journalism, academia, government, etc. The *liceo classico,* along with the *liceo scientifico* that emphasizes the practical and applied sciences, constitute the two major educational tracks that young Italians must choose by age 14 to determine whether they will pursue "classical" humanistic studies, or the alternative of practical, technical expertise and scientific research. Since the roots of the *liceo classico* can be traced back to the ancient Greek Academy of Plato and the Lyceum of Aristotle from the fourth century B.C. and the seven liberal arts of Medieval Scholasticism, Eco thus reflects an educational tradition that spans the full breadth of Western intellectual history and the synthesis of philosophy and religion which indicates the broad gulf between intellectuals in the humanistic tradition such as Eco and a popular audience.

GIOVENTU ITALIANA DI AZIONE CATTOLICA

Along with these intensive engagements in classical learning, Eco's educational development was closely integrated with his involvement in an increasingly militant role as a Catholic youth activist that can be traced to his experience with the Salesian oratory. Eco recalled that: "I joined the *Gioventu Italiana di Azione Cattolica* as a boy at age thirteen," and he characterized these years as "a period of great religious commitment and fervor."[18] The GIAC arose in the wake of the Risorgimento, the modern struggle for Italian statehood that liberated Italy from foreign domination in the nineteenth century. The forerunner of the GIAC, the *Societa della Gioventu Cattolica* (Society of Young Catholics) was founded in 1867 immediately after the initial triumph of the Risorgimento, by students at the University of Bologna. Their motto was Prayer, Action, Sacrifice, and they dedicated themselves to the following four principles: (1) obedience to the Pope, (2) religious education, (3) a life dedicated to Christian values, and (4) charity to the weak and poor. These tenets make them similar in doctrine and practice to a lay version of the Jesuit Order. And like the Jesuits, the *Gioventu Cattolica* became involved in religious and political controversies that continued into the period of Eco's involvement. The tendency toward social activism of these youth-oriented Catholic organizations aroused ongoing concerns and conservative backlash from the papacy which, as we will consider in the next chapter, had a major impact on Eco's identity as a Catholic lay activist and his early development as an intellectual.

THE AESTHETICS OF THOMAS AQUINAS

Moving from these broad associations of Eco with the long tradition of the social practices of the Salesian Order and his early schooling in the *liceo classico*, we can consider now the core focus that Eco pursued as an intellectual and Catholic youth activist through his acknowledged devotion to the "clean style of argument" and "religious world" of Thomas Aquinas. Aquinas represents historically the most comprehensive attempt by the Catholic Church to synthesize philosophy and religion. His ideas continue to be a foundation for contemporary adherents to the Catholic faith especially in preparation for the priesthood. Eco's particular focus, however, was on the aesthetics of Aquinas which was innovative, and, as Eco noted, "very controversial"[19] at that time because medieval scholars had traditionally held that Aquinas did not have a theory of aesthetics. Aquinas was, in his own time, also innovative and sometimes controversial in his attempt to synthesize Christian theology with the recovery of the ideas of Aristotle in the thirteenth century.

In his earliest published work, *The Aesthetics of Thomas Aquinas*, Eco describes Aquinas's project in the thirteenth century as an attempt to provide a complete description of the cosmos, like the architecture of the cathedrals, in which "everything was in its proper place."[20] The challenge confronting Aquinas in the thirteenth century was to resolve the longstanding tensions in Medieval Christianity between the revelation of God in biblical scripture, and the classical inheritance of analytical reason from the pagan philosophy of Plato and especially from the writings of Aristotle that had recently been appropriated from Arabic sources and then revised through new translations from the Greek into Latin that were thought to be more faithful to the original ideas of Aristotle.

The grand synthesis of philosophy and religion undertaken by Aquinas thus involved the reconsideration of the ancient inheritance from the Greeks stretching back over nearly 1,700 years. For this reason, it will be helpful to consider a concise portrait of the historical legacy of Western philosophy from the ancients that Aquinas confronted as both a theologian and philosopher during the late Middle Ages, and from which Eco derived his focus on Aquinas's notion of aesthetics. Exploring the long arc of intellectual development from the ancients serves as well for understanding more broadly Eco's particular practice as a contemporary intellectual with an encyclopedic knowledge of the Western intellectual tradition. As Peter Bondanella points out in the preface to his *New*

Essays on Umberto Eco: "The breadth and scope of Eco's writings qualify him as what the Italians call a *tuttologo* – someone who knows something important about virtually everything."[21] This expansive view across the ages is a central theme, for example, in Eco's first novel *The Name of the Rose* as well as in his later novels. The synthesis of philosophy and religion by Aquinas is especially useful as well for considering how the problem of language arose from the very beginning of Greek philosophy which serves as a useful framework for understanding Eco's pioneering efforts in the contemporary field of semiotics that analyzes our linguistic relation to the world.

THE UPWARD AND THE DOWNWARD PATH

A highlight of any tourist visit to the Vatican Museum in Rome is the Room of the *Segnatura* to see the marvelous frescoes by the Renaissance artist Raphael. The Room of the *Segnatura* was just one of the papal apartments that Raphael was commissioned to paint, but it has special significance because it originally served as the library and study of Pope Julius II, the great warrior pope and patron of both Raphael (1483–1520) and Michelangelo (1475–1564) two of the most celebrated artists of the Renaissance. At the same time that Raphael was commissioned to paint the Room of the *Segnatura*, Michelangelo was working on the ceiling of the Sistine Chapel (1508–1512). For the Room of the *Segnatura*, as inspiration for the Pope at his private study, Raphael depicted on opposite walls the realm of spiritual knowledge and the realm of worldly knowledge. Spiritual knowledge is represented by the fresco of the *Disputation of the Sacrament* that depicts the holy altar with the communion wafer representing the holy sacrament. Christ and God the father are directly above, and, on either side are biblical figures such as Adam and Moses and theologians including a prominent portrait of Thomas Aquinas. On the opposite wall, worldly knowledge is represented by the famous fresco of *The School of Athens* that depicts the philosophical inheritance from the ancient Greeks with Plato, at the center, pointing upward, and Aristotle, beside him, pointing downward toward the earth. On either side of them are major figures in ancient Greek philosophy and science such as the astronomer and geographer Ptolemy (100–170 C.E.); the mathematician, Pythagoras (c. 570–c. 495 B.C.); and the ancient scholar of geometry, Euclid (323–283 C.E.).

The contrasting gestures of Plato and Aristotle in Raphael's *The School of Athens* provide the clearest possible visual representation of what can be called the upward and downward paths to knowledge. These foundational pathways served subsequently as the twin pillars of medieval Scholasticism that confronted Aquinas in the thirteenth century. Although Christianity had displaced the so-called pagan philosophy derived from the Greeks, the early Christian theologians, such as Augustine (354–330 A.D.), saw the value of incorporating the Greek philosophical inheritance into Christian theology as a way of linking spiritual and worldly knowledge. The upward path of Plato was readily integrated into Christian theology because Plato's gesture toward otherworldly perfect forms was understood as pointing to the spiritual realm of God. Aristotle's downward focus was also incorporated for understanding worldly knowledge and for determining the truth of propositions through his method of logical analysis.

But difficulties arose over time concerning the relation between worldly and spiritual knowledge because of the logical analysis of Aristotle that threatened to undermine the foundations of Christian theology. This was the challenge that Aquinas confronted in the thirteenth century. The legacy of the upward and the downward paths that arose from classical antiquity of the fourth century B.C., and the way they were integrated into Christian theology by Aquinas in the thirteenth century, nearly two millennia later, was the inspiration for Eco's origins as a medievalist. And, as we will consider, these two contrasting approaches to knowledge continue to pose fundamental questions in contemporary philosophy about the problem of language that Eco pursued in his later development as an intellectual.

THE WIZARD OF "IS"

Plato's gesture upward to the truth of our being can be seen to arise from his assertion in Book Five of the *Republic* that the good or ideal state can only come about if led by philosophers because of their singular ability to understand the truth of the world as the basis for ordering the human community:

> Until philosophers rule as kings in cities or those who are now called kings and leading men genuinely and adequately philosophize, that is, until political power and philosophy entirely coincide, while the many natures

who at present pursue either one exclusively are forcibly prevented from doing so, cities will have no rest from evils, Glaucon, nor, I think, will the human race.[22]

Plato's privileging of the philosopher as the only one qualified to rule over human society can be seen as one of the earliest assertions of the highly specialized knowledge and elitist social role of the intellectual. Plato believed that there were broad innate differences in human capacity that called for a clear division of labor in the ideal state. The philosopher, according to Plato, was the only one with the specialized intellectual capacity for understanding the ultimate truth and thus for governing the ideal human community. It should be noted, however, that, even in ancient Greek philosophy, there was an alternative view by intellectuals such as Lycophron who argued against the assumption of an innate superiority on the part of the elite: "Now the nobility of good birth is obscure, and its grandeur a matter of words."[23]

What special capacity, then, did the philosopher possess? Plato asserts that the state must be led by philosophers because they are the only ones with the knowledge of what "is." Although the meaning of the word "is" may seem absurdly apparent, it presented a fundamental problem for the ancients that both Plato and Aristotle tried to resolve. The problem has continued into our own times, for example, through a trivial but instructive example. Former President Bill Clinton famously responded in a deposition in 1998, concerning the Monica Lewinsky scandal, that: "It depends on what the meaning of the word 'is' is." His response, of course, was strongly ridiculed from the political opposition as an absurd instance of legalistic semantics.

While the meaning of the word "is" may seem readily apparent, it posed a fundamental problem in the establishment of philosophical rationalism by the ancient Greeks. As the translators of the Hackett edition of the *Republic* indicate, the ancient Greek word for "is," *einai*, was inherently ambiguous because it could mean (1) the distinction between actual existence and non-existence, (2) the specific quality or character of things, or (3) the distinction between true and false assertions about things. The ambiguity in the meaning of the word "is" can be seen as a central concern for Plato in the *Republic* that led him toward the upward path to knowledge. Besides its inherent ambiguity, the problem with the word "is" was linked to longstanding doubts in the ancient world about the reliability of our senses for determining the truth because of visual distortions such as mirages, and because of the change and dissolution of things over time through erosion and decay. How could humans determine the truth of what "is" if things in the sensory world were always subject to change and dissolution over time? A major consideration for Plato was also the difference in perception between individuals about the character and meaning of things that seemed to be the cause of constant discord in the human community. The way that language reflects our experience of the world was thus a central problem in the development of ancient Greek philosophy.

In the *Republic*, Plato attempts to work through the problem of knowledge in the following way. He first asks: "does the person who knows know something or nothing?" to which the response is, of course, "something." Plato then asks, "Something that is or something that is not?" And the response is: "Something that is, for how could something that is not be known?" Plato then concludes that "No matter how many ways we examine it, what is completely is completely knowable, and what is in no way is in every way unknowable." So the task for the seeker of knowledge is to focus on what "is" because it is "completely knowable." The key word here is "completely" because the problem in the quest for knowledge, according to Plato, is that there are things in between what is and what is not: "Now, if anything is such as to be and also not to be, won't it be intermediate between what purely is and what in no way is?"

For Plato, what "is" must be completely knowable. But there are things that appear to have being and not have being because they are perceived in different ways by different people. The central distinction for Plato is between "knowledge," which is of those things that have one, unchanging state of true being, and "opinion" which is of those things that can be perceived as both having and not having being according to the way they are perceived. As Plato points out: "... of all the many beautiful things, is there one that will not also appear ugly? Or is there one of those just things that will not also appear unjust? Or one of those pious things that will not also appear impious?"[24] Knowledge, according to Plato, is the awareness of what "is" in the sense of being purely and completely knowable. As a result, he dismisses opinion as a lower or intermediate level of understanding because it is based on differences in perspective. Those things that can be perceived as both having and not having particular states of being, based on different points of view, are not reliable for understanding our true being as humans and for organizing the ideal state.

Plato asserts that knowledge must be the perception of the realm of pure existence uncorrupted by the imperfections of the sensory world and the differences in perspective between individuals. This is why he asserts that the pathway to knowledge can only be pursued by the philosopher. But how does the philosopher determine the difference between "knowledge" and "opinion"? According to Plato, the philosopher is able to achieve an awareness of true knowledge through the process of "dialectic" which is a purifying regimen of questioning, analysis, and contemplation that frees the philosopher through an ascending path from the lower realm of sensory knowledge and opinion to the upward path to the perfect forms. As Plato explains in the *Republic*, the realm of true being is ultimately known through a mystical experience like a religious epiphany that separates the philosopher from the experience of others. This epiphany of knowledge was described by a later devotee of Neoplatonism (the subsequent development of Plato's ideas), in the autobiography of the fourth century theologian Augustine (354–430 C.E.), who, however, found it to be a fleeting experience which caused him to convert to Christianity.

Because the realm of true knowledge is so far removed from the world of the senses and opinion, Plato depicts the state of most humans through his famous metaphor of the darkened cave in which humans are chained to a wall on which the shadows of objects are cast. Behind them and outside the cave is the sun that illuminates the true realm of pure knowledge that is only attainable by the philosopher. The realm of true knowledge, according to Plato, is, in fact, so far removed from the everyday sensory experience of most humans that it will be difficult for the philosopher, once having attained the experience of the truth, to return to the world of shadows. He also asserted that the experience of the ultimate truth would make the philosopher appear alien and suspicious to the majority of humans imprisoned in the cave. This is one of the earliest expressions of an inevitable divide between the philosopher as an intellectual with specialized knowledge and the masses that are perceived as inevitably ignorant and deluded.

Aristotle and the Downward Path

Aristotle's contrasting gesture toward the earth in Raphael's fresco *The School of Athens* represents the alternative downward path to knowledge. Aristotle attempted to resolve the problem of the word "is" by defining the ways in which we express our relation to the objects of our sensory experience through an analysis of the medium of language. The challenge for Aristotle was to overcome the problem of generating reliable truths from our sensory experience of the world that led Plato to focus on ideal forms. In particular, he had to resolve Plato's distinction between knowledge and opinion. Aristotle took up these problems in what he called the *Analytics* which involved defining the basic components of language and determining how they were organized to generate reliable truths that could be demonstrated on the model of mathematics. Aristotle's *Analytics* was consequently based on a fundamental assessment of how human language functions to organize our sensory relation to the world.

Plato and the Problem with Names

Plato had previously considered the role of language in the pursuit of knowledge in the dialogue entitled *Cratylus* only to dismiss it as an unreliable focus for understanding. In the *Cratylus*, Plato responds to a series of questions concerning the origin and function of names for designating the things that we experience in the world beginning with a discussion of the origin and meaning of both personal names such as "Agamemnon" and "Apollo" and the names of types of things such as "man" and "horse." Plato considers names as the most basic component of language in referring to things in the world: "a name is an instrument of teaching and distinguishing natures."[25] But because the names of things become altered over time through derivations he ultimately dismissed the naming function of language as a faulty instrument of knowledge: "For we should remember that if a person goes on analyzing names into words, and inquiring also into the elements out of which the words are formed, and keeps on always repeating this process, he who has to answer him must at last give up the inquiry in despair."[26] This view is reaffirmed toward the end of the dialogue when the problem of "opinion" versus "knowledge" is reconsidered in relation to the naming function of language:

> But if this is a battle of names, some of them asserting that they are like the truth, others contending that *they* are, how or by what criterion are we to decide between them? For there are no other names to which appeal can be made, but obviously recourse must be had to another standard which, without employing names, will make clear which of the two are right, and this must be a standard which shows the truth of things.

Plato concludes that: "the knowledge of things is not to be derived from names. No, they must be studied and investigated in themselves." As a result, Plato asserts that: "no man of sense will like to put himself or the education of his mind in the power of names."[27] Plato's dismissal of the naming function of language reaffirms his bias toward otherworldly forms that made his ideas readily acceptable in the medieval transition to Christian theology.

The One and the Many

Like Plato, Aristotle inquired into the function of language by considering names as the designators of the things of the world. But while Plato considered primarily the origins of names and their variability over time that made them unreliable for determining the truth, Aristotle considered names as tools for designating the broad range of states of being through an analysis of the function of the word "is." According to Garrett Thomson and Marshall Missner: "Aristotle argues that Plato's theory of forms is partly a result of a confusion concerning the term 'is.' These arguments are based on Aristotle's insight that the word 'is' has different uses which are reflected in the categories."[28] In the *Physics*, which was Aristotle's answer to Plato's problem of change over time in the sensory world, Aristotle asserts that: "Thinkers of the more recent past...were much agitated lest things might turn out to be both one and many at the same time. Some, like Lycophron, did away with the word 'is'; others sought to remodel the language, and replace 'That man is pale' 'That man is walking' by 'That man pales' 'That man walks,' for fear that by inserting 'is' they would render the one many – as if things were said to be or be one in only one way."[29]

The problem of the meaning of the word "is," according to Aristotle, involved the way in which it was applied in reference to things. Plato believed that the disorder of human society resulted from the inability of humans to understand that things could only have ONE, stable, unified meaning. If things had MANY diverse meanings based on different perspectives, how could human society agree on the truth? As a result, there would be no basis for a just and ideal society. That's the problem that Aristotle, above, refers to as the "one and the many." It is a problem that persists as a fundamental concern in contemporary philosophy because a function of our language capacity is our ability to group things together according to similar characteristics under ONE concept. But our language can attribute MANY different characteristics to things. So how do we determine the truth of things when they can be considered from multiple perspectives?

Aristotle's 10 Categories

Aristotle attempted to resolve the confusion about the word "is" by defining in the most general and comprehensive way the different states of being that can be referred to with the word "is." He could thus overcome the confusion about the meaning of the word "is" by showing that it had several meanings in relation to things while having a unified character as a component of language. Aristotle's attempt to clarify the problem of how language referred to the things of the world led to his formulation of 10 categories for describing the most general and fundamental conceptions of what "is" as substance, quantity, quality, relation, place, time, position, possession, action, and passivity.[30] This legacy was so powerful that it endured into the eighteenth century when it was reformulated into 12 categories by the German philosopher Immanuel Kant (1724–1804), and then in the nineteenth century by the American philosopher Charles Sanders Peirce (1839–1914) who reduced the number of categories to three. Peirce was one of the founders of semiotics who was a major influence on Eco's semiotic theory.

But Aristotle also links names with verbs as components of sentences or propositions that can be evaluated as statements about the world. As Aristotle specifies in *On Interpretation*, the things of the world designated through names are linked to states of being through statements: "First we must settle what a name is and what a verb is, and then what a negation, an affirmation, a statement, and a sentence are" because "falsity and truth have to do with combination and separation."[31] Names by themselves are just designators of observable or conceptual states of being. Verbs link these states of being with particular things. While Plato believed that the diverse perceptions of things made them unreliable for determining the truth, Aristotle devised a way of evaluating the truth or falsity of statements about the world through the analysis of propositions which indicates how Aristotle tried to resolve the problem of language by defining its components and how they function in relation to each other.

Aristotle's Four Causes

Besides his response to the problem of naming things and determining the truth of statements about them through language as a way of satisfying the challenges raised by Plato, Aristotle sought to respond to the problem of motion and change over time that made Plato reject the sensory world as unreliable. In the *Physics,* Aristotle conceived of four causes that determine the dynamics of change in the world, from potentiality to actuality, and from coming into being and passing away, while retaining a unified character:

> Plainly, then, these are the causes, and this is how many they are. They are four, and the student of nature should know about them all, and it will be his method, when stating on account of what, to get back to them all: the matter, the form, the thing which effects the change, and what the thing is for.[32]

The four causes were traditionally referred to as: material, formal, efficient, and final. The material cause is the passive, primordial, physical substance from which things come into being such as the marble from which sculptures are made. The formal cause is the structuring mode by which things acquire their outward aspect and function. The efficient cause is what brings about something which can be natural forces or the work of a human artisan. The final cause is the ultimate purpose or function of a thing that can also be conceived of as its fulfillment of change from potentiality to actuality. Aristotle's **formal cause** became a central concept that was taken up by Aquinas in the thirteenth century and, in turn, greatly influenced Eco's focus on aesthetics in our own time.

Thomas Aquinas and the Knowledge of the Beautiful

Aristotle's major works were mostly inaccessible in Europe for almost a thousand years until they were recovered from Muslim scholars and were revised through translations from the original Greek into Latin in the late Middle Ages. Their rediscovery was the catalyst for Aquinas's great synthesis of the upward path of Plato and Christian theology and the downward path of Aristotle which was the legacy that Eco chose to pursue as a student and Catholic youth activist.

Eco's intellectual engagement during this time as a "militant Catholic intellectual" was consistent with the study of Aquinas who, as a fellow

Italian and canonized doctor of the Church, would have provided an especially useful model for linking religious ideals with a rigorous analysis of the sensory world. Eco's contribution to the study of Aquinas was an exploration of the previously discounted role of aesthetics and beauty in medieval philosophy. Previous scholars of the Middle Ages had long held the view that medieval philosophers did not have a theory of aesthetics, so Eco's focus on the aesthetics of Aquinas was regarded at that time as controversial. Eco found in Aquinas's adoption of Aristotle's conceptions of matter and form, from his four causes, the basis for a medieval aesthetics which was also influenced by his mentor, Luigi Pareyson (1918–1991), at the University of Turin.

What Is "Aesthetics"?

Since Eco's first published works as a scholar were on *The Aesthetics of Thomas Aquinas* (1956) and *Art and Beauty in the Middle Ages* (1959), it will be helpful to first clarify what is meant by the terms "aesthetics" and "beauty" in relation to Aquinas and Christian theology and how these ideas influenced Eco's development as a contemporary intellectual. "Aesthetics" is commonly associated in contemporary usage with the arts and a sense of sophistication or refinement in the appreciation of style, design, composition, etc. It can also be thought of in sociological terms as the engagement with cultural artifacts, paintings, architecture, cinema, theater, music, etc., that are produced by and intended especially for the educated taste of elite society as a means of stimulating the senses and arousing an expanded consciousness about our relation to the world.

"Aesthetics" can thus be used in a variety of ways that may seem overly broad and imprecise. To understand the term "aesthetics" better, we can consider its roots. For example, the term "anaesthetic" is readily understood as a procedure for patients before surgery to temporarily numb the senses, or to temporarily render the patient unconscious to eliminate the sensation of pain. Thus "aesthetics" refers specifically to our sensory experience of the world. But isn't all of our experience of the world mediated through our senses? Not according to the long tradition arising from the ancients of contemplative knowledge that was thought to be separate from the world and internal to our cognitive faculties. Consider, for example, the legacy of Plato's rejection of sensory knowledge as inferior to the pure ideas attained by the philosopher. According to Raymond Williams (1921–1988), a prominent contemporary contributor to cultural studies, "aesthetics" comes from the Greek *aisthesis* that originally referred to "material things...perceptible by the senses, as distinct from things which were immaterial or which could only be thought."[33] As we considered in Chapter 1, the linguistic capacity of humans allows us to think of things "offline" without them being present as sensory stimuli. This capacity made it possible for humans to engage in internal reflection as a thought process separate from the sensory world. Contemplative thought beginning with the ancients was thus considered more profound and pure in an abstract way from the particulars of our sensory experience which is the focus of aesthetics.

In *The Aesthetics of Thomas Aquinas*, Eco notes that, although the term "aesthetics," was derived from the ancient Greek *aisthesis*, which meant "sense perception," it wasn't until modern times that "aesthetics" was first used to refer to a category of knowledge when it appeared in the work of the eighteenth-century German philosopher Alexander Baumgarten (1714–1762) in his two-volume treatise *Aesthetica* (1750–1758). Baumgarten described aesthetics as: "the science of sense knowledge, the theory of the liberal arts, the epistemology of the lower level of knowledge, the rules of thinking aesthetically, [and] the rules of reasoning by analogy." Aesthetics was thus conceived by Baumgarten as the domain of knowledge that was subordinate to the pure, conceptual domain of contemplative philosophy. While acknowledging that this definition would exclude medieval philosophers like Aquinas from participation in aesthetics, Eco asserts that, "if aesthetics refers to a whole range of issues connected with beauty – its definition, its functions, the ways of creating and of enjoying it – then the medievals did have aesthetic theories."

What Is Beauty?

Eco offers his own definition of aesthetics as: "the problem of the possible objective character, and the subjective conditions of what we call the experience of beauty."[34] Although the term aesthetics was not used by the medievals as a category of knowledge, Eco argues that the experience of beauty as sense perception in response to both natural and cultural objects was a prominent aspect of the medieval world. Eco cites the medieval historian E.R. Curtius's view that medieval scholars synthesized ancient Greek philosophy with Christian theology to develop an understanding of beauty unequivocally as "an attribute of God." But Curtius is also cited by Eco to point out the paradox that the medievals, far from lacking a concept of aesthetics in relation to the moderns, actually had a more comprehensive conception of beauty – as an intelligible reality in both art and nature – than the modern view that "over-values art."[35] Because medieval intellectuals considered beauty as an attribute of God, and God as the creative principle inherent in the universe, the evidence for God's creativity was found in nature as well as representations of the truth of God in art. Since the rise of the Enlightenment and modern science, the tendency of "modern" intellectuals is to think of beauty primarily as an aspect of works of art.

What, then, is meant in referring to things as "beautiful"? "Beauty" is also a concept that in everyday usage is often applied in a broad and imprecise manner. In our contemporary world dominated by popular culture, the beautiful can be considered as an individual's judgment of virtually anything, including natural objects, works of art, as well as the products of mass media consumerism, that arouse one's attention in an especially attractive, pleasing, or powerful way. Since the sense of the beautiful in our contemporary world of popular culture is democratically applied to each individual's judgment, it will vary extensively based on culture, class, age, gender, etc. So how can there be any unifying standard by which to determine the beautiful? For example, if the beautiful can be attributed to the products of popular culture such as pop songs and comic books as well as the products of elite culture such as classical music and literary novels, are there any standards of taste and judgment that can serve to distinguish what is beautiful? This is an important question for Eco that he derived from his foundational study of the beautiful in the ideas of Thomas Aquinas that motivated him to bridge between an analysis of popular and elite culture.

THE BEAUTY OF GOD'S CREATIVITY

Returning to the concept of beauty in the history of Western philosophy, we find that, for the medieval philosophers, there were specific, universal criteria for what constituted "the beautiful." According to Eco, medieval scholars "taught the Middle Ages to look upon things with a penetrating eye, to read the universe, to read nature, as if it were a vast store of symbols." They saw nature as pointing "toward God, and to God conceived of as Beauty revealing itself through harmonious design" and thus "openly and profoundly aesthetic."[36] A good example of the medieval perspective on the signs of God in nature can be found in the work of a fellow public intellectual and contemporary of Eco's, the French philosopher Michel Foucault (1926–1984), who uses an example from the *Traite des signatures* (1609) of Oswald Crollius, a sixteenth-century professor of medicine and alchemy, to describe how nature was perceived prior to the end of the sixteenth century through resemblances and similarities amongst the things of God's aesthetic creation:

> There exists a sympathy between aconite [a type of flower] and our eyes... This sign is easily legible in its seeds: they are tiny dark globes set in white skinlike coverings whose appearance is much like that of eyelids covering an eye. It is the same with the affinity of the walnut and the human head: what cures 'wounds of the pericranium' is the thick green rind covering the bones – the shell – of the fruit; but internal head ailments may be prevented by the use of the nut itself 'which is exactly like the brain in appearance'.[37]

According to Eco, if aesthetics can be understood as the sensory and cognitive participation in the experience of beauty, then, for medieval scholars such as Aquinas, beauty was understood as an essential "attribute of God." Rather than rejecting the sensory world as corrupt and unreliable as Plato did, Aquinas drew on the ideas of Aristotle to bring the downward path of the sensory world together with the upward path of contemplative knowledge and religion. As a result, as Eco noted, the medievals had a more comprehensive sense of beauty and aesthetics in every aspect of the world in relation to the modern age that focuses primarily on the elite world of art. As we will consider, because of his foundations as a medieval scholar, Eco adapts the conception, as noted above, of aesthetics as "the problem of the possible objective character, and the subjective conditions of what we call the experience of beauty" to the contemporary relation between elite and popular culture. When Eco later refers to works that have "aesthetic value,"[38] he means those that provoke a sense of "beauty" that arouses a higher or expanded consciousness of our relation to the world through a transformative experience. Beauty is the experience that arouses our awareness of the world and our potential for determining our own meaning as humans.

AQUINAS AND THE DOWNWARD PATH OF ARISTOTLE

How, then, did Aquinas, as the great synthesizer of ancient and medieval philosophy, draw on the ideas of Aristotle and the downward path to link it with the upward path to the truth of God? Aquinas adopted Aristotle's 10 categories of being: substance, quantity, quality, relation, place, time, position, possession, action, and passivity. And he appropriated Aristotle's four causes by which things come into being and undergo change: material, formal, efficient, and final. From this inheritance, Aquinas considered how Aristotle's categories of knowledge and his four causes could be applied to an understanding of God as the creative principle inherent in nature. Medieval scholars before Aquinas, such as his mentor Albertus Magnus (1200–1280) at the University of Paris, had already adapted the ideas of Aristotle to Christian theology based on the work of Muslim scholars who had preserved his writings from antiquity. The Muslim scholars reflected on Aristotle's 10 categories and determined that only "substance" was an "essential" attribute that was fundamentally associated with the being of all things. The other categories were regarded as "accidentals" or particular aspects of the character of things but not necessary to the essential being of a thing, for example, its color, size, etc. Medieval scholars then considered what other aspects of things, besides "substance," were essential because they spanned the full spectrum of being. These were called "transcendentals" because they were thought to be aspects of the sensory world that point beyond it to the creative essence of God.

"Beauty" was one of the transcendentals that Aquinas derived from earlier medieval scholars in their appropriation of the ideas of Aristotle. As a sign of God, "beauty" was understood, according to Eco, as "harmonious design." "Beauty" was also associated with two other transcendentals: "the good" and "the true." Plato had described "the good" as the mystical consciousness of the ultimate source of being. In the sensory world, we can think of "the good" as the striving of all things toward perfection or the highest fulfillment of their being. "The true" was the aspect of things that guided one's understanding toward "the good" which was identified with God. "Beauty" was thus a sign of things in the sensory world that led one toward "the good" and "the true" as attributes of God.

According to Eco, the idea of "the beautiful" as an attribute of things pointing to the truth of God was derived from the writings of John Scotus Eriugena (815–877), in the ninth century but it was first proposed as a transcendental by Saint Bonaventure (1221–1274) in the thirteenth century:

> Eriugena taught the Middle Ages to look upon things with a penetrating eye, to read the universe, to read nature, as if it were a vast store of symbols. For him, the relations between God and things were not solely causal, but were also like the relations between sign and signified. The created world is a

revelation. Nature is a theophany. In this theophanic harmony, objects are symbols, disclosures, indicators. It is their nature to point toward God and to God conceived of as Beauty revealing itself through harmonious design. It is a theophanic vision which is openly and profoundly aesthetic.[39]

Eco notes that Aquinas's approach to aesthetics was innovative for his time because he conceived of beauty not only in the appearance of objects but also in their way of being formed which revealed the creative nature of God in the world. The beautiful, for Aquinas, was thus understood in two ways. It was perceived through its outward aspect – its shape and composition – that revealed its beauty, according to Eco, as "organic wholeness." But Aquinas also conceived of beauty through its internal, dynamic unfolding toward its potential in accordance with divine creativity. In this way, Aquinas's notion of beauty is influenced by and develops Aristotle's conception of formal cause. The outward aspect of beauty is revealed through its aspect of form, and the inward aspect of beauty comes about through the dynamic formativity of its being as the creativity of God.

Aquinas as Medieval Existentialist

Aquinas differed from his medieval predecessors by conceiving of beauty as a living embodiment of God in the sensory world and not just as an objective character of things pointing to a mysterious source of creativity outside this world. Eco notes that medieval scholars prior to Aquinas regarded being as an "effect" of creation while God himself was "beyond being." According to Eco, Aquinas departed from this understanding by asserting that "God was being, goodness, and beauty, and that things participated in these attributes."[40] In other words, the formative creativity of God was physically present in the things of the world. Aquinas understood beauty as a form of revelation of the being of God through the dynamic relation between the things of the world and the individual who experienced them. Aquinas thus asserted that, besides the truth of God found in the writings of biblical scripture, one could experience God through the dynamic relation between the individual and the things of the sensory world created by and embodying the truth of God.

While Aquinas has often been regarded as simply a disciple of Aristotle who incorporated his philosophical conceptions into Christian theology, the real contribution of Aquinas to Western philosophy was to reorient the notion of being not as an objective fact, but, according to the medieval scholar James Anderson, as the "inner act of existence within the being itself."[41] In relation to this view, Aquinas's metaphysics constituted an "existentialist" philosophy long before the advent of modern existentialism by philosophers such as Kierkegaard (1813–1855) in the nineteenth century and its broad influence and popularity in the twentieth century through philosophers such as Nietzsche (1844–1900), and Sartre (1905–1980), etc. Beauty for Aquinas was the living, creative embodiment of God in the world of our senses, and the interaction of the individual with the beauty of God's creativity in the things of the world would transform the individual toward the truth of God. Because of this view, Eco notes that Aquinas "introduced the problem of the psychological and subjective desire for beauty" as an aspect of its essence.[42] Eco saw Aquinas consequently as a precursor of existentialism, the contemporary philosophical view that reality is determined by each individual's interaction with the people and things of the world. As previously mentioned in Chapter 2, existentialism can best be understood in relation to what distinguishes humans as a species. Since we are the species that constantly modifies our environment over time, and we, in turn, become modified as a species, our character as a species is determined by our direct interaction with the things of the world.

Eco's perspective on Aquinas as a medieval precursor of existentialism was also derived from the concept of form and formativity of his mentor at the University of Turin, Luigi Pareyson (1918–1991). Although his philosophical writings have not been extensively translated into English, and thus he is not as well known outside of Italy and Europe as Eco, Pareyson was a major contributor to the understanding of the relation between aesthetics and existentialism. Pareyson's existentialism is a contemporary instance of the downward path that, like the ideas of Aquinas, also points toward an upward path of spirituality. In this respect, Pareyson's existentialism is parallel to and compatible with the Christian notion of transcendence.

How is existentialism an aspect of the downward path? Existentialism conceives of the meaning of human existence as being determined not by abstract concepts of truth but rather through each individual's everyday physical and sensory interactions with the things of the world. From Plato and continuing into modern philosophy through figures such as Hegel, the upward path values pure ideas as a higher reality, whereas the downward path represented by existentialism through philosophers such as Pareyson focuses on the everyday sensory experience of the individual. Existentialism is inherently linked to the downward path because it focuses on individuals as a kind of work in progress who are formed by their interaction with other people and the material things of the world that make up human society and culture. Each individual has an outward aspect or form but also an internal formativity that occurs through the individual's response to the circumstances of the world beginning at birth. Each individual is thus an "aesthetic" being as an ongoing work of art based on the individual's self-formative adaptations or choices in responding to the social and cultural stimuli of the world. But, for Pareyson, there is also an upward path of transcendence or spirituality in existentialism. As Peter Carravetta suggests in a review article of a recent translation of selected writings by Pareyson:

> Perhaps what is important to bear in mind is the problem of reality and the responsibility of the single individual, issues which existentialism treated in depth but in the past few decades have been too often dismissed or forgotten. If it can be argued that Pareyson still harbors a "spiritual" component to his foundationless ontology (which can be traced...to Kierkegaard...) it is significant that he often also employs the language of transcendental phenomenology.[43]

Thus the existentialism that Eco found in the idea of aesthetics and beauty in Aquinas was also a reflection of the existentialism of his mentor Luigi Pareyson at the University of Turin. The importance of aesthetics and beauty for Eco, that he drew from the form and formativity of Aquinas and Pareyson, can be seen as the focal point for all of his subsequent work as a theorist and novelist in response to the particular circumstances that he confronted as a postwar Italian intellectual which we will consider in the next chapter.

NOTES

1. Eco, "Postscript" to *The Name of the Rose*, p. 510.
2. *The Name of the Rose*, p. 5. Although the preface appears to be written by the author, Umberto Eco, he doesn't identify himself as such, so the preface, itself, must be considered as part of the fictional text.
3. Eco, *Travels in Hyperreality*, pp. 64–65.
4. Eco, *Travels in Hyperreality*, p. 61.
5. Eco, *The Name of the Rose*, p. 509.
6. Eco, *The Aesthetics of Thomas Aquinas*, (Cambridge: Harvard University Press, 1988), p. viii.

7. Eco, "Postscript" to *The Name of the Rose*, pp. 510–511.
8. Eco, *The Aesthetics of Thomas Aquinas*, p. vii.
9. http://www.nationmaster.com/graph/rel_cat_as_per-religion-catholics-as-percentage.
10. Peter Bondanella, *Umberto Eco and the Open Text*, p. 2.
11. Porta Ludovica, "A Short Biography of Umberto Eco": http://www.themodernword.com/eco/eco_biography.html.
12. Carlo Romano, "The Unbearable Lightness of Umberto Eco," *The Chronicle of Higher Education*, February 29, 2016.
13. Lila Azam Zanganeh, "Umberto Eco: The Art of Fiction, No. 197," *The Paris Review*, Summer 2008, No. 185.
14. Porta Ludovica, Interviews: http://www.umbertoeco.com/en/eco-interviewed.html.
15. Eco, "Ur-Fascism," from *Five Moral Pieces*, translated by Alistair McEwen, (New York: Harcourt, Inc., 2001), p. 65.
16. *The Paris Review*, Umberto Eco, The Art of Fiction No. 197, interviewed by Lila Azam Zanganeh.
17. Eco, "Ur-Fascism," from *Five Moral Pieces*, pp. 65–66.
18. Pansa, Francesca, and Vinci, Anna, *Effeto Eco*, (Nuova Ecizioni dei Gallo, 1990), p. 24. Translations are my own.
19. Eco, *Confessions of a Young Novelist*, (Cambridge: Harvard University Press, 2011), p. 6.
20. Eco, *The Aesthetics of Thomas Aquinas*, pp. 211–212.
21. Bondanella, Peter, editor, *New Essays on Umberto Eco*, (Cambridge: Cambridge University Press, 2009), p. xi.
22. Plato, *Republic*, translated by G.M.A. Grube and revised by C.D.C. Reeve, (Hackett Publishing Company, Inc., 1992), p. 148.
23. Mario Untersteiner, *The Sophists*, translated by Kathleen Freeman, (Oxford: Basil Blackwell, 1954), p. 252.
24. These excerpts are drawn from Plato's *Republic*, translated by G.M.A. Grube and revised by C.D.C. Reeve, (Hackett Publishing Company, Inc., 1992), p. 152.
25. Plato, "Cratylus" translated by B. Jowett from *The Collected Dialogues of Plato*, edited by Edith Hamilton and Huntington Cairns, (Princeton: Princeton University Press, 1989).
26. Plato, "Cratylus," p. 456.
27. Plato, "Cratylus," pp. 472–474.
28. Garrett Thomson and Marshall Missner, *On Aristotle*, (Wadsworth Philosophers Series, Belmont, California, 2000), p. 11.
29. Aristotle, "The Analytics," from *A New Aristotle Reader*, edited by J.L. Ackrill, (Princeton: Princeton University Press, 1987), p. 83.
30. Aristotle, *A New Aristotle Reader*, p. 6.

31. Aristotle, "The Analytics," from *A New Aristotle Reader*, p. 12.
32. Aristotle, *A New Aristotle Reader*, p. 105.
33. Raymond Williams, *Keywords*, (Oxford: Oxford University Press, 1976), p. 31.
34. Eco, *The Aesthetics of Thomas Aquinas*, p. 2.
35. Eco, *The Aesthetics of Thomas Aquinas*, p. 6.
36. Eco, *The Aesthetics of Thomas Aquinas*, p. 24.
37. Foucault, Michel, *The Order of Things*, (New York: Vintage Books, 1973), p. 27.
38. Eco, *The Limits of Interpretation*, (Bloomington: Indiana University Press, 1990), p. 3.
39. Eco, *The Aesthetics of Thomas Aquinas*, p. 24.
40. Eco, *The Aesthetics of Thomas Aquinas*, p. 29.
41. Anderson, James, *An Introduction to the Metaphysics of St. Thomas Aquinas*, (Washington D.C.: Regnery Publishing Inc., 1997), p. xv.
42. Eco, *The Aesthetics of Thomas Aquinas*, p. 48.
43. Carravetta, Peter, "Form, Person, and Inexhaustible Interpretation: Luigi Pareyson," *Existence, Interpretation, Freedom, Selected Writings*, translated by Paolo Diego Bubbio, (Davies Group Publishers, 2009) from Parrhesia, Number 12, 2010, p. 4.

CHAPTER 4

The Exiled Heretic

Heresy has a long history in the Catholic Church. From the twelfth century, the Church instituted the Inquisition to investigate and condemn those who held views contrary to the strict interpretation of Church doctrine, often with horrific tortures such as water boarding – an invention of the Inquisition – resulting in forced confessions and ultimately execution. There was an aggressive campaign against heresy during the time of Eco's intellectual mentor, Thomas Aquinas, whose incorporation of Aristotle's ideas into Christian theology was temporarily subject to condemnation by the clergy of Paris. The Inquisition became especially active after the Protestant Reformation in the sixteenth and seventeenth centuries, for example, with the trial and execution of the philosopher monk Giordano Bruno (1548–1600), an important influence on Eco, who said at his sentencing that: "Perchance you who pronounce my sentence are in greater fear than I who receive it."[1] And most famously in the trial and condemnation of Galileo (1564–1642) who wrote that:

> an injunction had been judicially intimated to me by this Holy Office, to the effect that I must altogether abandon the false opinion that the sun is the center of the world and immovable, and that the earth is not the center of the world, and moves, and that I must not hold, defend, or teach in any way whatsoever, verbally or in writing, the said false doctrine[2]

The wars of national independence in the nineteenth century finally ended the reign of the Catholic Inquisition, but, as Eco and his fellow leaders of the GIAC discovered, its legacy continued during the ideological struggles of the Cold War.

In the introduction to his first published work on the aesthetics of Thomas Aquinas, Eco asserted that an understanding of the ideas and legacy of a philosopher can best be pursued through an historicist perspective: "I believe that a philosopher's significance appears most fully when he is placed in his own time, considered as a representative of his period, and when his ideas are seen as part of a problematic peculiar to that period." An especially formative period for Eco was the year 1954 when he was completing his thesis on Aquinas. In the preface to the republication of his doctoral thesis on Aquinas in 1988, he recalled that: "I began the work in 1952 in a spirit of adherence to the religious world of Thomas Aquinas, whereas now I have long since settled my accounts with Thomistic metaphysics and the religious outlook."[3]

As indicated previously, during the years that Eco pursued the study of Aquinas, he was a devoted participant, by his own admission, as a "militant" social activist in the Catholic lay youth group, *Gioventu Italiana di Azione Cattolica*(GIAC). But by 1954, when Eco was completing his study of Aquinas, Pope Pius XII became increasingly critical of the activities of the new leadership of the GIAC that included a prominent role by Eco. The Pope's oppositional stand against the leadership of the GIAC precipitated a personal crisis of faith that, as Eco has indicated, was also motivated by an intellectual transition.

THE POPE AND POSTWAR ITALIAN POLITICS

The tension between the Pope and the new leadership of the GIAC in the fifties can be traced back to the ideological climate of Italy following WWII that, in turn, arose out of the earlier circumstances of the Italian independence movement. The reign of Pope Pius XII began in 1939, at the start of WWII, and continued until 1958 during the turbulent postwar years of Italian reconstruction. As a result, the Pope had to contend with the struggles over Church authority following Mussolini's fascist takeover of the Italian government in 1922, and his later alliance with Hitler in 1940. This was followed by the demoralizing German occupation of Italy from 1943, the horrible reprisals against the Italian resistance movement, and the deportation and execution of more than 7,500 Italian Jews as victims of the holocaust. The Pope also witnessed the widespread destruction of Italian urban centers and infrastructure including sacred historical monuments and churches. Pius XII reigned as well during the difficult and fragile reorganization of the Italian state after the fall of Italian Fascism and the liberation of Italy by the Allied forces in 1945.

The postwar reconstruction of Italy was a period of great political anxiety for the papacy because of the ideological tensions of the Cold War. Italy was heavily contested in the struggle between the Soviet Union and the USA because of the political power of the Italian Communist Party. Just after WWII, the Italian Communist Party had the largest membership of any communist party in the West. It had developed a broad popular following mostly in northern Italy as a result of its anti-corruption campaigns, its opposition to Mussolini, and its prominent involvement in the resistance movement against the German occupation. After the war, it became the second largest political party in Italy, and its leaders were major contributors in reestablishing the Italian state. During the postwar period, the Italian Communist Party was also receiving substantial monetary support from the Soviet Union. In response, the USA embarked on an extensive campaign of foreign aid and investment to rebuild the Italian economy and to counter what was perceived to be a direct threat to the Italian state and the papacy by the Italian Communist Party.

American involvement in postwar Italy was intended to support the centrist Christian Democrats while working covertly to undermine the Italian Communist Party. According to the historian Martin Clark: "As the elections to Italy's first post-war parliament grew nearer, the USA increased its anti-Communist investment: shiploads of food, promises of Marshall Aid,... guns and ammunition for the police, even posters and leaflets." The Church was also directly involved in a political partnership with the Christian Democrats, and, according to some accounts, a covert alliance with members of the Mafia,[4] to assist in the opposition to the Italian Communist Party. Martin Clark recounts that "Priests and bishops threatened excommunication for anyone who voted Communist," and "The Pope himself... warned that 'he who gives his support, his service and his talents to those parties and forces that deny God is a deserter and a traitor.'"[5] As a result, Pope Pius XII became even more rigidly conservative than his predecessors. He saw the necessity of aggressively engaging in secular politics because of the perceived threat to Church authority posed by the Italian Communist Party, and his hyper-vigilant stance against the Party made him especially wary of any leanings toward leftist reforms by Catholic youth groups.

THE CATHOLIC YOUTH PROBLEM

The Pope's opposition to Eco and the new leadership of the GIAC was also consistent with a longer history of ambivalence by the papacy in relation to Catholic lay youth organizations. The Church had initially encouraged and attempted to accommodate lay Catholic youth groups immediately following the Risorgimento, the movement for Italian national independence that began in 1815 and culminated in 1870. But the Church also maintained a conservative and wary attitude toward the role of these youth groups in social causes and secular politics. The tension between the papacy and Catholic youth groups thus developed from the beginning of the modern Italian state. The roots of this tension are grounded in the circumstances of the Italian independence movement that was precipitated to a great extent by the consciousness of a younger generation who found their aspirations for liberation directly opposed by the papacy. One of the founders of the independence movement, Giuseppe Mazzini (1805–1872), had organized a secret group called *La Giovane Italia* (Young Italians) as early as 1831. It was aligned in 1835 with a broader youth movement for national independence throughout Europe called *Giovane Europa*. Giuseppe Garibaldi (1807–1882), the charismatic freedom fighter of the Risorgimento, aligned himself with Mazzini's *Giovane Italia* in 1833. As a result, youth groups were a major impetus for the revolutions of independence in Italy and throughout Europe in the nineteenth century.

But when the fiery orator of the Risorgimento, Giuseppe Mazzini, first announced the declaration of Italian independence in Rome in 1849, Pope Pius IX (who reigned from 1846 to 1878), called on the French to intervene militarily to suppress the independence movement. Besides being threatened by the secular ideology of modern statehood, the papacy was intent on defending its status as a sovereign state and a major landholder in Italy. This was based originally on the Church's claim of a donation of land from the first Christian Emperor Constantine from around 315 A.D. (determined to be a forgery in the fifteenth century), and then expanded under Charlemagne in the ninth century.[6] In 1859, prior to the dissolution of the Papal States through the eventual success of the Italian independence movement, the lands held by the Papacy extended from Rome to Bologna and totaled about 16,000 square miles making the Papal States equivalent in area to the Netherlands. The Pope thus saw any call for Italian national independence as a threat to the Church as well as the Papal States' longstanding status as a sovereign nation.

After a valiant resistance lasting two months that included the participation in direct fighting by Italian youth that resulted in numerous casualties by the young revolutionaries, the French military's overwhelming force defeated the first wave of the Italian independence movement in 1849. But the defeat only temporarily thwarted the aspirations of a broad youth-centered movement for independence. The French intervention at the instigation of the pope had just perpetuated the centuries-long indignation of the Italian people against foreign occupation that was the core motivation for independence. The youth movement for independence was consequently betrayed by the Pope's call for military intervention by the French, which prompted Garibaldi to call for the papacy to be eliminated: "The papacy, being the most harmful of all secret societies, ought to be abolished."[7]

However, after the eventual success of the independence movement in 1867, despite Garibaldi's denunciation of the papacy, Italian youth remained fiercely devoted to the Church. Immediately after the initial establishment of the modern state of Italy in 1867, but before the final confrontation against the papal forces that conquered Rome in1870, Italian youth signaled their continuing loyalty to the papacy by requesting the establishment of the first Catholic lay youth organization. The *Societa della Gioventu Cattolica Italiana* (The Society of Young Italian Catholics) was established through the initiative of students at the University of Bologna whose intention was to dedicate themselves to religious education, Christian values, and charity to the weak and poor. Thus even though the papacy had adamantly opposed the independence movement and was denounced by Garibaldi for betraying it, Italian youth continued to identify themselves with the ideals, as they perceived them, of the Catholic Church. The first and foremost principle of the *Societa* was, in fact, obedience to the Pope. The *Societa della Gioventu Cattolica Italiana* was officially recognized by the Pope in 1868, with the provision that it was specifically prohibited from direct political involvement.

Defending Against Modernism

The relation between the Catholic lay youth organization and the papacy, however, began to fracture early in the twentieth century. In 1904, just 36 years after its founding, the *Societa della Gioventu Cattolica* was disbanded along with a parent organization called *Opera dei Congressi* and replaced by *Azione Cattolica* (Catholic Action) by Pope Pius X who reigned from

1903 to 1914. The Pope was concerned about what he characterized as the "intransigence" and "innovative" leanings of the earlier organizations. He also condemned "modernism" and "relativism" as heresies that he associated with leftist, liberal tendencies in Italian politics. As an index of the immense gulf between the arch-conservatism of the Catholic Church and the temper of the times, the Pope's denunciation of "modernism" was countered in 1909 by a youth-oriented movement in the arts called "Futurismo." The artists of the Futurist movement enthusiastically and defiantly embraced modernism with an aesthetic manifesto that called for a radical break from the past through the glorification of youth, and the emancipatory potential of the new technology of the automobile, the airplane, and the locomotive.

In Italy at the turn of the century, there was consequently a polarizing tension between the conservatism of the Church and the liberal and progressive tendencies of Italian youth. But, after the disbanding of the *Societa della Gioventu Cattolica Italiana,* the *Azione Cattolica* became the parent organization for Catholic lay organizations which still drew the enthusiastic participation of both men and women of all age groups. In 1931, a new Catholic lay organization for young students was founded under the *Azione Cattolica* that was the origin for the GIAC. When Eco joined the group in 1945, immediately after WWII, it had survived the anti-clerical attacks by Mussolini's Fascist movement and was broadly established throughout Italy. In recognizing the new lay Catholic youth organizations, the Pope, however, reasserted the strict prohibition against any engagement in political action.

The Youthful Crusaders

In 1945, at age 13, Eco became a member of the GIAC, and he described his growing involvement with the group as a period of "great religious commitment and fervor."[8] Eco's religious enthusiasm and active participation in the Catholic youth group continued when he went to the University of Turin in 1949 and became engaged as "a militant Catholic intellectual."[9] At that time, the organization's chapters extended throughout Italy with a membership numbering more than two million at the *liceo* (high school) and university level, and their numbers were growing each year.[10] During the postwar years, according to Eco chroniclers Francesca Pansa and Anna Vinci, for an ostensibly non-political group, the GIAC had become pervaded with a "crusading spirit" following an address to a crowd of 100,000 youth in 1947 by then president Carlo Carretto (1910–1988):

> We must evangelize the people and help them to accept the uncompromising nature of essential problems. It is not possible to be with Christ in the Church and against Christ in the piazza or in the political arena.[11]

This fusion of religion and politics, according to Pansa and Vinci, was reflected in the success of the Christian Democrats in the parliamentary elections of 1948. But, in 1951, while Eco was pursuing his studies at the University of Turin, a new leader of the GIAC was beginning to alter its course in relation to the changing circumstances of the postwar period. The newly elected president, Mario Rossi, sought to depart from the political "intransigence" of the past toward a more "autonomous" and humanistic approach. Rossi asserted that "society is atheistic not because of a lack of faith in God, but because of a lack of love for humanity."[12] This emphasis is similar to what Eco experienced under the tutelage of the Salesian approach of Don Bosco that was based on loving kindness rather than strict imposition of religious doctrine. After his first two years at the university, Eco assumed a prominent role in the new leadership of the GIAC, and his religious pursuits expanded into political activism when, as he recalls, he was invited to take part in "the central direction [of the GIAC] in Rome."[13] According to Eco, the political tendencies of the new leadership at that time were "democratic-socialist" and "somewhat similar to certain third world Catholic groups":

> As young leaders of the organization, we were moving steadily toward a position that could be defined as leftist, toward social reform, aid to the oppressed, and, in a curious way, with the reading of St. Thomas and Gramsci.[14]

St. Thomas was, of course, his religious and intellectual mentor Thomas Aquinas. Antonio Gramsci (1891–1937), on the other hand, was a secular Italian intellectual who was opposed to the Church as one of the founders of the Italian Communist Party. Gramsci's imprisonment and death under Mussolini made him a martyr for the resistance movement, and he has continued to be highly influential for his innovative analysis of the role of intellectuals in relation to the masses. As we considered in Chapter 2, Gramsci famously asserted that: "all men are intellectuals." While imprisoned for eight years under the Fascist regime of Benito Mussolini, Gramsci wrote extensively in what are called his *Prison Notebooks* about the problem of society's lack of awareness of its willing conformity to the structures of power embedded in social practices which he called "hegemony" from the Greek term *hegemon* for leader or ruler.

Gramsci advocated for the responsibility of the intellectual to draw attention to the mechanisms of power that pervaded society. Eco's citing of both St. Thomas Aquinas and Antonio Gramsci indicates that the group was motivated by a synthesis of religious and secular ideals involving engagement in political action toward social reforms that would benefit the poor and disadvantaged and the working class in general. As their earlier leader Carlo Carretto had advocated, they wanted to be "with Christ" not only "in the Church" but also "in the political arena." While not directly identifying with the Italian Communist Party, they were influenced, as Eco indicates, by Gramsci's strongly leftist, liberationist ideas in a way that they considered compatible with the Christian concept of charity to the poor. Unfortunately these ideals went directly against the Pope's prohibition against political engagement by the lay Catholic youth organizations, and their leftist tendencies aroused the Church's vigilant reaction against leftist reforms that seemed to be aligned with the objectives of the Italian Communist Party.

Eco described this period as one of "profound conviction" and "high spirits" in embracing the possibilities of "modernization."[15] Unfortunately, as indicated previously, the Church associated "modernism" with the threat of secularism, moral relativism, and the leftist liberal objectives of the Italian Communist Party. As a result, the optimistic and progressive outlook of the new leadership of the GIAC was increasingly confronted by the conservative stance of the parent organization, *Azione Cattolica*, and directly opposed by the hyper-vigilant stance against leftist leanings of Pope Pius XII. Peter Bondanella, a professor emeritus of Italian, Comparative Literature and Cinema Studies at Indiana University, has suggested that Eco and Rossi were inspired by "the more liberal policies of the French clergy of the period" and sought to push the Catholic Church in the direction of liberal reforms by "attempting to transcend the heavily conservative religious, social, and cultural policies represented by the then reigning pontiff, Pius XII."[16]

Although the French clergy are not specifically mentioned by Eco, a fellow leader, Enzo Scotti, suggests that the French cardinal Jacques Maritain (1882–1973) was a prominent influence on the leadership of the group during this time. Scotti recalls that the new leadership of the GIAC was inspired by Maritain's attempt to move beyond the insular, defensive posture of the Church in response to the threat of atheism and Marxism, and beyond the traditional sphere of Church practice by confronting the social conditions of the marginalized working class.[17] This approach is, again, highly consistent with the benevolent attitude toward the poor and working classes of the Salesians of Don Bosco who had been a prominent influence on Eco as a young student. In response to these influences, Scotti recalls that the new leaders of the GIAC were trying to "shift the focus of the organization outside the Church and into the workplace, the school, and the university." This shift in focus precipitated a "breakdown" between the new leadership of the GIAC and the traditional conservatism of the Church that Eco chroniclers Pansa and Vinci characterized as "inevitable."[18]

Eco's companions during this time remember his contribution to the movement as "a great capacity for dialogue and openness to diverse ideas as well as a great devotion to research and freedom of inquiry."[19] Scotti recalls that the distinguishing character of this period was the dynamic engagement in "multiple interests." Pansa and Vinci note that the leaders of the movement were interested not only in politics but also in the cinema, literature, music, and the theater. Citing interviews with Eco's companions during this time, Pansa and Vinci describe the defining character of the movement as: "The plurality of interests, curiosity towards life, and a great attention and participation in things that Eco, especially, nourished and transmitted to others."[20] Scotti remembers Eco's "exceptional intellectual vivacity and his great capacity to capture the attention of people." According to Scotti, Eco "gave life to the realization of a spirited journal, not only in its graphic design but also through its content that would bring us an occasional rap on the knuckles from the general president of the *Azione Cattolica*."[21]

Some of Eco's earliest writings as a social activist were published during this time in *Gioventu Cattolica*, a publication of the Catholic youth group. For example, in an article from 1954, Eco demonstrated an early interest in the relation between literature and popular culture in the form of the detective novel: "If we could rummage through the library of a celebrity, a statesman, a scientist, it's possible we would find there a series of popular detective novels...[which are] not just an indulgence for the young but a temptation for all." In this same article, Eco states that literature is characterized by its "pedagogical value."[22] The distinguishing qualities that Eco would later develop in his mature practice as an intellectual, as Scotti suggests, were already apparent when he was a 20-year-old student at the University of Turin: an exploration of "multiple interests" and "a focus on the modern world from the perspective of a strong synthesis of secular and religious views..."[23]

DOCTRINAL DEVIATIONS

Despite the religious ideals that motivated the social activism of Eco and the other leaders of the GIAC, their actions were regarded by the Pope as a direct violation of the prohibition against political activity and inconsistent with the conservative values of the Church. As mentioned previously, both the parent organization *Azione Cattolica* and the Pope had expressed concerns about the direction of the new leadership of the GIAC. After openly reproaching the organization's president, Mario Rossi, in 1953, the Pope finally forced him to resign the following year when Eco was completing his thesis on Aquinas. The *Osservatore Romano*, the official newspaper of the Vatican, reported that the resignation was due to "'doctrinal deviations' represented by 'disobedience' to the Pope, alliances with French clerics, and certain leftist tendencies."[24]

After Rossi's ouster by the Pope in 1954, Eco and his fellow companions, in allegiance to Rossi, also resigned from the organization. Eco recalls that Pope Pius XII removed Rossi as president because he considered him "too leftist," and, as a result, "all of us young leaders of the central and regional level of the organization resigned."[25] According to the testimony of his companions, Eco had favored dialogue during this time instead of oppositional alliances because of his strong ties to the Church. But, nevertheless, the social reforms advocated by Eco and the other leaders of the GIAC were perceived by the Pope as unacceptable deviations from Church doctrine. Their efforts toward social reforms to alleviate poverty and economic exploitation were perceived as being too closely aligned with the leftist objectives of the Italian Communist Party. According to Eco, the rift between the Pope and the leadership of the GIAC caused a crisis in the organization that endured for many years. While constituting a political confrontation for the leaders and activists in the GIAC, for Eco it also became a "philosophical and religious crisis." As he recalled in an interview for the *Paris Review*:

I had a Catholic education and during my university years I ran one of the national Catholic student organizations. So I was fascinated by medieval scholastic thought and by early Christian theology. I started a thesis on the aesthetics of Thomas Aquinas, but right before I finished it my faith suffered a trauma. It was a complicated affair. I belonged to the more progressive side of the student organization, which meant that I was interested in social problems, social justice. The right wing was protected by Pope Pius XII. One day my wing of the organization was charged with heresy and communism. Even the official newspaper of the Vatican attacked us. That even triggered a philosophical revision of my faith. But I continued to study the Middle Ages and medieval philosophy with great respect, not to mention my beloved Aquinas.[26]

The charge of heresy may seem like a disproportionally severe and oddly archaic judgment by the Church in the twentieth century, especially against young, devoted student Catholics who were pursuing what they considered to be core Christian values of assistance to the poor and oppressed. The Pope's expulsion from the Church of Eco and his fellow leaders of the GIAC in 1954 as "communists" and "heretics" reflected, however, the continuation of the Church's campaign against the Italian Communist Party during the postwar elections when the Pope threatened excommunication for anyone who voted Communist and specifically warned that anyone supporting those who deny God would be considered a "deserter and traitor." Unfortunately, despite the devout, religiously motivated activism of Eco and his companions, their attempts to link their faith to liberal social reforms could only be seen by the papacy as a direct threat to the Church due to its long tradition of ultra conservatism that was intensified by the Cold War tensions of postwar Italy.

Although Eco and the new leadership of the GIAC in 1954 considered themselves devout Catholics, their activism in support of the poor and oppressed was perceived by the Church through the lens of the "Red Scare" of the fifties. Eco's expulsion from the Church as a heretic and communist in 1954 occurred the same year as the Army-McCarthy hearings in the USA. Senator Joseph McCarthy (1908–1957) aroused a climate of fear about the threat of Communist infiltration of the Army, the State Department, and other institutions of American society that resulted in the blacklisting and expulsion of prominent figures from government and the film industry. Because of McCarthy's broad accusations without evidence, he was later discredited and censured, but he is representative of the political paranoia and demagoguery of that period. In describing the expulsion from the Church in 1954 of himself and the other leaders of the GIAC, Eco used the term "*cacciati*" which means those who are "driven out" or "banished."[27] Eco recalled that this incident was "very painful" for him and resulted in his complete withdrawal from political activism for a period of eight years.[28]

THE AESTHETICS OF AQUINAS RECONSIDERED

During the same period as Eco's ouster as a student activist from the Catholic Church, he also confronted an intellectual crisis in his exploration of the aesthetics of Aquinas. For Eco, Aquinas was both a religious and intellectual mentor. What appealed to Eco in the work of Aquinas were his analytical clarity and his conception of beauty as a reflection of God's creative presence in the world. As indicated previously, Aquinas conceived of beauty as an existential pathway to God reflected in the formative character of things. Eco cites the following passage from Aquinas's work to indicate how he conceived of beauty:

> Beauty...has to do with knowledge, for those things are called beautiful which please us when they are seen.

The beautiful for Aquinas is determined by the form of things:

> Now since knowing proceeds by imagining, and images have to do with form, beauty properly involves the notion of formal causes.[29]

Eco takes up Aquinas's conception of beauty as form by asserting that: "Everything has within it the conditions of beauty, but it appears beautiful to us only if we concentrate our attention upon its formal structure."[30]

> Looking at an object aesthetically means looking at its structure, physical and metaphysical, as exhaustively as possible, in all its meanings and implications, and in its proportionate relations to its own nature and to its accidental circumstances. It means, that is, a kind of *reasoning about* the object, scrutinizing it in detail and in depth. Only then can it be appreciated in its harmony and its formal structure.[31]

Eco thus asserts that the experience of the beauty of God's creation can occur only through the full understanding by the human beholder of the object in all its "completeness and perfection."[32] This is an important point for Eco because it asserts that the aesthetic quality of things does not consist in its outward appearance, or expressive content, but through its formative effect on the individual.

In relation to Aquinas's conception of beauty, however, Eco ultimately concluded that the full understanding of "its structure, physical and metaphysical" by the human beholder would not be possible. The "completeness and perfection" of the things of God's creation could only be understood by God as the creator. Eco also concluded that it was necessary to move beyond the historical circumstances of Aquinas's conception of beauty to recognize that "It is only the productive processes of human makers that we can trace and comprehend."[33] Eco found that Aquinas's system attempted to accommodate an eternal and unchanging conception of perfect being, understood as the creative expression of God, with the aspiration for perfect being of human society and the human intellect. The contradiction in the system, according to Eco, arose from the "humanist culture of late medieval times" which "destroyed the system from within."[34]

This crisis in the historical transition between worldviews can be seen as a core theme in Eco's first novel *The Name of the Rose* that depicts the tensions between the conservative Catholicism of the monastery and the threat posed by the rise of the cities, commerce, the money economy, etc. Aquinas's conception of beauty was sufficient for providing an understanding of the relative simplicity of the agricultural economy of the medieval world that was not yet affected by the dramatic expansion of the human-centered world of the cities. The continuing alteration of the natural and social world by human enterprise created the conditions in the late Middle Ages for, according to Eco, "a new conception of art and beauty" based on "a conception of the artist as an inventor and creator, someone who no longer submitted to the eternal laws."[35] This view can be traced to the Italian humanist-historicist tradition derived from the seventeenth-century Italian philosopher Giambattista Vico (1668–1744). Aquinas's system attempted to accommodate an eternal and unchanging conception of perfect being with the earthly world that was constantly being modified by human culture. In other words, Aquinas attempted to bring together the upward path of Plato and Christian theology with the downward path of Aristotle focused on the world of our senses, and Eco ultimately concluded that this project was no longer viable in relation to the contemporary world dominated by the forces of modern science, the industrial revolution, multiculturalism, and the mass media, as well as the autonomous role of the artist.

Although Eco became totally disillusioned with the "religious outlook" after being driven from the Church as "a communist and heretic" in 1954, and he came to recognize that Aquinas's conception of beauty was no longer viable in the contemporary world, he managed to complete his thesis on Aquinas the same year. Under the title, *Il problema estetico in Tommaso d'Aquino*, it was so well received that it became his first published work in 1956 (published in English in 1988 as *The Aesthetics of Thomas Aquinas*). His university studies thus established his early reputation as an intellectual with a strong foundation in the late Middle Ages and the aesthetics of Aquinas. But, according to Peter Bondanella, 1954 was also the year that Eco "set aside both Thomistic metaphysics and a religious outlook on life for a more secular attitude."[36] Eco's expulsion from the Church and his turn to more secular concerns caused him, according to Bondanella, to be "thrown pell-mell from the rarified atmosphere of the Italian university, a cathedral devoted to the often monastic pursuit of learning, into the everyday world of popular culture."[37] He consequently embarked on an extended reflection on his intellectual foundations in relation to the social and cultural challenges of his time. His departure from academia to confront a secular world occurred at a time when Italy was rapidly being transformed by the impact of the mass media and consumerism and thus vastly different from the medieval world that he continued to inhabit intellectually with a sense of nostalgia.

THE TELEVISION YEARS

So where does one go in modern, secular society after being exiled from the Catholic Church as a heretic and communist, and after graduating from academia with a focus on medieval aesthetics that Bondanella describes as "esoteric" and not readily accessible "even for well-educated readers"?[38] It's certainly not the case that Eco was totally isolated from the "secular" world as a university student which was evident from the characterization of his engagement in the Catholic student group by his fellow leaders of the GIAC as involving "multiple interests," such as the "cinema, literature, music, and the theater." But Eco's exit from the Church and his temporary departure from academia coincided with the start of the great transformation of Italian society by the mass media, and just before Italy's dramatic postwar economic recovery, known as the "economic miracle," that began in 1958. After more than a decade of intensive rebuilding of its heavily damaged urban centers and infrastructure from WWII, Italy was shedding its former identity as a relatively underdeveloped agricultural nation by becoming a major industrial power. A sustained period of economic growth and expanded prosperity caused a cultural revolution due to the impact of the mass media and consumerism. Despite the objections that Pope Pius X had raised in 1904 against the evils of modernization, Italian society was quickly becoming "modernized" into a heavily secularized society dominated by the mass media and popular culture.

Eco's intellectual practice of bridging between an elite and a popular audience thus developed in response to the particular conditions of the postwar cultural revolution in Italy. Eco went directly from his "cloistered" focus on the medieval aesthetics of Thomas Aquinas, to working as an assistant in the beginning years of Italian television in 1954. In describing himself as a "medievalist in hibernation" in the *Postscript to the Name of the Rose* (1984), Eco explained that: "I know the present only through the television screen whereas I have a direct knowledge of the Middle Ages."[39] To appreciate Eco's frequent use of playful irony, we can first consider that his transition from academia found him in a "direct" role in the inaugural year of public television broadcasting in Milan by RAI (*Radiotelevisione Italiana*), the Italian state broadcasting monopoly, similar to the BBC in England. His first position as an intellectual outside academia was in a pioneering role as a producer of cultural, educational programming offered for the first time to a mass audience through the new medium of television. Reflecting on his early work in Italian television, Eco remembered a long apprenticeship during which he learned "how to correctly deliver a notice with the minimum number of words possible" and how to "analyze political facts."[40]

According to Peter Bondanella, Eco's work in Italian television was focused on educational programming that consisted of "cultural programs to book reviews, children's shows, and dramatic reconstructions of historical events." Bondanella cites as an example that Eco assisted in the production of "A version of the popular American program 'You Are There' that was devoted to imaginary interviews with important historical figures at a crucial moment in their past." Because Eco started in public television during its infancy and before the advent of videotape, these programs were, as Bondanella indicates, "live" and "improvisational."[41]

Although program content was scripted, it had to be performed live, in "real" time, as it was being broadcast to the Italian public, with rudimentary modes of production and at a primitive stage of technological development. Television programming in its infancy, according to Eco, was supposed to give the spectator "the impression of reality." In order to achieve this, on one occasion they filmed a succession of photographs of museum artifacts mounted on tripods to create the effect of "walking slowly along the galleries of the Louvre."[42] Concerning the "improvisational" aspect of these early years of television, Eco recalled that a technician accidentally knocked over a series of tripods so that the director had to blackout the image while they remounted the tripods.

But, apart from the handicap of early broadcasting technology, Eco found himself confronting a greater challenge from the Italian mass public audience that was not receptive to the kind of cultural programming that was the initial hope of television as an educational medium. Instead the Italian television audience was already being determined by the culture of mass consumerism. Similar concerns in the USA prompted Federal Communications Commission (FCC) chairman Newton Minnow's famous description of television programming in 1961 as a "vast wasteland."[43] Eco's experience at RAI in the inaugural years of television broadcasting left a strong impression on him of the way in which television bridged between "real" and "imaginary" worlds. For Eco, television functioned as a "window on the world" as well as "an imaginary interior space" which is similar to the way in which "poetry had to anchor itself to the external world."[44] He noted how events in the external world were subordinated to the fictional aspects of television production. The audience, Eco suggested, "was a mysterious entity whose tendencies and social composition were unknown." Direct contact with the audience occurred only through telephone complaints by viewers that "television was showing them a reality they knew nothing about and one that they were not at all interested in seeing."[45] In contrast to the kind of programming that Eco was producing on culture, the arts, history, etc., the most popular program during the early years of Italian television was a quiz show called "*Lascia o Raddoppia*" ("Double or Nothing") that was similar to the hugely popular American quiz show "The 64,000 Dollar Question." The host of the quiz show, which Eco contributed questions for, was Mike Bongiorno who became a celebrity in Italy and the focus of a highly unflattering critique by Eco that became a touchstone in the relation between intellectuals and popular culture that will be taken up in

Chapter 7. The other program that was especially popular with the new Italian television audience was a half-hour show called "Carosello" that featured brief commercial announcements inserted between a medley of children's stories and cartoons. "Carosello" was initially the only outlet that the Christian Democrats, who controlled RAI, would allow for commercial messages. It had great appeal for young children and their parents. Ironically, however, for the Christian Democrats, it gradually undermined the role of the Church through the lure of cultural consumption.

INTELLECTUALS AND THE ITALIAN CULTURAL REVOLUTION

Eco's early years in Italian television occurred during the period of Italy's postwar cultural revolution which formed the foundation for his later development as a public intellectual who bridges between elite and popular culture. Italian society during the fifties and sixties was undergoing profound changes due to the impact of the mass media and consumerism in ways that completely overturned the traditional role of elite intellectuals and their relation to the masses. According to David Forgacs, Cambridge University scholar of Italian Studies, Eco began his practice as an intellectual in the public sphere at the very moment when Italy was being radically altered from the "elitist, traditional, and conservative" world of "humanistic liberalism" into "an urbanized, industrial society in which cultural consumption arose through an expanding, interactive exchange between producers and consumers." From the turn of the century, Forgacs indicates, "Italy was still primarily an underdeveloped agricultural society just beginning its awkward transition to an urban industrial economy." Even in the thirties and early forties, according to Forgacs, "nearly half of Italy's working population still earned its living from agriculture, [and] the nascent consumer culture was almost exclusively an urban phenomena" that left "whole areas of the country, and whole social groups...unaffected."[46] In the early 1900s Italian publishers were just beginning to adapt to the effects of "urbanisation, and increasing literacy" by attempting to appeal to a more general readership and a growing demand for what was called "*letteratura amena*" or "light reading."[47] As evidence of the elitist attitude of traditional Italian intellectuals at this time, there were already concerns that their privileged status as arbiters of cultural standards was being threatened. According to Forgacs, Italian intellectuals were beginning to complain that: "the age when it was shameful to write for money had passed," and that publishers were beginning to adopt "the mentality of the mass public."[48]

The changing relation between traditional intellectuals and the masses that began at the turn of the century was dramatically altered after WWII. In postwar Italy, the elitist role of Italian intellectuals was radically transformed through the advent of Italian television in 1954 which Eco experienced firsthand as a production assistant. Eco's direct involvement in the mass media occurred at its pivotal point in rapidly changing the content and technological mediation of Italian postwar society and culture. The analysis of the impact of the mass media in Italy by David Forgacs and Robert Lumley in 1996 in *Italian Cultural Studies* concluded that Italian television was "one of the principal agents of the 'great transformation' in cultural consumption." The advent of television in Italy caused "the erosion of cultural differences between localities and classes and the triumph of consumerism and acquisitiveness."[49] As the historian of Italy Paul Ginsborg put it "No innovation of these years had a greater effect on everyday life than television."[50]

Obviously television had a major impact in all countries where it was first introduced in the fifties, but the effect was especially profound in Italy because Italian society, as indicated above, was just beginning to fully adapt to industrial production and the mass media. One of the ironies of Eco's participation in its inaugural years was that television caused the displacement of other media such as book publishing (that Eco took up in 1959), and newspapers and magazines (that Eco began to write for in 1960). Eco's transition from academia to a role in the fledgling development of Italian television occurred at a time when the privileged status of traditional Italian intellectuals, through the medium of books and periodicals, was being threatened by the new forces of the mass media and consumerism. As Donald Sassoon's 1997 study of postwar Italy points out, because of the impact of Italian television, "The overall standard of cultural consumption of the average Italian is remarkably low" with a general Italian readership of only 51 percent compared to 74 percent in Britain. This was due to the "unusually high degree of access to television" by young Italians.[51] The advent of television caused a broadening cultural divide in Italy that also affected the status of Italian journalism. The journalistic profession in Italy is highly prestigious, but Italian newspapers have traditionally served as organs for elite corporate interests and political parties. Italian newspapers, according to historian Martin Clark, are "written to be decoded by the elite, not absorbed by the public."[52] But besides the elitist insularity of Italian journalism, the reason for the low level of readership, according to Clark, is that "Italy is a latecomer in the field of mass literacy and mass education" and that "When this was achieved, the age of television had already come."[53] Instead of being drawn to the prestigious mainstream press, the Italian mass media audience was attracted to what Clark calls the "political glossies" that are characterized by a mix of glitzy photographs and celebrity gossip.

THE AMERICANIZATION OF ITALY

The other major impact of the advent of television in Italy was the Americanization of Italian culture. According to Donald Sassoon, Italian society was adopting "the model of social behaviour and the consumption habits described in American situation comedies" and that "the very class structures of Italian society became 'Americanized'."[54] The medium of television was the single most dominant force in diminishing the development of a broad Italian readership, and it facilitated the importation, or more accurately, the "invasion" of American culture in postwar Italy. The confrontation of Italian intellectuals with the perception of an American cultural invasion was what motivated Eco, as noted in Chapter 1, to engage in a critical analysis of American consumerism in his travels to the USA in 1975. In a study of the impact of the mass media in Italy during the fifties and sixties, Donald Sassoon suggested that: "There are, in fact, two Italies." While most Italians receive their cultural content from the mass media, "A relatively tiny elite reads voraciously a high quality press as well as the books on display in the well-stocked bookshops which are a common feature of urban centres."[55]

Although the mass media have had a major impact on societies throughout the world, their historical impact on Italy has had an especially significant role in the challenges that it posed for postwar Italian intellectuals. Because the economic miracle in Italy caused such precipitous and profound social and cultural changes, and because the phenomena of mass consumption were perceived, for better or worse, as the result of the American cultural invasion of Italy, the radical transformation of Italian society during the fifties and sixties can be seen as a virtual laboratory for the study of the social impact of cultural consumption caused by the mass media. Eco's later academic focus, as indicated in Chapter 1, on the "aesthetics" of popular culture venues such as wax museums can be understood in response to the historical circumstances of postwar Italy in which the phenomena of the mass media were perceived as a threat to the traditional role of the intellectual and a problem that called for new methods of critical analysis. According to the Italian Studies scholar JoAnn Cannon, "the debate on the role of the intellectual in society has had a particularly prominent and privileged position in Italy."[56]

The intensive Italian reflection on the role of the intellectual has also occurred in response to two prominent figures in Italian cultural analysis. As mentioned previously, Antonio Gramsci was a key figure in setting out the social responsibility of the intellectual in raising an emancipatory consciousness of the mechanisms of power and oppression. Gramsci conceived of the intellectual as a "permanent persuader" whose work is dedicated to the needs of the oppressed. This perspective was countered by the intellectual practice of the writer Elio Vittorini (1908–1966) who called for a scientific analysis of culture that was not influenced by politics in order to explore the full range of human needs and aspirations. In response to these alternative legacies, many intellectuals, such as Eco, attempted to practice in both spheres by bridging between theoretical or aesthetic works that were traditionally aimed at a sophisticated, mostly academic audience, and through public commentary that attempted to communicate a cultural awareness to a popular audience. But Italian intellectuals also joined together in an antagonistic role to confront the problem of the mass media and consumerism through the Italian Neo-avant-garde whose impact will be considered in the next two chapters.

During this accelerated period of cultural transformation, Eco began to develop his signature practice as a public intellectual by taking up positions in the popular mass media as well as the elite world of book publishing and academic theory. As previously indicated, immediately after graduating from the University of Turin in 1954, Eco started working as an assistant in the state-sponsored Italian television network RAI (*Radiotelevisione Italiana*) in the inaugural year of Italian television. He was, however, discouraged by this experience because a popular audience was not being drawn to the cultural programming he was developing and instead acquired a taste for quiz shows and consumer advertising. Eco's engagement with a mass audience shifted to print media in 1960 when he began to write regular essays and commentaries for Italian newspapers and magazines. Apart from his engagement in the popular media, Eco took up a position in the elitist domain of Italian book publishing as an advisor to the Italian publisher Bompiani in 1959. His engagement with the intellectual elite also included a return to academia in 1961 first as a lecturer in aesthetics at the University of Turin and eventually as the founder of the school of semiotics at the University of Bologna in 1975 which was the first of its kind. Except for his brief, five-year stint as an assistant for cultural programming in the very first years of Italian television, 1954–1959, he maintained these relationships with a public and an elite audience throughout the further development of his career.

NOTES

1. Giordano Bruno from Dorothea Waley Singe, *Giordano Bruno: His Life and Thought*, (New York: Schuman, 1950).
2. Galileo Galilei, from *Dialogue Concerning the Two Chief WorldSystems*, (1632).
3. Eco, from the preface to the republication of his doctoral thesis *The Aesthetics of Thomas Aquinas* for an English readership in 1988.
4. For example John Dickie, *Mafia Republic*, (London: Hodder and Stoughton Ltd., 2013), pp. 327–328.
5. Clark, Martin, *Modern Italy 1871–1982*, (London: Longman Group Limited, 1984), p. 324.
6. The document supporting that claim was demonstrated to be a forgery in the fifteenth century through the textual analysis of Lorenzo Valla (1407–1457).
7. Guerzoni, Giuseppe, *Garibaldi: con documenti editi e inediti*, Florence, 1882, Vol. 11, p. 485.
8. Pansa, Francesca and Vinci, Anna, *Effetto Eco*, (Nuova Edizioni dei Gallo, 1990), p. 24. Translations are my own.
9. Bondanella, Peter, *Umberto Eco and the Open Text*, (New York: Cambridge University Press, 1997), p. 2.
10. Pansa and Vinci, *Effetto Eco*, p. 21.
11. Pansa and Vinci, *Effetto Eco*, p. 21.
12. Pansa and Vinci, *Effetto Eco*, p. 22.
13. Pansa and Vinci, *Effetto Eco*, p. 21.
14. Pansa and Vinci, *Effetto Eco*, p. 24.
15. Bondanella, Peter, *Umberto Eco and the Open Text*, p. 2.
16. Bondanella, Peter, *Umberto Eco and the Open Text*, p. xii.
17. Pansa and Vinci, *Effetto Eco*, p. 28.
18. Pansa and Vinci, *Effetto Eco*, p. 25.
19. Pansa and Vinci, *Effetto Eco*, p. 22.
20. Pansa and Vinci, *Effetto Eco*, p. 25.
21. Pansa and Vinci, *Effetto Eco*, p. 26.

22. Pansa and Vinci, *Effetto Eco*, p. 23.
23. Pansa and Vinci, *Effetto Eco*, p. 28.
24. Pansa and Vinci, *Effetto Eco*, p. 22.
25. Pansa and Vinci, *Effetto Eco*, p. 22.
26. *The Paris Review*, "Umberto Eco, The Art of Fiction" No. 197, interviewed by Lila Azam Zanganeh.
27. Pansa and Vinci, *Effetto Eco*, p. 117.
28. Pansa and Vinci, *Effetto Eco*, p. 24.
29. Eco, The *Aesthetics of Thomas Aquinas*, p. 56.
30. Eco, *The Aesthetics of Thomas Aquinas*, p. 191.
31. Eco, *The Aesthetics of Thomas Aquinas*, p. 196.
32. Eco, *The Aesthetics of Thomas Aquinas*, p. 197.
33. Eco, *The Aesthetics of Thomas Aquinas*, p. 204.
34. Eco, *The Aesthetic of Thomas Aquinas*, p. 205.
35. Eco, *The Aesthetics of Thomas Aquinas*, p. 214.
36. Bondanella, Peter, *Umberto Eco and the Open Text*, p. 8.
37. Bondanella, Peter, *Umberto Eco and the Open Text*, p. 8.
38. Bondanella, Peter, *Umberto Eco and the Open Text*, p. 7.
39. Echo, "Postscript" to *The Name of the Rose*, p. 14.
40. Pansa and Vinci, *Effetto Eco*, p. 42.
41. Bondanella, Peter, *Umberto Eco and the Open Text*, p. 6.
42. Pansa and Vinci, *Effetto Eco*, p. 43.
43. Newton N. Minow, "Television and the Public Interest," address to the National Association of Broadcasters, Washington, D.C., May 9, 1961.
44. Pansa and Vinci, *Effetto Eco*, p. 43.
45. Pansa and Vinci, *Effetto Eco*, p. 43.
46. Forgacs David and Lumley, Robert, editors, "Cultural Consumption, 1940's to 1990's," from *Italian Cultural Studies, An Introduction*, (Oxford: Oxford University Press, 1996), p. 277.
47. Forgacs and Lumley, "Cultural Consumption, 1940's to 1990's," from *Italian Cultural Studies, An Introduction*, p. 44.
48. Forgacs, David, *Italian Culture in the Industrial Era, 1880–1890: Cultural Industries, Politics, and the Public*, (Manchester: Manchester University Press, 1990), p. 41.
49. Forgacs, David and Lumley, Robert, editors, "Cultural Consumption, 1940's to 1990's," from *Italian Cultural Studies, An Introduction*, p. 281.
50. Ginsborg, Paul, *A History of Contemporary Italy*, (London: Penguin Books, 1990), p. 240.
51. Sassoon, Donald, *Contemporary Italy, Economy, Society and Politics since 1945*, (London: Addison Wesley Longman Limited, 1997), p. 164.
52. Clark, *Modern Italy, 1871–1982*, p. 367.
53. Clark, *Modern Italy*, p. 162.

54. Sassoon, Donald, *Contemporary Italy*, p. 262.
55. Sassoon, Donald, *Contemporary Italy*, p. 163.
56. Cannon, JoAnn, *Postmodern Italian Fiction*, (London: Associated University Presses, 1989), p. 21.

CHAPTER 5

The Art of Adventure: Eco, Joyce, and the Open Work

Eco's discouraging experience in the inaugural years of Italian television was fortunately offset by providing him with connections to a new generation of Italian intellectuals who were attempting to respond to the impact of popular culture and mass media consumerism. Two floors above Eco's office at RAI was the studio for Luciano Berio (1925–2003) an early experimental composer in electronic music. This chance encounter led to dinner discussions with Berio and his American wife Cathy Berberian (1925–1983) who was a mezzo-soprano and also a composer (as well as a notable eccentric who collected pornographic porcelain). Through these discussions, Eco discovered that they shared his avid appreciation for the radically unconventional writings of the Irish novelist James Joyce (1882–1941) who was the focus of Eco's writings at that time. Their mutual interest developed into a collaboration on a spoken-word composition entitled *Thema: Omaggio a Joyce* (Theme: Tribute to Joyce, 1959) that consists of a collection of vocalizations drawn from Joyce's novels. In 1962 Eco also collaborated separately with Cathy Berberian, whom he affectionately nicknamed "Magnificathy," in the Italian translation of two works by American authors with playful approaches to the intersection between elite and popular culture: the cartoonist and author Jules Feiffer (*Passionella and other stories*, 1959), and the comedian and movie director Woody Allen (*Getting Even*, 1971, published in Italian as *Saperla Lunga* 1973, "to know better"). Cathy Berberian was also an early inspiration for Eco in considering the cultural connections between elite and popular culture. He mentions in the "Postscript to the Name of the Rose," for example, that "it took the initiative of Cathy Berberian to show us that the Beatles, linked with Purcell, as was only right, could also be performed in recital with Monteverdi and Satie."[1]

As a result of their collaborations, Berio asked Eco to submit an article on the characteristics of modern avant-garde works for his review publication "Incontri musicali" (Musical Encounters). Eco provided Berio with an essay that he had submitted the year before (1958) to the International Congress of Philosophy. Eco's article subsequently attracted the attention of Italo Calvino (1923–1985) who was the most famous Italian writer of his time through numerous writings translated for an international audience, including his unconventional novel about the experience of reading entitled *If On A Winter's Night a Traveler* (1979). Calvino was so impressed with Eco's essay for Berio that he asked Eco whether he would consider a collection of related essays for publication. Eco recalled that, although he had not initially intended such a book, he subsequently made plans for a theoretical exploration that he described as "a kind of systematic study of the concept of 'openness'."[2] That idea led to the development of his first theoretical writings on contemporary culture that were published in 1962 as *Opera Aperta*, (published in English in 1988 as *The Open Work* which includes essays from other publications by Eco).

After these initial contacts, Eco developed strong ties with a number of Italian avant-garde intellectuals who formed an association known as the Gruppo 63 from their inaugural meeting in Palermo, Sicily in that year. The focus of the Gruppo 63 was a militant engagement in new modes of analysis and artistic expression in opposition to the Italian cultural establishment as well as the impact of mass media consumerism that they saw as the degradation of culture. What was especially significant about the approach of the Gruppo 63 was its emphasis on language as a mode of engagement that came to be the core focus of Eco's practice as an intellectual.

From Future's Past: Eco and the Middle Ages of James Joyce

When Eco left academia in 1954 to find his way in the emerging culture of mass media consumerism, he was introduced to the modern, exploratory aesthetics of the Italian Neo-avant-garde through his work in the inaugural years of Italian television. But Eco's connection to the avant-garde preceded his acquaintance with Berio, Berberian, Calvino, and his fellow intellectuals and artists of the Gruppo 63. Eco's initial introduction to the avant-garde came about ironically through his foundations in the Middle Ages and Aquinas. Eco was first introduced to the aesthetics of the avant-garde through the writing of the Irish novelist James Joyce (1882–1941) who, like Eco, was inspired by the aesthetics of Thomas Aquinas. Eco notes in the introduction to the third edition in Italian of *Opera Aperta* (published in 1997), that when he began as a production assistant in the inaugural years of Italian television, he had been working on the writings of James Joyce which then led to his collaboration with Berio and Berberian on the spoken word composition entitled *Homage to Joyce*.[3] Consequently Joyce provided Eco with an intellectual pathway from the medieval aesthetics of Aquinas to the modern world of the avant-garde and became the original inspiration for Eco's collection of essays entitled *The Open Work*.

Eco does not specifically state when or how he first happened to become acquainted with the writings of Joyce except to indicate in the introduction to *The Aesthetics of Chaosmos: The Middle Ages of James Joyce* in 1981 (originally published in Italian in 1962 as "Le Poetiche di Joyce" in *Opera Aperta*): "Joyce was also an Italian author [Joyce had written articles for the Italian newspaper, *Il Piccolo della Sera* in Trieste] and some of his highest praise came in the very beginning from the Italian literary milieu (Svevo, Benco, Montale ...)."[4] Although Joyce's fictional writings are closely focused on his life in Dublin, his connection to Italy and the Italian literary milieu occurred when Italy became his adopted home as an exile from Ireland. After leaving Dublin in 1904, Joyce moved to Trieste where he lived and worked intermittently as a teacher of English over a period of 12 years while pursuing his writing career, by drawing upon his experience as a student of Italian from an early age.

Trieste was then still part of Austria until the end of WWI, with a mixed population of Italians and Slovenians. Joyce, however, was drawn in particular to the Italian community and Italian culture as evidenced by his adoption of the Italian language, apart from his writings in English. Even his children's names, Giorgio and Lucia, reflected his love of Italian culture. As J.C.C. Mays notes in the introduction to the publication of a lecture that Eco delivered on Joyce in Dublin in 1991, Italian "was the language [Joyce] used for what was nearest to him." Although he wrote in English and was conversant in French and German, Mays notes that: "Italian remained the medium of his ordinary and most intimate living."[5] As a teacher of English in Trieste, Joyce became a close friend of the Italian writer Italo Svevo (1861–1928) whose works he helped to publish. And, as Eco indicates, Joyce's writings attracted the attention of other Italian writers who became some of his earliest admirers.

When Eco first began to write about contemporary aesthetics in the late fifties, however, Joyce's work was still largely unknown in Italy. *Ulysses* (1921), Joyce's third novel, had only appeared in Italian translation in 1960 and his fourth and final novel *Finnegans Wake* (1939) was only available, as Eco noted, through "incomplete and tentative translations."[6] According to Peter Bondanella, Eco's turn to Joyce as inspiration also constituted a clear departure from the legacy of Benedetto Croce (1866–1952), Italy's preeminent intellectual of the first half of the twentieth century. Croce was referred to as the "lay pope" of Italy because of his dominance over the Italian cultural establishment that Eco and the Gruppo 63 were resisting. In contrast to Eco and the new postwar generation of Italian intellectuals of the Gruppo 63, Croce had emphasized the canonical works of the "masters," and he was not receptive to the avant-garde pretensions of *Finnegans Wake* which he described as Joyce's "incomprehensible English novel."[7]

Eco's attraction to Joyce was based on their shared foundations in the medieval world, and, in particular, the aesthetics of Aquinas as a pathway to the contemporary avant-garde. As Eco indicated: "To me Joyce was the node where the Middle Ages and the avant-garde meet." But he also acknowledged that the link between the Middle Ages and modern avant-garde aesthetics was "paradoxical."[8] How could the theological mindset of the Middle Ages be applicable to the problem of aesthetics in the contemporary world dominated by the secular forces of multiculturalism and mass media consumerism? Eco found in Joyce what he called "a dialectic of order and adventure, a contrast between the world of the medieval summae and that of contemporary science and philosophy."[9] The medieval summae were summaries of theological knowledge written by monks such as Aquinas that provided a totalized description of the Christian cosmos as an enclosed world with finite boundaries and a fixed center represented by the creator God from whom all meaning was derived. The totalized cosmos of the medieval summae, however, came to be increasingly displaced by the development of modern science, for example, through figures such as Copernicus, Galileo, Kepler, and

Newton who found evidence in the sensory world that undermined the Christian conception of the Earth as the center of a finite cosmos. Although Eco had greatly admired the concept of beauty that he found in the summae of Aquinas, he came to recognize, as he completed his thesis, that the vision of Aquinas was no longer applicable to the contemporary human-centered world of modern science, multiculturalism, and mass media consumerism that he confronted in 1954.

Joyce, however, provided Eco with a way to transition from the medieval world striving for a comprehensive order, and the modern world of multiple perspectives. Eco found that Joyce had adapted Aquinas to the contemporary world through the influence of two other prominent Italian intellectuals: Giordano Bruno (1548–1600) and Giambattista Vico (1668–1744). Giordano Bruno was a Dominican monk who sought to explore the order of the universe free from the constraints of the Church. His conception of an unbounded universe of multiple worlds without a center, along with other highly unconventional views, however, put him in direct conflict with Church doctrine. As a result, he was imprisoned for seven years by the Inquisition in Rome where he was subjected to interrogation and torture, and he was eventually burned to death as a heretic. A statue was erected in 1889 in Rome's Campo de' Fiori, the site of his execution, to commemorate Bruno as a heroic martyr for freedom of thought. For Joyce and Eco, Bruno's ideas served as a model of the religious quest for meaning adapted to an unbounded world of infinite possibilities. Giambattista Vico, as we considered in Chapter 2, was an eighteenth-century Italian scholar who asserted that the proper focus of knowledge is not speculations on the meaning of God's creativity reflected in the natural world, but rather on the way that humans project their own meaning on the world through human culture. His ideas became one of the core foundations of what is called the Italian "humanist-historicist" tradition because of his emphasis on knowledge through the interpretation of human culture as a form of collective art, and history as a constant recycling of the old and the new.

Eco asserts that, in Joyce, "we find the influence of Aquinas, thrown into crisis but not completely destroyed by the reading of Bruno...".[10] He notes also that Joyce adopts Vico's idea that "fallen man, having lost any hope of being helped by Nature, looks to a superior thing for salvation," and that Joyce "couples this Viconian striving for salvation with the Brunian idea of the discovery of a god within the unity of the world and not beyond it."[11] Eco sees these ideas reflected in Joyce's final novel *Finnegans Wake* through its "circular schema, borrowed from Vico's cyclical vision of history."[12]

Finnegans Wake also includes numerous puns with references to Aquinas, as "aquinatance" for example[13]; and Vico, as "vicus of recirculation" in the opening paragraph.[14] There are also references to Bruno, as "Nolan" because of his birthplace in Nola, Italy, and as "Fratomistor Nawlanmore and Brawne" because Bruno in Italian also means brown.[15]

Although Eco and Joyce are separated in time by half a century (Joyce was born in 1882, 50 years before Eco, and died in 1941 when Eco was nine years old), their personal and intellectual paths share core similarities. They were both raised and educated as Catholics in countries where the Church is dominant culturally and politically in relation to contemporary, secular society. They were both devout adherents to the faith who became disillusioned and eventually exiles from the Church. Most significantly, their religious and intellectual aspirations were both based on the aesthetics of Aquinas. Both Joyce and Eco went through a similar crisis in attempting to accommodate their religious beliefs and intellectual foundations to a contemporary secular worldview while remaining faithful to the aesthetics of Aquinas.

Although Joyce was not formally expelled from the Church like Eco, he chose a life of exile to free himself from its institutional and cultural constraints. His motivation for leaving his homeland and the Church was expressed very explicitly in a highly personal and impassioned letter to his future companion Nora Barnacle in 1904: "My mind rejects the whole present social order and Christianity – home, the recognized virtues, classes of life, and religious doctrines. How could I like the idea of home?" While expressing his general disillusionment with Irish society, he was especially vehement about his rejection and principled defiance towards the Catholic Church:

> Six years ago I left the Catholic Church, hating it most fervently. I found it impossible for me to remain in it on account of the impulses of my nature. I made secret war upon it when I was a student and declined to accept positions it offered me. By doing this I made myself a beggar but I retained my pride. Now I make open war upon it by what I write and say and do. I cannot enter the social order except as a vagabond.[16]

In his first novel, *Portrait of the Artist as a Young Man*, Joyce had already announced his break from the Church:

> He would never swing the thurible before the tabernacle as priest. His destiny was to be elusive of social and religious orders. The wisdom of the

priest's appeal did not touch him to the quick. He was destined to learn his
own wisdom apart from others or to learn the wisdom of others himself
wandering among the snares of the world.[17]

But he also felt alienated from the secular culture outside the Church:

> but yet it wounded him to think that he would never be but a shy guest at the
> feast of the world's culture and that the monkish learning, in terms of which
> he was striving to forge out an esthetic philosophy, was held no higher by the
> age he lived in than the subtle and curious jargons of heraldry and falconry.[18]

Eco and Joyce were exiles from the Church, but they retained their
allegiance to the thought of Aquinas and the religious worldview of the
Middle Ages by transforming their faith into a philosophical and aesthetic
practice. As Eco indicates: "Joyce abandons the faith but not religious
obsession,"[19] and that "Joyce reaches aesthetics through theology."[20]
According to Eco, Joyce's foundations in the Middle Ages "were still
and always would be his vocation and destiny."[21] Joyce served to inspire
Eco as "the last of the medieval monks"[22] by applying the medieval
conception of beauty to the modern world. Through the influence of
Joyce, Eco found a way to affirm his religious faith and medieval foundations in the aesthetics of Aquinas which became the basis for his unique
practice as a public intellectual.

Joyce and Eco rejected the Catholic Church while holding on to a
vision of the world determined by aesthetics that they derived from
Aquinas and the Italian humanist-historicist tradition of Giordano Bruno
and Giambattista Vico. While abandoning their religious and intellectual
quest in relation to what they perceived as the distant, mysterious, transcendent God of the Catholic Church, Joyce and Eco looked instead to the
creative play of meaning expressed in human culture. As Eco indicates, "If
you take away the transcendent God from the symbolic world of the
Middle Ages, you have the world of Joyce."[23] For Eco, Joyce transforms
the aesthetics of Aquinas into the cultural aesthetics of the contemporary
world:

> Joyce departs from the summa to arrive at *Finnegans Wake*, from the
> ordered cosmos of scholasticism to the verbal image of an expanding universe. But his medieval heritage, from which his movements arise, will never
> be abandoned.[24]

The Aesthetics of Chaosmos

After the religious and intellectual crisis that Eco experienced at the completion of his university studies, he found in Joyce's *Finnegans Wake*, in particular, the inspiration for his conception of a modern "open work" that, as we will consider, became the manifesto for the Italian Neo-avant-garde. Eco describes *Finnegans Wake* as "the most terrifying document of formal instability and semantic ambiguity that we possess."[25] Using *Finnegans Wake* as a model, Eco offered an analysis of modern avant-garde aesthetics as a "chaosmos": a relation between the ordered cosmos of conventional culture, and the disordered chaos that lies at its boundaries. Eco notes that: "the Joycean dialectic, more than a meditation, offers us the development of a continuous polarity between Chaos and Cosmos, between disorder and order, liberty and rules, between the nostalgia of Middle Ages and the attempts to envisage a new order."[26] But chaos, in this instance, does not mean confusion and disarray. In Greek mythology, chaos meant the unformed, open void that preceded the emergence of the ordered material world. In relation to contemporary aesthetics, chaos refers to what lies beyond the boundaries of conventional culture that is open to infinite possibilities because it is "disordered," not subject to the constraints of order. Venturing into the chaos provides the creative freedom of infinite possibilities, but it requires the cosmos of conventional order in order to explore its possibilities. Otherwise there would be no basis from which to orient oneself and communicate anything understandable and meaningful.

In relation to Joyce's aesthetics of chaosmos, the medieval world of Aquinas was a fixed, completely enclosed cosmos within which the meaning of human existence was entirely determined in relation to a transcendent God as the author of creation. In other words, there was no outside to the Christian cosmos, and everything within it was fixed and predetermined in relation to a single creative or aesthetic origin. In contrast, Eco describes the contemporary world as a "dialectic of order and adventure [that] puts order into crisis but defines the very condition of adventure."[27] The contemporary world, in contrast to the Middle Ages of Aquinas, has been thrown into crisis through the impact of the human-centered world arising from the Renaissance, and further destabilized by the Enlightenment domination of science and technology, as well as the global recognition of a plurality of religions and cultures. Instead of a transcendent Christian God as the sole author of creation, all of human

THE AESTHETICS OF CHAOSMOS 111

culture can be seen as the source of the infinite diversity of contemporary aesthetic expression. Human culture is constantly involved in exploring possible states of being whose evolving character is determined by reaching beyond the historically ordered cosmos into the chaos of infinite possibilities. The historical circumstances of human cultures provide the ordered cosmos from which new states of being arise through the openness of chaos that allows for what Eco calls the aesthetics of "adventure."

In Joyce's *Finnegans Wake*, Eco found the most radical expression of the aesthetics of "adventure" that deliberately violates and playful disrupts the conventional order through which language generates meaning. Joyce uses words and expressions drawn from the ordered cosmos of conventional culture and alters them to create a dense, multilayered opening into the cultural chaos of possibility. Although Joyce had been exploring the use of unconventional literary styles in his previous novels, his adventure into chaosmos took its most destabilizing form with *Finnegans Wake* (1939) which Joyce described as "the story of a night" in contrast to his previous novel *Ulysses* (1922) that was "the story of a day."

> In writing of the night I really could not, I felt that I could not use words in their ordinary connections. Used that way, they do not express how things are in the night, in the different stages – conscious, then semi-conscious, then unconscious. I found that it could not be done with words in their ordinary relations and connections. When morning comes, of course, everything will be clear again.[28]

Joyce had already stretched the boundaries of literary convention with his previous novel *Ulysses* through the use of a variety of literary styles including stream of consciousness and innovative wordplay as well as an unconventional narrative based on the experience of a single day. *Finnegans Wake*, in comparison, represents a much further venture beyond the boundaries of conventional language. In *Finnegans Wake*, the reader is confronted with an artistic work without a clearly specified framework for determining its meaning apart from an invitation to infinite interpretations. Consequently Joyce's writings reflect a progressive exploration of not just the subject matter that can be expressed through literature, but more importantly the boundaries of conventional language as the medium through which we project our meaning on the world. Joyce's *Finnegans Wake* became the inspiration and principal model for Eco's conception of the contemporary "open work" that, as mentioned previously, became the manifesto of the Italian Neo-avant-garde. Joyce's radical focus on language rather than content became the core strategy that the Italian Neo-avant-garde adopted a generation later.

According to Eco, the chaosmos of Joyce's writings disrupts the "univocal, stable vision of the world,"[29] that he and Joyce had found in the aesthetics of Aquinas, in order to reflect the human-centered contemporary world of science, technology, mass media consumerism, and multiculturalism. As we considered in Chapter 4, Eco, through the influence of Vico, determined that "It is only the productive processes of human makers that we can trace and comprehend."[30] The summae of Aquinas attempted to accommodate an eternal and unchanging conception of perfect being, understood as the creator God, with the aspiration to creative transcendence of human society and the human intellect. But, as Eco indicated, Aquinas's worldview was unable to accommodate the "humanist culture of late medieval times" which "destroyed the system from within."[31] Aquinas's conception of beauty was sufficient for providing an understanding of the relative simplicity of the medieval world that was not yet affected by the dramatic expansion of the human-centered world of urban society and commerce. As Eco indicated, the accelerating alteration of the natural and social world by human enterprise created the conditions in the late Middle Ages for "a new conception of art and beauty" based on "a conception of the artist as an inventor and creator, someone who no longer submitted to the eternal laws."[32] But, while moving beyond the aesthetic vision of Aquinas, Joyce and Eco retained Aquinas's religious notion of transcendence. Joyce and Eco were devout Catholics heavily influenced by Aquinas's attempt to bring together Catholic theology with Aristotle's analysis of the world of our senses. But as exiles from the Catholic Church, they needed to adapt Aquinas's ideas for orienting oneself in the contemporary world of dynamic change and instability due to the rapid pace of technological innovation and the impact of multiculturalism and mass media consumerism. How could the closed cosmos of Aquinas's theology serve as a way of understanding the modern aesthetics of the contemporary world represented by what Eco calls the "open work"?

After his expulsion from the Catholic Church as a heretic in 1954, Eco asserted that "...I have long since settled my accounts with Thomistic metaphysics and the religious outlook."[33] But his conception of modern aesthetics, like Joyce's, can be seen as arising from a similar religious quest for meaning adapted from the medieval theology of Aquinas. Eco's assertion that "Joyce abandons the faith but not religious obsession"[34] and that "Joyce reaches aesthetics through theology"[35] reflects his own religious and intellectual transition. For an intellectual in the humanities such as Eco, the focus of inquiry is to explore as fully as possible the meaning of human existence. As we considered in Chapter 2, the role of the intellectual in the humanities is closely linked to the traditional religious quest for ultimate meaning. The worldview of Aquinas was attractive to Joyce and Eco from a religious and intellectual perspective because it provided a totalized view of the ultimate meaning of human existence through a model of analytical clarity and broad explanatory power based on a conception of beauty. Aquinas joined rational analysis with scriptural interpretation to bring together faith in a transcendent God that could be experienced as beauty in the world of our senses. Aquinas's totalized understanding of the medieval cosmos thus represented for Joyce and Eco a profound unification of reason and religion through the perspective of aesthetics.

While the Middle Ages in the popular imagination is typically seen as both barbaric, for its brutal warfare and subjugation of the peasant class, as well as romantic and heroic for its mystical conception of love and valor, for Joyce and Eco, it was a time when all of our sensory experience of the world could be experienced from the perspective of art and beauty. As Eco indicates, the medieval world saw beauty everywhere as "an attribute of God" in contrast to the modern world that "over-values art."[36] Consequently the medieval world, that came to be characterized as the "dark ages" following the rise of the Renaissance and the Enlightenment, had paradoxically a much more comprehensive view of beauty. From the medieval perspective on aesthetics, it is ironically the contemporary world that would be regarded as dark and barbaric.

But what if Aquinas's conception of beauty as a sign of God's creative presence in the world of our senses was applied instead to the signs of human creativity in the contemporary world of art as well as technology and mass media consumerism? According to Aquinas's conception, the interaction with the beauty of God's creation would transform the individual toward the truth of God. The beautiful, from this perspective, was not just an aspect of things that was attractive to one's senses. For Aquinas, the sensory interaction with the internal formative character of things would cause the transformation of the beholder toward the truth of God. As indicated previously, Aquinas's view of aesthetics was thus seen by Eco and other medieval scholars as a precursor to the modern philosophy of existentialism that conceives of reality as being determined by each individual's interaction with the things of the world. This view is consistent with what we considered in Chapter 2 as a core aspect of our distinguishing character as humans. Since we are the species that constantly modifies our environment over time, we, in turn, are constantly modified through our interaction with the things of the world.

Aquinas's vision of beauty in all things was appealing to Joyce and Eco from a religious and intellectual perspective even though they found that it could not accommodate the historical and cultural circumstances of the contemporary world. But, if the human-centered world of modern technology and mass media consumerism is considered from an existentialist perspective, then the medieval worldview that saw beauty in all of our experience of the world as "an attribute of God," could be applied instead to the cultural products of human creativity. Like Aquinas's view that all of our sensory experience of the world could lead us to the truth of God, our response to works of art as well as technological innovations and the products of mass media consumerism can draw us toward the "truth" of our potential as humans. Joyce's conception of the synthesis of a religious quest with the aesthetics of form is evident in an excerpt from his second novel *Ulysses*:

> Thought is the thought of thought. Tranquil brightness. The soul is in a manner all that is: the soul is the form of forms. Tranquility sudden, vast, candescent: form of forms.[37]

But one can sense as well his isolation as an intellectual and artist in the contemporary world:

> Endless would it be mine, form of my form? Who watches me here? Who ever anywhere will read these written words?[38]

Joyce was at least aware of the possibility that the multilayered puns and obscure references in *Finnegans Wake* would draw the attention of the academic elite:

> I've put in so many enigmas and puzzles that it will keep the professors busy for centuries arguing over what I meant, and that's the only way of insuring one's immortality.[39]

From the perspective of existentialism, art and beauty can be seen in every aspect of our experience of the world from the seemingly most banal products of technology and popular culture to the works of elite culture. The aesthetic quality of all things engages us not only as an external object of our senses but also more importantly through its formative effect on our relationship to the world. The critical awareness of the formative effect on us of cultural products became the project of both Joyce and Eco. The existential perspective on the impact of art and beauty provided Joyce and Eco with a way of adapting the religious sense of transcendence of Aquinas to the circumstances of the contemporary world. The automobile, for example, affects our relationship to space and time, alters the urban environment, privatizes the act of transportation, etc. Digital technology has had a profound impact on our access to information, consumerism, global relations, social interaction, etc. These are all existential factors caused by the products of human culture that transform us through our sensory interaction with the things of the world. The ability to understand the impact of these cultural products and messages is what inspired Eco to become a public intellectual.

THE *FORMA FORMANTE* OF LUIGI PAREYSON

Eco's conception of the aesthetics of Aquinas as a medieval precursor of existentialism that gave him a transitional pathway to the contemporary world was also consistent with the philosophical perspectives that he derived from Luigi Pareyson (1918–1991), his mentor at the University of Turin. In *Estetica: Theoria della Formativita* (Aesthetics: A Theory of Formativity, 1988) Pareyson's approach to the question of aesthetics, like that of Aquinas, is based on an existential perspective:

> Philosophy as such has a character that is at the same time concrete and speculative: Its affirmations have value only if they are the result of a reflection on experience, and only if they arise at the point of contact with experience which succeeds in providing a method of interpretation and criteria for assessing its value.[40]

The emphasis on experience thus becomes the core of his approach to aesthetics:

> The aesthetics proposed in this book is not a metaphysics of art, but an analysis of the aesthetic experience: not a definition of art considered

abstractly in itself, but a study of the person who makes the work of art in the act of making it.[41]

Pareyson also asserts that aesthetics should no longer be considered as just one branch of philosophy, but instead as the foundation for ALL of philosophy:

> aesthetics is not a part of philosophy, but all of philosophy is focused on the problem of beauty and art.[42]

Philosophy, from this perspective, appropriates the religious perspective of Aquinas that beauty and art surround us as the creative expression of human culture. Since Pareyson sought to focus on aesthetics, not based on abstract concepts, but from the perspective of the actual lived experience of the world, he asserts that aesthetics is the proper foundation for **ALL** of philosophy. In other words, contemporary philosophy, consistent with the model of modern science, should not be based on abstract concepts detached from our direct sensory experience of the world, but instead draw its understanding of human experience from an analysis of the sensory world of human culture. Because aesthetics is concerned with our sensory experience of the world, all philosophical inquiry should thus be rooted in, as Pareyson asserts, "the problem of beauty and art." Pareyson's conception of aesthetics is thus developed as the foundation of philosophy which is drawn from the actual experience of the artist as well as the response of the individual in determining the meaning, value, and transformative potential of the work of art. Since philosophy, according to Pareyson, should be considered from the perspective of the experience of "beauty and art," the striving of philosophy for meaning and understanding would encompass all of the products of human culture.

> Formativity is thus essentially a kind of reaching for meaning, because it is able to imagine multiple possibilities, and, at the same time, to find among them the best one, the one that is determined by the same process as its formativity.[43]

Pareyson's emphasis on actual lived experience of the world can be seen as a way of reestablishing the validity of philosophy in the wake of the rise of modern science. The empirical method of modern science grounds its knowledge and verifies its findings on the analysis of data from the material world of nature. Instead of proposing broad generalizations about the natural world, science begins with the gathering of sensory data that is then analyzed to determine the truth. To pursue the same validity, Pareyson asserts that philosophy should be based on an analysis of the sensory experience of interacting with the products of human culture, an idea, as indicated earlier, first proposed by Giambattista Vico in *The New Science*, 1725.

Concerning Pareyson's focus on experience as a way of reasserting the validity of philosophy, it's instructive to find that he conceived of the aesthetics of human activity as a union of the upward and the downward path that was considered in Chapter 3. As Pareyson points out, this notion of two fundamental paths of understanding spans "the entire history of philosophy from Plato and above all from Aristotle."[44] Pareyson, in fact, uses the exact same language, although in a somewhat different way, to describe how these ideas come together in his conception of aesthetics:

> aesthetics is a good example of the point of encounter of the two ways of philosophical reflection: the upward path, that draws universal results from the meditation on concrete experience, and the downward path, that uses these results for interpreting experience and resolving problems.

PAREYSON'S INFLUENCE ON ECO'S PRACTICE AS A PUBLIC INTELLECTUAL

Beyond the emphasis on aesthetics from an existential perspective, it's especially useful to note at this point, how influential Pareyson's theory of aesthetics was for Eco, and how his ideas allowed Eco to adapt his foundations in the medieval aesthetics of Aquinas to the modern world of mass media consumerism. From the aesthetics of Pareyson, Eco could retain the focus on art and beauty as a reflection of God's creativity but apply it instead to the creativity of human culture. In this way, it would take the form of the creative potential of the human experience historically and culturally. Recall that Eco's contribution to the study of Aquinas was a focus on aesthetics which was the medieval view of art and beauty as a way of being drawn to the truth of God through the medium of one's senses. This perspective rooted Aquinas's conception of art and beauty in the everyday experience of each individual. And Aquinas, according to Eco, saw reflections of God's creativity in every aspect of human experience. As previously mentioned, Eco noted that paradoxically the medieval world had a more comprehensive view of aesthetics than the modern world that "overvalues art." Eco could adapt Aquinas's concept of art and beauty in all of our sensory experience to the contemporary world by drawing on Pareyson's assertion that:

> there is art in all of human activity... from the humblest artisanry to the greatest inventions, wherever there is the formative act, there is thus a striving or will towards the becoming of a work of art.[45]

"Art" in this sense represents every aspect of the human modification of the world as *homo faber* according to the imagination drawn from our being as *homo sapiens* rather than being restricted to the work found in museums and art galleries. Consequently Pareyson's aesthetics can help us to understand why Eco as an academic engaged in the scholarly analysis of the products of elite culture would also be drawn to an analysis of the products of mass consumption for a popular audience. If there is "art in all of human activity," then the full spectrum of cultural products from comic books to comic opera are worth considering for understanding the creative expression and the impact of human culture.

Since, according to Pareyson, aesthetics covers the full spectrum of human activity, he asserts that an understanding of the products of human culture should be based on new modes of interpretation:

> The process of knowing and understanding [the formativity of human society] is thus through an interpretation. This calls for on one hand a general theory of interpretation considered from the foundational perspective of how culture generates meaning[46] and therefore it relates to every human activity and operation, and on the other hand an explanation of the multiple interpretability of works of art and how the making of a work of art cannot be understood as either unique or arbitrary for it always involves a specific person who from a personal point of view tries to bring the work alive as he or she wishes.[47]

Pareyson's call for "a general theory of interpretation" can thus be seen as the impetus for Eco to become a pioneering contributor to semiotics during its early years as an emerging field of study, as well as his focus on the interpretation of texts that will be considered in Chapter 9.

But if, as Pareyson asserts, there is "art in all of human activity," what criteria can be used to judge the relative merit of the diverse products of human culture? What then distinguishes the "multiple interpretability of works of art" as a cultural expression? Pareyson describes the making of art through his conception of "formativity":

> formativity means first of all 'to make'... But it's necessary to emphasize that 'to make' truly involves a 'formativity' only when it doesn't limit itself to carrying out something already conceived or to realizing a project already established, or to applying a technique already predisposed, or to following already established rules, but in the very act of making it, invents the way of making it, defines the rules of the work while making it, and conceptualizes while executing it and fashions it in the same act of realizing it. Formativity therefore means 'to make,' but a kind of making that, in the process of making, invents the means of its own making.[48]

An excellent example of Pareyson's notion of artistic formativity can be seen in a brief quote from an interview with Tom Elling, the director of photography for the Danish director Lars Von Trier's film "Breaking the Waves." Elling explained that in the process of filming: "We don't know what we're doing until we do it."[49] From this perspective, Pareyson's conception of aesthetic formativity provides a foundation for Eco's notion of the aesthetics of "adventure" that he found in Joyce and the Italian Neo-avant-garde. As Eco indicates about the focus on language in the writings of Joyce, they involve a "radical conversion from 'meaning' as content of an expression, to the form of the expression as meaning..."[50] According to Pareyson, authentic works of art, or what Eco calls "works with aesthetic value"[51] are formed by exploring beyond what has already been conceived, and beyond established techniques and rules by making up its own techniques as well as the means for determining its meaning. The meaning of what Eco calls "works with aesthetic value" is their formativity.

Eco's practice as a public intellectual who communicates his ideas about the full spectrum of cultural products for both an academic and a popular audience can consequently be understood as arising from his religious and intellectual foundations in the medieval aesthetics of Thomas Aquinas adapted to contemporary aesthetics through the work of James Joyce, as well as the contemporary aesthetics of formativity drawn from Luigi Pareyson. Eco's emergence as an exemplary public intellectual who, as he puts it, attempts "to translate into language accessible to all" the ideas that he draws from both elite and popular culture is consistent with Pareyson's conception of the role of contemporary philosophy:

> conforming to the idea that in order for philosophy to deal with [the problem of experience] it must and can use a common language – not technical jargon – and thus it can be read by all, even those who don't have a background in philosophy so long as they can focus on the less general aspects and more on what is closest to their own experience.[52]

Eco's difficult transition from his university studies on medieval aesthetics to the modern world of mass media consumerism was thus aided by adapting the medieval aesthetics of Aquinas to the Italian humanist-historicist tradition of Bruno and Vico, and by reconceiving the focus of modern aesthetics through the writings of Joyce and the theoretical perspectives of Pareyson. These influences provided Eco with a pathway to the development of his particular practice as a public intellectual. Joyce offered a way of transforming the spiritual quest of the Middle Ages into a secular quest for transcendence through the aesthetics of modern avant-garde works. The influence of Joyce and the Italian avant-garde led to his first theoretical writings on contemporary art as "open" works that will be considered below. The emphasis on language as a formative medium that he found in the writings of Joyce and the Italian Neo-avant-garde would have been an initial catalyst toward his development as a prominent scholar in language theory as the foundational model for a theory of signs or semiotics that Eco has described more broadly as a theory of culture. From Pareyson's idea that "there is art in all of human activity," Eco would find a foundation for critical analyses of the products of popular culture such as soccer matches and James Bond movies. This approach would extend to the full range of cultural products such as pop songs, blue jeans, cell phones, television programs, etc. These were the topics that Eco explored through his numerous columns in Italian newspapers and magazines for a broad popular audience. Pareyson's call for a "general theory of interpretation" as well as an exploration of the "infinite interpretability" of works of art from an individual perspective would serve as the impetus for his *A Theory of Semiotics* in 1975 as well as his focus on *The Role of the Reader* (published in English in 1979) that will be taken up in Chapter 9.

OPERA APERTA

Now that we have considered the influence of Joyce in providing Eco with a link from the medieval aesthetics of Aquinas to the contemporary world, and the influence of Pareyson's concept of formativity on Eco's focus on language and interpretation as a public intellectual who explores the full range of cultural products with a public audience, we can briefly examine how Eco's idea of a "systematic study of the concept of 'openness'" resulted in his first writings on contemporary aesthetics in 1962 entitled *Opera Aperta* (The Open Work). In "The Poetics of the Open Work," Eco first set out his conception of modern aesthetics: "A work of art... is a complete and *closed* form in its uniqueness as a balanced organic whole, while at the same time constituting an *open* product on account of its susceptibility to countless different interpretations which do not impinge on its unadulterable specificity."[53] As noted previously, Eco's conception of the "open work" became highly influential in Italy in the sixties by becoming the manifesto of the Italian Neo-avant-garde. His theory of the open work continues to be one of his most useful and explanatory writings in providing an understanding of the mechanisms of contemporary works of art as well as aesthetic works in general. This essay also provides an early demonstration of Eco's encyclopedic knowledge and virtuosity in drawing upon a variety of perspectives. Following the inspiration of Joyce, Eco finds examples of modern "open" works from avant-garde musical composers such as Luciano Berio (1925–2003), Henri Pousseur (1929–2009), and Pierre Boulez (1925–2016), and from authors of written works such as Franz Kafka (1883–1924), and Stephane Mallarme (1842–1848), as well as artists of visual works such as the mobiles of Alexander Calder (1898–1976). In addition, he links the "open" character of these works of art to the radically altered worldview derived from modern quantum physics in Albert Einstein's (1879–1955) rethinking of time and space, Werner Heisenberg's (1901–1976) "uncertainty principle," and Niels Bohr's (1885–1962) discovery that elementary matter can behave as both particles and waves.

Open works are further linked to the "perceptive ambiguities" proposed by modern philosophers such as Edmund Husserl (1859–1938) and Jean-Paul Sartre (1905–1980) who concluded that "'openness' is at the heart of every act of perception."[54] These diverse points of reference that span the fields of art, science, and philosophy are considered as well in relation to the long arc of historical modes of interpretation from ancient philosophy beginning with Plato, through medieval writers such as Dante, and the precursors to modern open works in the "fluid" worldview of the Baroque, and the "blurred sense and vague outlines" of "Romanticism."[55]

Eco conceives of the distinguishing character of modern aesthetic works as their openness to multiple interpretative pathways that require the performer or audience to actively collaborate in generating their meaning. Instrumental works by Pousseur and Boulez, for example, consist of segments that call upon the performer to arrange them in a sequence of their choice. In other words, the performer collaborates with the composer in generating the formative organization and thus the meaning of the composition because the work is "open" to many choices and a broad range of interpretive perspectives. Eco cites examples of "openness" in literary works such as the puns and word linkages in Joyce's *Finnegans Wake* that offer a kaleidoscope of interpretative configurations. Similar to the choices made available to the performer of open works of musical composition, in the case of literary "open" works, the reader must assume the role of "performer" by choosing among a wide variety of interpretive possibilities.

A potent expression of the conceptual basis for the aesthetics of "openness" is the quote cited by Eco from the French poet Mallarme: "To name an object is to suppress three-fourths of the enjoyment of the poem, which is composed of the pleasure of guessing little by little: to suggest... there is the dream."[56] The modern "open" work functions through deliberate ambiguity that requires the active "guessing" on the part of the audience. This deliberate ambiguity offers a broad range of free choices that both allow for and also require the participation of the audience as an essential aspect of the meaning of the work. The aesthetics of modern open works thus emphasize form over content because, in essence, the form **is** the content. The function of modern open works is to create a formative effect on the audience by generating a "higher" or "expanded" awareness of our interrelationship with the world.

As we will consider in the next chapter, Eco and the Italian Neo-avant-garde were attempting to respond to the alienation of the intellectual and artist by the impact of popular culture and consumerism by calling attention to the role of language as the formative medium of art and culture. As a result, the artists and intellectuals of the Italian Neo-avant-garde attempted to foreground the formative aspect of their work by requiring the audience to be involved collaboratively in its creation. Through this interrelational formativity, the individual would be drawn to a "higher" or "expanded" consciousness of their collaborative role in the aesthetics of human culture. In reference to literary works, for example, Eco indicates in the "Postscript" to *The Name of the Rose* that: "A text is meant to be an experience of transformation for the reader."[57] To generate this formative effect, contemporary open works require the collaborative participation of the audience in exploring multiple paths of interpretation.

But haven't works of art always been subject to multiple interpretations in relation to the aesthetic taste and cultural circumstances of the individual? Eco responds to this question by providing a comparative historical background on the emergence of modern "open" works that traces the role of the interpreter in relation to the work of art over the course of Western history. Eco indicates that, beginning with ancient Greek society, there was an awareness of the relation between the work of art, for example in painting and architecture, and the way it would be perceived by the audience. This gave rise to the technique of perspective that created a sense of symmetry in the design of architectural columns. It had the effect, however, of creating a single, privileged point of view. In the Middle Ages, similarly, there was an understanding that diverse modes of interpretation were available to the reader of biblical scripture for example. But, as Eco points out, these modes of interpretation were strictly limited. Citing a passage from Dante, Eco notes that there were three prescribed paths of interpretation during the Middle Ages: "the moral, the allegorical, and the anagogical."[58] The interpretive possibilities were thus rigidly predetermined which closed off the interpretative freedom of the reader. This closed system, as Eco indicates, reflected the "hierarchy" and "authoritarian" character of the "ordered cosmos" of the medieval worldview.[59]

Eco points to the Baroque period of the seventeenth century as "the first clear manifestation of modern culture and sensitivity" by confronting "(both in art and in science)... a world in a fluid state..."[60] But, as Eco points out, even though "Baroque form is dynamic," its interpretive possibilities were "codified by modern criticism and organized into aesthetic canons."[61] Although the fluid dynamics of Baroque art made it open to multiple perspectives, it was still subject to a limited and predetermined interpretive scheme. The Romanticist aesthetics of "late-nineteenth-century Symbolism," according to Eco, signaled "the first occasion when a conscious poetics of the open work appears" with "infinite suggestive possibilities."[62]

Art of the Ambiguous and the Strange

The key terms for understanding Eco's conception of the open work are "dynamism,"[63] "indefiniteness,"[64] "ambiguity,"[65] "indeterminacy,"[66] "defamiliarization,"[67] and "suggestiveness."[68] The modern open work is "dynamic" in the sense that it calls for the active interplay between the audience and the work of art in pursuing its fluid, constantly changeable ways of generating meaning. As Eco indicates with the example of the mobiles of the artist Alexander Calder, it is a "work in movement" that "offers the interpreter, the performer, the addressee a work *to be completed*."[69] The open work is incomplete because of its deliberate "indefiniteness." It allows for multiple interpretations by not defining for the audience a prescribed set of interpretative outcomes. Instead the audience is offered an "opening" into an interpretative playfield that is created through deliberate "ambiguity." The symbolic components of an open work are intentionally ambiguous or vague so that multiple potential meanings can be drawn from them without a prescribed set of interpretive guidelines. Because the paths of possible interpretations are not predetermined by the artist in open works, it creates an "indeterminacy" of meaning. The open work also intentionally violates the conventional uses of language and art as a mode of "defamiliarization." It opens up new possibilities of meaning by making the familiar appear strange, for example, in the unconventional wordplay in Joyce's *Finnegans Wake*. Familiar words such as "Neanderthal," "meander," and "tale" are defamiliarized by joining them together as "meandertale,"[70] to suggest a story of primitive origins that can wander in many directions. While creating an opening to infinite possibilities, however, the open work retains a formative character that limits the free collaboration of the audience. In effect, the open work fosters an opening into new modes of understanding, but its structured formativity provides the means for making this experience possible. The open work thus functions through a formative "suggestiveness." It empowers the audience to recognize its own potential as an active participant in the aesthetic project of cultural collaboration and development, but it does so in relation to the experience of the artist that is embedded in the making of the work of art.

But how can Eco's conception of the open work help us to understand more generally the function of works of art? Doesn't the conception of openness just perpetuate the interpretive game that is familiar to anyone, for example, from high school and college literature courses? The student is encouraged to engage in interpretation as a kind of guided guesswork. The literary text functions as a form of concealment through the use of vague and allusive symbolic references of supposedly dense significance. Identifying and interpreting the meaning of these symbolic clues can be puzzled through by considering the historical and cultural background of the author and the author's modes of stylistic expression. But it's apparent in these interpretive exercises that there is an academically sanctioned set of interpretations that can be supported by citing excerpts from the text. The accepted interpretations arise from the authority of the writer of the text and the scholarly expertise of the instructor of the course. Sometimes there is simply the suggestion of unresolved but supposedly instructive questions. For example, can Shakespeare's *Hamlet* be understood as the exploration of the underlying theme of poison as a metaphor for the corruptive effect of power? In this way, the interpretation of works of art is an exercise in attempting to decipher the meaning of symbols concealed by the artist that are drawn from their cultural and historical background either consciously or unconsciously. The full meaning of these works would consequently require an intensive engagement in scholarly analysis but as a predominantly passive participant.

Eco, however, offers an explanation of the mechanisms of aesthetic works in general that empowers the audience as an active participant in the making of the work. Eco's theory of the open work alleviates the audience from being passively subordinated to the artist or author in a game of concealment and decipherment. While there were specific guidelines for interpretation of aesthetic works over the course of Western history, as indicated previously, the modern open work frees the audience from those constraints as well as subordination to the intentions of the artist. It should be acknowledged, however, that the experience of the artist, such as Joyce, is an important consideration in exploring the meaning of aesthetic works because the artist's unique experience of the world is embedded in the work. And there are certainly many instances of subtle concealment to be found in aesthetic works that Eco has pointed out, for example, in the work of Joyce. But Eco's theory of the open work allows the audience to assume a collaborative role in the interpretive "performance" of the work. The deliberate ambiguity of open works creates an interpretive space so that the audience can and must find their own interpretive path. The interpretation is thus not predetermined by the role of the artist. Eco states in the "Postscript" to *The Name of the Rose* that: "the author should die once he has finished writing. So as not to trouble the path of the text."[71] And, for emphasis, he states twice on the following page that: "The text is there, and produces its own effects."[72] The text consequently has an autonomous role in generating meaning, and the deliberate ambiguity of open works requires the collaboration of the audience. The openness of these works to the collaborative interpretation of the audience, however, was later clarified in Eco's writings on interpretation theory that emphasize the "limits" of the audience's collaborative freedom. The problem of understanding how the author's history and culture are embedded in the text is also taken up by Eco in his interpretation theory that will be considered in Chapter 9.

As we will consider more fully in Chapter 8 on language theory, the author cannot know and cannot control all of the potential interpretive pathways of the text because language itself functions through ambiguity. As noted with the puns in Joyce's *Finnegans Wake*, words and sentences have multiple meanings. For example, "date" can refer to a fruit, a particular day in time, a meeting of potential romantic partners, etc. Eco notes, in reference to Joyce's *Finnegans Wake* that: "Formal logic has suggested that natural languages have no logic. In fact, they are not ruled by a formal logic but by a rhetoric, a logic of substitutions."[73] As a function of language, substitutions mean that words can have multiple meanings, as indicated before, in relation to the concepts that they refer to (for example the word "pen" can substitute for the act of writing and "sword" for the act of fighting as in "the pen is mightier than the sword"). Because of the many possible substitutions between words and things, language is open to infinite interpretive pathways. But the inherent ambiguity of language would result in gibberish, as Eco notes, without "an underlying network of possible connections established by a previous cultural convention."[74] In other words, language is a powerful medium of thought because of its inherent ambiguity that allows for infinite substitution, innovation, and expansion, but it can only generate meaning through reference to some recognizable relations of understanding. Eco points out that because of the intensive reflection on language in Joyce's *Finnegans Wake*, it functions as a "grandiose epistemological metaphor."[75] Epistemology explores the most fundamental philosophical question of what and how we can know. The defamiliarizing use of language in *Finnegans Wake* causes the reader to become aware of the constraints as well as the potential freedom of language as a medium for understanding what and how we can know.

Eco's theory of the open work empowers the audience to "complete" the work because it is created as an interpretive vehicle that is independent from the artist. For example, the novel, as Eco points out, is "a machine for generating interpretations."[76] Eco was influenced by Joyce's conception that the stylistic form and not the intentions of the author is the guiding principle in interpretation. He cites Joyce's principle of the "impersonality of the work of art"[77] which Joyce derived from ancient and medieval conceptions that "the work is an object which expresses its own structural laws and not the person of the author."[78] This is an important consideration because Eco's practice as an intellectual has involved the attempt to communicate his ideas to both an academic and a popular audience. His work can be seen as central to the humanistic tradition of attempting to foster an emancipatory consciousness. Modern open works are intended to arouse the audience to a higher consciousness through the transformational effect of the work of art. The problem in this project arises when trying to bridge between dense and radically unconventional aesthetic works such as Joyce's *Finnegans Wake* and the cultural background of a popular audience.

NOTES

1. Eco, *The Name of the Rose*, p. 529.
2. From the introduction to Eco's *The Open Work*, (Milan: Bompiani, 1997), pp. v–vi.
3. Eco, *Opera Aperta*, (Milan: RCS Libri S.p.a., 1997), p. v.
4. Eco, *The Aesthetics of Chaosmos, The Middle Ages of James Joyce*, translated by Ellen Esrock, (Cambridge: Harvard University Press, 1989), p. xi.
5. J.C.C. Mays, from the introduction to *Talking of Joyce*, (Dublin: University College Dublin Press, 1998), p. 2.
6. Eco, *The Aesthetics of Chaosmos*, p. xi.
7. Bondanella, *Umberto Eco and the Open Text*, p. 24.
8. Eco, *The Aesthetics of Chaosmos*, p. xi.
9. Eco, *The Aesthetics of Chaosmos*, p. 2.
10. Eco, *The Aesthetics of Chaosmos*, p. 2.
11. Eco, *The Aesthetics of Chaosmos*, p. 64.
12. Eco, *The Aesthetics of Chaosmos*, p. 7.
13. Eco, *The Aesthetics of Chaosmos*, p. 72.
14. James Joyce, *Finnegans Wake*, (New York: Penguin Books, 1999), p. 3.
15. Joyce, *Finnegans Wake*, p. 50.
16. From the biography of James Joyce by Richard Ellmann, (Oxford: Oxford University Press, 1982), p. 169.

17. Joyce, *Portrait of the Artist as a Young Man*, (New York: Bantam Books, 1992), p. 153.
18. Joyce, *Portrait of the Artist as a Young Man*, p. 174.
19. Eco, *The Aesthetics of Chaosmos*, p. 3.
20. Eco, *The Aesthetics of Chaosmos*, p. 5.
21. Eco, *The Aesthetics of Chaosmos*, p. 79.
22. Eco, *The Aesthetics of Chaosmos*, p. 81.
23. Eco, *The Aesthetics of Chaosmos*, p. 7.
24. Eco, *The Aesthetic of Chaosmos*, p. 3.
25. Eco, *The Aesthetics of Chaosmos*, p. 61.
26. Eco, *The Aesthetics of Chaosmos*, p. 3.
27. Eco, *The Aesthetics of Chaosmos*, p. 72.
28. Eco, *The Aesthetics of Chaosmos*, p. 62.
29. Eco, *The Aesthetics of Chaosmos*, p. 37.
   From Max Eastman, "Poets Talking to Themselves," Harper's Magazine, no. 977 (October 1931).
30. Eco, *The Aesthetics of Thomas Aquinas*, p. 204.
31. Eco, *The Aesthetic of Thomas Aquinas*, p. 205.
32. Eco, *The Aesthetics of Thomas Aquinas*, p. 214.
33. Umberto Eco, *The Aesthetics of Thomas Aquinas*, translated by Hugh Bredin, (Cambridge: Harvard University Press, 1988), p. vii.
34. Eco, *The Aesthetics of Chaosmos*, p. 3.
35. Eco, *The Aesthetics of Chaosmos*, p. 5.
36. Eco, *The Aesthetics of Thomas Aquinas*, p. 6.
37. Joyce, *Ulysses*, (New York: Random House, 1986), p. 21.
38. Joyce, *Ulysses*, p. 40.
39. From Richard Ellmann, *James Joyce*, (New York: Oxford University Press, Revised Edition, 1982), p. 521.
40. Pareyson, Luigi, *Estetica: Teoria della Formativita*, (Milan: Bompiani, 2005), p. 8.
41. Luigi Pareyson, *Estetica: Teoria della Formativita*, p. 9. Translations from the Italian are my own.
42. Pareyson, *Estetica: Teoria della Formativita*, p. 15.
43. Pareyson, *Estetica*, (Milan: Gruppo Editoriale Fabbri, Bompiani, Sonzongo, Etas, S.p.A. 1988), p. 61. Translation is my own.
44. Pareyson, *Estetica: Teoria della Formativita*, p. 8.
45. Pareyson, *Estetica: Teoria della Formativita*, p. 19. Note that the text in Italian reads as follows: "c'e l'arte di ogni attivita umana dalle techniche piu umili sino alle invenzione piu grande... ovunque c'e esercizio di formativita, e quindi esigenza di arte." In consultation with the art historian Riccardo de Mambro Santos at Willamette University, I was advised that the term "techniche" would be translated literally as "techniques" from an Italian

art history perspective, and the phrase "esigenza di arte" would be translated as the "need of art" or "will of art" in reference to the Austrian art historian Alois Riegl's concept of "kuntswollen" which is difficult to translate into English. Since I am writing more broadly for a general audience as well as an academic one, I tried to convey the sense of these expressions by translating "techniche" to "artistry" and "esigenza di arte" to a striving or will toward the becoming of a work of art.
46. The text in Italian reads as follows: "considerata come originaria" which would translate literally to "considered as originary" which seems a bit vague to me in English. "Originary" means causing the existence of something, primal, productive, etc., so I tried to paraphrase that sense in my translation as "considered from the foundational perspective of how culture generates meaning."
47. Pareyson, *Estetica*, p. 11.
48. Pareyson, *Estetica*, p. 59.
49. From the documentary *Tranceformer: A Portrait of Lars Von Trier* (1997) included in the DVD of *The Element of Crime* (1984).
50. Eco, *The Aesthetics of Chaosmos*, p. 37.
51. Eco, *The Limits of Interpretation*, p. 3.
52. Pareyson, *Estetica*, pp. 9–10.
53. Eco, *The Open Work*, (Milan: Bompiani, 1997), p. 4.
54. Eco, *The Open Work*, p. 16.
55. Eco, *The Open Work*, pp. 7–8.
56. Eco, *The Open Work*, p. 8.
57. Eco, "Postscript" to *The Name of the Rose*, now included in current editions of the novel (New York: Harcourt Brace & Company, 1983), p. 524.
58. Eco, *The Open Work*, p. 5.
59. Eco, *The Open Work*, p. 6.
60. Eco, *The Open Work*, p. 7.
61. Eco, *The Open Work*, p. 7.
62. Eco, *The Open Work*, pp. 8–9.
63. Eco, *The Open Work*, p. 18.
64. Eco, *The Open Work*, p. 9.
65. Eco, *The Open Work*, p. 16.
66. Eco, *The Open Work*, p. 15.
67. Eco, *The Open Work*, p. 11.
68. Eco, *The Open Work*, p. 9.
69. Eco, *The Open Work*, p. 19.
70. Eco, *The Aesthetics of Chaosmos*, p. 69.
71. Eco, "Postscript" to *The Name of the Rose*, p. 508.
72. Eco, "Postscript" to *The Name of the Rose*, p. 507.
73. Eco, *The Aesthetics of Chaosmos*, p. 67.

74. Eco, *The Aesthetics of Chaosmos*, p. 67.
75. Eco, *The Aesthetics of Chaosmos*, p. 74.
76. Eco, "Postscript" to *The Name of the Rose*, p. 505.
77. Eco, *The Aesthetics of Chaosmos*, p. 15.
78. Eco, *The Aesthetics of Chaosmos*, p. 17.

CHAPTER 6

The Gruppo 63 and the Italian Neo-avant-garde

Although Eco became increasingly disillusioned with the potential of television to bring an expanded cultural consciousness to the masses, through his association with a new generation of Italian intellectuals that became the Gruppo 63, he began to pursue a movement for reasserting the role of the intellectual and artist in confronting the encroachment of popular culture. Eco characterized the Gruppo 63 as "the cultural sickness of the generation of consumer prosperity" whose goal was "to smash the very media of communication."[1] As a result, they engaged in a militant role as aesthetic provocateurs through an emphasis on language as a way of countering the impact of the new industry of mass media consumerism. Citing his fellow Gruppo 63 member Angelo Guglielmi, Eco asserted that the challenge confronting Italian avant-garde intellectuals in the sixties was "an alienation which the writer can only fight against by working with signs and language rather than things and contents."[2] For the Gruppo 63, language became the battleground for the soul of culture, and, for Eco, the study of language became the core of his intellectual practice.

THE ORIGINS OF THE AVANT-GARDE

As cultural provocateurs, the intellectuals of the Gruppo 63 were following in a long tradition that, as Renato Poggioli indicates in *The Theory of the Avant-Garde*,[3] originated in France in the nineteenth century through French poets such as Rimbaud (1854–1891) and Verlaine (1844–1896) who engaged in a counter-culture movement in opposition to the French cultural establishment. The term "*avant-garde,*" however, was originally derived from the French military to refer literally to an "advance guard," a force deployed ahead of the main body of troops. In the late nineteenth century, with the expansion of the industrial revolution and urban society, *avant-garde* shifted in meaning as an adjective designating a revolutionary alliance of political and artistic movements. As Poggioli indicates citing the French writer Baudelaire (1821–1867), the use of the term *avant-garde* to refer to artistic and political movements was typical of the French penchant for metaphors drawn from the military.[4] By the early twentieth century the term *avant-garde* shifted again to designate radically innovative and experimental artistic movements that attempted to free themselves from the constraints of conventional society. It's useful, however, to keep in mind the initial alliance between art and revolutionary politics because, during the period leading up to and following the French Revolution of 1789, intellectuals and artists were in the vanguard of the radical break from the traditional establishment. These associations have continued for intellectuals and artists in contemporary society who see their role as raising an emancipatory consciousness that is inherently political and revolutionary.

The roots of the avant-garde as an artistic movement, however, can be traced even earlier to Romanticism from the early nineteenth century. As Poggioli indicates, "romanticism was the first cultural-artistic manifestation of prime importance." Romanticism went beyond a shared focus on style and technique and engaged in a movement "as a group of artists intent on a common program."[5] In other words, Romanticism involved a group of artists who were motivated by the need to arouse a political, liberatory consciousness in response to specific historical conditions. The intellectuals of Romanticism were reacting against the impact of the industrial revolution and urban development arising from the Enlightenment emphasis on reason and technology. The Romanticist movement emphasized the alternative of the "heart over the head," the emotions and creative impulses over rational analysis. Romanticism was thus a reaction by a new generation of humanistic intellectuals against an emerging new class of scientific and technical "intelligentsia" from the Enlightenment. The English poet and painter William Blake (1757–1827) is especially representative of this reaction through his famously disparaging portrait of the scientist and mathematician Isaac Newton (1642– 1727) who is depicted measuring the ground at his feet with a compass while oblivious to the beauty of nature behind him. Blake's opposition to Newton motivated his declaration that "Art is the Tree of Life, Science is the Tree of Death."[6]

From the eighteenth and nineteenth centuries, the historical circumstances that were antagonistic to the humanistic intellectuals of the Romanticist movement were the degradation of nature and the human spirit by industrialization spawned by science and technology. But while the response of the Romanticist movement in art and literature was innovative and broke with tradition in emphasizing the expression of the individual's imaginative and emotional instincts, it did not focus primarily on violating the conventional boundaries of art in the same radical manner as the later avant-garde.

After Romanticism and the alliance between artists and revolutionaries in the nineteenth century, the first wave of avant-garde movements in the twentieth century occurred in Italy through the Futurist movement. Following a longstanding avant-garde tradition, Futurism was instigated through the publication of a manifesto in 1909 by the Italian intellectual Filippo Tommaso Marinetti (1876–1944) who called on a new generation of artists to engage in a political and artistic movement focused on a violent break from the past. The Futurist artists, in contrast to the Romanticist movement, enthusiastically embraced the new science and technology of the automobile, locomotive, airplane, etc., as a means of liberation from the past. But after the demoralizing, mechanized warfare of WWI cast doubt on the emancipatory potential of the new technology, the Futurists were succeeded by avant-garde artists of the Dadaist movement such as Marcel Duchamp (1887–1968) whose objective was to antagonize the bourgeois cultural establishment's conception of art. His famous submission in 1917 of a "ready-made" urinal as a work of art was intended as a direct provocation against the sense of aesthetic refinement held by the affluent elite of industrialized society.

THE INTELLECTUAL ELITE AND CULTURAL POPULISM

After WWII, the challenge confronting Eco and the Italian Neo-avant-garde intellectuals and artists of the Gruppo 63 was both to break free from the Italian cultural establishment that preceded them and to aggressively confront the encroachment in the cultural domain of the impact of popular culture through mass media consumerism. The historical development of the avant-garde movement is a key aspect for understanding the contemporary relation between intellectuals and popular culture because it represents an attempt to reassert the role of the intellectual elite through a coordinated attack against the forces of popular culture. Eco and his fellow members of the Gruppo 63 were descendents of a long historical tradition as the privileged creators and arbiters of cultural expression who were being displaced by the new market forces of mass media consumerism that gave rise to "popular" culture. Prior to the rise of modern industrial society and mass media consumerism, "culture" had always referred exclusively to the distinguishing character of elite society. The "natural" superiority of elite society over the common, laboring classes was based on the inherited birthright of the aristocracy (from the Greek "aristos" for "best" and "arete" for "excellence") and the cultural refinement that distinguished them through breeding and education which was expressed through their manner of speaking, taste in the arts, architecture, fashion, etc. Elite culture was the product of artists and intellectuals either born into the elite or those drawn from the laboring classes whose talent and ingenuity earned the patronage of the elite. The elite intellectuals' specialized knowledge of philosophy, history, and the arts made them the privileged arbiters and creators of cultural expression. Over the long span of human history "popular" and "culture" were thus contradictory terms. The general "populace" did not possess "culture" because being "cultivated" was the social distinction held by the elite. From this perspective, the contemporary notion of culture determined by the relation between producers and the masses through the market forces of consumerism would be regarded as an inherent contradiction and the expression "popular culture" would constitute an oxymoron.

It should be noted, however, that long before the rise of mass media consumerism in the twentieth century, there had always been an undercurrent of "popular" culture through the long tradition of folk music and folk tales of the peasant and laboring classes. But "folk" culture was not recognized by the cultural elite until the interest in fairy tales from the end of the seventeenth century,[7] and the idealization of the organic "purity" of folk culture by Romanticism as a reaction to the industrial revolution. Folk culture also became a focus during the rise of European nationalism from the eighteenth century that aroused an interest in national culture and the roots of national ethnic identity. Classical folk tales such as *Cinderella*, *Sleeping Beauty*, and *Snow White* originated from the oral culture of the peasant class. They were collected in written form by the Brothers Grimm in the nineteenth century, which provided the source for the broadly popular animated films for a mass audience by Walt Disney while filtering out the rougher details of the original folk versions. There are also many examples of classical composers such as Johannes Brahms (1833–1897) and Franz Liszt (1811–1886) who integrated folk tunes in their work. Folk traditions, however, were recognized as having cultural value by the elite because of their organic expression of national, cultural roots. In contrast, especially from the twentieth century, the commercial interests of producers attempting to appeal to the taste of the masses through the forces of the mass media have displaced the traditional role of folk culture as well as the cultural elite. As Eco noted in *The Open Work*, the transition to popular culture caused artists and intellectuals to become alienated as a class:

> Popular culture spreads when elite culture is still very much in touch with the sensibility and language of society as a whole. Artists begin feeling a different vocation as the industry of mass culture acquires ascendency and society is invaded by easily consumable messages. Art begins to elaborate the project of an avant-garde (even though the term may not yet have been coined) when popular novels are satisfying the masses' needs for escape and cultural elevation, and when photography starts fulfilling both the commemorative and the practical functions that were once the province of painting. According to many, the crisis was first felt in the middle of the nineteenth century.[8]

Until the nineteenth century, "culture" thus designated the traditional distinction between elite society and the masses. From this historical perspective, how could "culture" be determined by the popular masses in modern society, not as a judgment of refined taste, but solely through the market forces of consumerist demand promoted by the mass media? To cultivate means to foster the growth or development of something toward its potential. Besides their birthright and breeding, distinctions of dress, speech and manners, members of elite society were "cultivated" through their specialized education that gave them exclusive access to the knowledge of philosophy, literature, and the arts which provided them with the cultivated taste and judgment to appreciate and maintain elite culture.

EDUCATION AND CULTURAL CLASS DISTINCTIONS

The educational traditions that came to distinguish the elite arose over the long span of Western history. From the time of the ancient Greeks, education was directed toward preparing the elite members of society for their role as civic leaders. It included a cultural background drawn from literature through the works of Homer, for example, as well as the ability to reason and engage in public debate, and knowledge of the techniques of warfare held by Greek men. Roman society adopted the model of the Greeks and transformed it into the traditional seven liberal arts. The liberal arts provided the body of knowledge necessary for maintaining the privileged status of the "liberal" class which meant the "free" citizens of the ruling elite whose education was intended to prepare them to assume and maintain their inherited role as civic leaders in relation to the proletarian class of slaves and laborers. When these traditions were taken up in the Middle Ages, they were integrated with Christian theology into what was called Scholasticism. Through the highly restricted access to literacy during the Middle Ages, education became, for the most part, the exclusive domain of the clergy until the late Middle Ages and the establishment of the universities beginning in the eleventh century.

During the Renaissance, the liberal arts tradition was taken up outside the clergy by artists and intellectuals who reappropriated classical literature and the arts from the ancient Greeks and Romans. The Renaissance reappropriation of the ancient inheritance was the foundation for what we now call the "humanities" because of the emphasis on the human experience in contrast to the theological focus on the spiritual life of Scholasticism. The humanistic studies were based on the ancient liberal arts foundation of the *trivium* of grammar, logic, and rhetoric, but with a greater emphasis on the study of Latin and Greek, and expanded to include history, moral philosophy, and literature, all of which dealt with an understanding and guidance for aspiring to the highest potential of the human experience. This is the tradition that Eco inherited.

With the rise of the Enlightenment age of reason in the eighteenth century and the assertion of the principle of human equality, as well as the increasing complexity of urban life, education gradually began to expand beyond the traditional elite. As indicated in Chapter 2, the Enlightenment eventually caused the broad proliferation of education and the creation of specialized fields of knowledge including scientific and technical applications. During the twentieth century, as a legacy of the Enlightenment, education in developed, industrialized countries expanded on a massive scale. Students enrolled in higher education rose from around two percent at the turn of the century to between 40 and 50 percent by mid-century in the USA and Europe with Italy, however, just below 30 percent.[9] Consequently the class of individuals engaged in specialized intellectual pursuits became a major force in class relations. Industrialization and the expansion of education also caused the development of a greater distribution of wealth that brought about the rise of an educated middle class as well as a laboring class with a higher standard of living that was eventually the catalyst for the development of consumerism through the mass media that caused the "popular culture" revolution.

The technological development of mass communication media such as radio and television, and more recently the internet, has provided broad access to information and entertainment for much of the world's population. But consumerism and the mass media, while providing the potential for vastly expanded access to products, information, and entertainment, have also, at least from the perspective of elite intellectuals, contributed to a degradation of culture. The negative impact on culture, from an elite perspective, arises because of the need of producers to appeal to the taste of a broad popular audience rather than trying to cultivate more broadly the "refined" taste of the traditional elite. The rapid advances in modern technology, the proliferation of the mass media, and the impact of consumerism have thus brought mixed benefits, and the perception of the degradation of culture was the motivation for the reaction by intellectuals and artists that took the form of the Neo-avant-garde in Italy in the sixties.

KITSCH AND THE FUNCTION OF "HIGH" ART

In the essay entitled "The Structure of Bad Taste" from the English version of *The Open Work* (originally published in Italian in 1964 in the collection of essays on the mass media entitled *Apocalittici e Integrati* which will be discussed in the next chapter) Eco explores the relationship between the cultural function of works of art and works for popular consumption such as *The Da Vinci Code* that attempt to appeal to the taste of a mass audience while appropriating the symbols of "high" art. Despite the seemingly snooty title, Eco offers a fairly even handed and highly useful analysis of the relationship between art and the products of mass consumption by drawing on the ideas of the art critic Clement Greenberg (1909–1994) from his 1939 essay "Avant-garde and Kitsch." *Kitsch* is a German word that originated in the late nineteenth century to refer to inexpensive decorative objects for the home such as paintings and figurines marketed for mass consumption. From an elitist perspective, these objects would be considered "cheap" and "tacky" because they don't reflect a "cultivated" taste in decorative aesthetics, and because they are so broadly accessible for a mass audience. But to characterize these products as "kitsch" could be dismissed as petty elitist snobbery for disparaging the harmless desire of popular consumers for objects that provide some decorative flair for the home. Greenburg, however, uses the term "kitsch" more precisely to refer to the impact of the new mass media consumerism of the twentieth century in appropriating the symbols of "high culture" in a way that undermines the cultural function of art. In this sense, the usage of the term "kitsch" as an indicator of bad taste provides a powerful explanatory analysis of the dynamics of cultural consumption across the social spectrum.

Eco introduces the concept of kitsch as follows:

> As an easily digestible substitute for art, Kitsch is the ideal food for a lazy audience that wants to have access to beauty and enjoy it without having to make too much of an effort.[10]

Kitsch can be seen as a result of the industrial revolution that generated a middle class of consumers and the mass media that aroused their desire for cultural products. According to Clement Greenberg:

> The peasants who settled in the cities as proletariat and petty bourgeois learned to read and write for the sake of efficiency, but they did not win the leisure and comfort necessary for the enjoyment of the city's traditional culture. Losing, nevertheless, their taste for the folk culture whose background was the countryside, and discovering a new capacity for boredom at the same time, the new urban masses set up a pressure on society to provide them with a kind of culture fit for their own consumption. To fill the demand of the new market, a new commodity was devised: ersatz culture, kitsch, destined for those who, insensible to the values of genuine culture, are hungry nevertheless for the diversion that only culture of some sort can provide.[11]

This great profusion of mass produced cultural products not only led the intellectuals and artists of the avant-garde to engage in a militant resistance by antagonizing a popular audience with works that were intentionally "unacceptable," but it also led to the desire by the emerging mass of popular consumers to appropriate the products of "high" culture in an accessible way. Since the industry of mass consumption was attempting to accommodate an emerging middle class that lacked the sophistication of the elite, it promoted these products by making them intellectually accessible to a popular audience. As Eco indicates:

> The culture industry appeals to a generic mass of consumers (for the most part quite unaware of the complexities of specialized cultural life) by selling them ready-made effects, which it prescribes along with directions for their use and a list of the reactions they should provoke.

From this perspective, we can understand more fully Eco's response in *Travels in Hyperreality*, discussed in Chapter 1, when he noted during his visit to the USA in 1971 how the wax museum exhibit of Da Vinci's *The Last Supper* included a taped voice that told the audience in specific terms how to experience the full emotional and religious aura of the wax figures and the "mystery" of art.

"Kitsch" constitutes "bad taste" by appropriating the symbols and stylistic expression of art while undercutting its function which is to provoke an aroused consciousness of our relation to the world. While artistic works generate a higher consciousness of the world by imposing interpretive challenges on the audience, in contrast, kitsch functions through predetermined effects that the consumer is instructed to experience in a passive manner. An example of an especially banal form of kitsch would be the cheap figurine reproductions of Michelangelo's statue of David. Admittedly they can serve as harmless souvenirs of the experience of the original, but they effectively undercut the function of aesthetics by marketing an object solely as an iconic work of art without engaging with its potential for arousing a reflection on its aesthetic function as a vision of a humanistic ideal. The kitsch figure of David would represent a consumerist appropriation of a symbol of high art that would undercut the full engagement in its meaning.

Rather than a prescribed set of effects, art opens up the potential for experiencing the world in an altered way that requires the collaborative "effort" of the audience to produce its multiple possibilities of meaning. Eco acknowledges that there are objects that provide decorative effects for the home that may be considered "cheap" when they are marketed for mass consumption, and "cheesy" when they draw on cliched, commonplace themes. But, as Eco indicates, these are "mass products that aim at the production of effects without pretending to be art."[12] Mass products constitute kitsch, according to Eco, only when they try to imitate the formative character of art and allow it to be appreciated in a lazy way that diminishes its aesthetic potential.

Eco describes the social forces involved in the attempt by mass consumerism to mimic the taste of the aesthetic elite by drawing on the ideas of the American writer and social critic Dwight MacDonald (1906–1982) from *Against the American Grain: Essays on the Effects of Mass Culture* (1962). The rise of mass consumerism, according to MacDonald, has resulted in the "high" cult of the artistic elite, represented by the contemporary avant-garde, being confronted with what he calls "masscult" and "midcult." Masscult represents the revolutionary impulse to "homogenize" culture by "breaking down the old barriers of class, tradition, and taste, dissolving all cultural distinctions." Midcult, in contrast, aspires to appropriate the status symbols and sophistication of the aesthetic "high" cult but without acquiring the sophistication to appreciate it.[13] According to this analysis, it is the midcult that is guilty of bad taste by being drawn to the kitschy debasement of the artistic expression of the cultural elite. But Eco suggests that MacDonald's analysis privileges the aesthetic elite in an overly simplified way that engages in a form of cultural "snobbery." Eco asserts that "Good and bad taste thus become flimsy categories."

> Mass society is so rich in determinations and possibilities, that it acquires an immensely elaborate network of mediations and reactions between a culture of discovery, a culture of mere consumption, and a culture of popularization and mediation, none of which can be easily reduced to a simple definition of Beauty or Kitsch.[14]

Eco also acknowledges that

> All of these supercilious condemnations of mass taste, in the name of an ideal community of readers involved solely in discovering the secret beauties of the cryptic messages produced by high art, neglect the average consumer (present in just about all of us) who at the end of the day may resort to a book or a movie in the hope that it may evoke a few basic reactions (laughter, fear, pleasure, sorrow, anger) and, through these, reestablish some balance in his or her physical and intellectual life.

Eco cites the example of the Mona Lisa "embroidered on a pillow"[15] as a typical example of a particularly banal form of consumerist kitsch. But Eco also notes numerous examples of kitsch by artists and writers, such as the science fiction author Ray Bradbury in his novella about Picasso. These artists engage in kitsch through the use of stylistic borrowings from works of art as an overly ostentatious way of aspiring to an aesthetic virtuosity. Because kitsch can apply to artists as well as consumers, Eco offers a redefinition of kitsch as the stylistic or thematic borrowing from other aesthetic works for use in a work where it strives for similar effects in a way that is inconsistent with the original. The stylistic borrowing of the writer Ray Bradbury in his story about Picasso, according to this definition, would qualify by attempting to rise to the aesthetic level of "high" art through a pretentious stylistic effect.

THE DA VINCI CODE AND THE LITERATURE OF MASS CONSUMPTION

Eco's analysis of the relationship between "midcult" and "kitsch" is useful for reflecting on the comparison between Dan Brown's *The Da Vinci Code* and Eco's *The Name of the Rose* that we initially considered in Chapter 1. Critics drew clear distinctions between these novels by touting Eco's novel as the "thinking man's *Da Vinci Code*,"[16] while asserting that Dan Brown's novel "plays to the worst and laziest in humanity."[17] As the bestselling novel of the twenty-first century, however, *The Da Vinci Code* can be seen as a prime example of how a work of broad popular consumption can engage in mysteries involving aspects of elite culture such as Renaissance art and occult religious conspiracies traced to the distant past. So how would Eco's analysis of the products of popular culture apply to Dan Brown's *The Da Vinci Code*? Dan Brown made no pretense about trying to appeal to the "cultivated" taste of an intellectual elite. He set out specifically to reach the broadest possible popular audience through a simplified style and storyline based on a model of a bestselling popular novel. But Dan Brown's novels became phenomenal bestsellers as well by exploring aspects of art, history, and secret societies that, as he indicated, were drawn from his lifelong interest in intellectual puzzles and the relation between science and religion. The appeal of his novels to a mass popular audience can be attributed, as Eco points out, to the "average consumer (present in just about all of us)" who will find some benefit in exploring these ideas in an accessible way as vehicles of entertainment, but they would also attract a broad following among what Dwight MacDonald calls "midcult" consumers who want to appropriate the cultural symbols of the elite. The question would be whether novels such as *The Da Vinci Code* are a disservice to a popular readership that is obviously drawn to intellectual questions, that are otherwise the domain of the "cultivated elite," by treating them in a superficial way as kitsch that closes off the potential for raising a higher consciousness.

As indicated previously, Eco and his fellow intellectuals and artists of the Gruppo 63 were reacting to the invasion of American popular culture through the rise of mass media consumerism. As a result, they developed an antagonistic attitude to, among other things, popular escapist literature. To counter the impact of popular culture and mass media consumerism they sought to focus on language in an attempt to frustrate the expectations of a popular audience for escapist entertainment. Eco noted in the "Postscript" to *The Name of the Rose* that part of the strategy of the Italian Neo-avant-garde was to provoke a popular audience with "shock and outrage" in works "where the logical and temporal consequences of traditional action were omitted and the public's expectations might have seemed violently frustrated."[18]

But Eco later observed that, ironically, a popular audience eventually overcame the antagonistic strategy of the avant-garde and came to enjoy just those provocative aspects that were intended to antagonize them with "the greatest pleasure,"[19] which is consistent with Dwight MacDonald's conception of the aspirations for elite culture of midcult consumers. This revealed to Eco an interesting interrelationship between elite art and a popular audience. The "unacceptability" to a popular audience of avant-garde works was "a guarantee of value" only during the early years of the Italian Neo-avant-garde, and that "unacceptability had now been codified as entertaining." He also concluded that the distinctions drawn by avant-garde intellectuals and artists between "a work for popular consumption and a work of provocation" needed to be "re-examined."[20] He noted that "it will be possible to find elements of revolution and contestation in works that apparently lend themselves to facile consumption [which will be considered in the next chapter], and it will also be possible to realize, on the contrary, that certain works, which seem provocative and still enrage the public, do not really contest anything..."[21] As a result, Eco came to reevaluate the elitist, intellectual attitude of the Gruppo 63 concerning the relation between elite and popular culture. The "unacceptability" to a popular audience of works of art was no longer "a guarantee of value," which also meant that the broad popularity of a work for mass consumption could no longer be taken as an indicator of its lack of aesthetic value.

So what criteria could be used to determine the cultural value of contemporary works of popular consumption such as *The Da Vinci Code*?

Despite the strongly negative critical response to *The Da Vinci Code*, it can be considered as both a "work for popular consumption" and "a work of provocation" at least from the perspective of raising scandalous speculations about traditional religion by suggesting historical evidence for an epic struggle between a covert agency of the Catholic Church and a secret society linked to the artist Da Vinci that was safeguarding a purported female descendent of Christ and Mary Magdalene. In relation to the core values of conventional society, the historical claims of *The Da Vinci Code* cast doubt on the very foundations of Christianity, celibacy, and the role of women in the Church. But the phenomenal popularity of *The Da Vinci Code* could also be attributed to a marketing approach to a popular audience drawn to "escapist" literature and tabloid-style scandals. So what, then, distinguishes "escapist" literature from the aesthetic value of art if mass consumption is no longer a reliable distinction?

One of the factors cited by reviewers in distinguishing *The Name of the Rose* from *The Da Vinci Code*, was specifically the difficult challenges Eco's novel posed for a general readership because of its dense references to medieval Church doctrine and numerous passages of untranslated Latin, French, and German. Supposedly these difficult challenges would pose a problem for "uncultivated" readers, but they did not, however, make the novel inaccessible to a popular readership. Instead those challenges aroused the curiosity of a broad popular audience to inquire further into the meaning of the novel. But the controversies associated with the historical claims of *The Da Vinci Code* also aroused the curiosity of a broad popular readership. Both novels were highly popular entertainment vehicles that explored the mysteries of the past, and thus both could be considered "escapist" literature. Both novels also engaged readers in questions about the role of religion and ideology in determining the meaning of our existence.

In the "Postscript" to *The Name of the Rose*, Eco asked whether there could be "a novel that was not escapist and, nevertheless, still enjoyable."[22] He quoted from the French literary theorist and fellow semiotician Roland Barthes (1915–1980), who suggested that contemporary novelists may not be able to reach "the lobotomized mass-media illiterates," but that they "should hope to reach and delight" beyond the "professional devotees of high art." Eco also cited the American literary critic Leslie Fiedler (1917–2003) for wanting "to break down the barrier that has been erected between art and enjoyability."[23] Perhaps the question of how to assess the relative value of *The Da Vinci Code* and *The Name of the Rose* can be pursued from the perspective of Eco's conception of the "open" work as an intellectual challenge to the reader.

Finnegans Wake as the Exemplar of Aesthetic Openness

Concerning the relation between the intellectual and popular culture, and the "openness" of a work of art, it can be useful to consider how Eco looks at the opposite ends of this spectrum. Eco's supreme model for an open work, as previously discussed, is Joyce's *Finnegans Wake* which he describes as "the most terrifying document of formal instability and semantic ambiguity that we possess."[24] In other words, it represents the far end of the aesthetic spectrum in the extent of its "defamiliarization" of language, and its "openness" in requiring the active participation of the reader. As a result, it holds a privileged position as a monument to the aesthetics of the avant-garde in venturing far beyond the conventional uses of language which raises a question concerning its "unacceptability" for a general audience. As Eco has indicated, Joyce imagined the audience for *Finnegans Wake* as "an ideal reader affected by an ideal insomnia."[25]

But because of the level of ambiguity and intensified defamiliarization of language in *Finnegans Wake*, it is generally regarded as inaccessible to all but a small minority of readers. Although *Finnegans Wake* has become a literary classic, it was initially criticized even by many friends and critics of Joyce as "impenetrable." For example, the author H.G. Wells, who described his own desire to use "language and statement as simple and clear as possible," wrote personally to Joyce that "you have turned your back on common men, on their elementary needs and their restricted time and intelligence."[26] Concerning the response by a popular readership to *Finnegans Wake*, the following posts, submitted by two different individuals from an archived internet chat site concerning the question of how to read *Finnegans Wake*, are instructive:

> Literally, every other word is a literary pun or a literary reference. If you've been a prolific, deep reader of the Western Canon for twenty or thirty years, you will probably "get" 1/3 to 2/3 of the references, and you will be able to understand the bare bones without stopping to look up a reference. If you haven't been devouring literary classics for thirty years, you will have to stop to look up stuff so often that you'll become befuddled.

Don't read it. It's not for reading. It's for putting on your bookshelf to impress Lit majors. They'll have heard of it but will have never read it either.[27]

For an academic with an encyclopedic knowledge of the "Western Canon" such as Eco, *Finnegans Wake* would represent a literary playground. But for a popular readership, it would constitute the exemplary model of the avant-garde notion of "unacceptibility" because of its dense literary references and unconventional use of language. However, despite its early detractors and skeptics *Finnegans Wake* has become a literary monument of the avant-garde. But it also points out the cultural divide between the intellectual with a broad knowledge of elitist cultural references, and a popular audience with probably at most a college education that in today's academic environment would include a progressively diminished exposure to the humanities. As a result, *Finnegans Wake* would be inaccessible without an extended research effort into its profusion of allusive cultural references.

If Joyce's *Finnegans Wake* represents the far end of the aesthetic spectrum of "openness," Eco's *The Name of the Rose* might be considered as a middle ground. In comparison, then, where would we place Dan Brown's *The Da Vinci Code*? *The Da Vinci Code* obviously did not attempt to challenge conventional expectations for a work of fiction as a way of arousing a "higher" critical consciousness like Joyce's *Finnegans Wake*. Dan Brown acknowledged that he was influenced by the "simplicity of the prose and efficiency of the storyline" of a popular bestseller. In other words, it was written specifically to appeal to the broadest possible popular audience. Typical of the detective genre, the mystery at the heart of the novel is resolved at its conclusion in a completely unambiguous way. Concerning its impact in raising a critical consciousness, it certainly prompted questions about hidden symbols in Renaissance art, and the historical role of celibacy and women in the Catholic Church, while generating a controversy concerning the validity of its historical claims. But, although the novel aroused the curiosity of a broad popular audience about these aspects of high art and occult history, there was little beyond these inquiries for the reader to do in participating in the determination of its meaning.

But would this be a fair assessment of a novel that was written specifically as an entertainment vehicle for a broad popular audience by raising controversial questions about an icon of Renaissance art and the origins of the Catholic

Church? Does this kind of popular, escapist entertainment that appropriates the symbols of highbrow art do a disservice to a popular readership by not challenging them to a more active engagement with the text? Or is it useful just for generating a curiosity about the meaning of art, literature, secret knowledge, etc.? Eco has criticized Dan Brown for taking old and discredited ideas about intellectual conspiracies and repackaging them: "It's all old material that's been covered a thousand times before. Brown was very good at taking trash lying around and turning it into a page turner. But it makes me laugh that people take it seriously."[28] According to this critique, Dan Brown's novels could be faulted for being thematically unoriginal, for giving credence to discredited historical conspiracies, and for creating a passive response on the part of the readers. We can consider these assessments further when we look at Eco's interpretation theory and the role of the reader in Chapter 9.

Notes

1. Eco, "The Death of the Gruppo 63," from *The Open Work*, pp. 237–240.
2. Eco, "The Death of the Gruppo 63," p. 241.
3. Poggioli, Renato, *The Theory of the Avant-Garde*, (Cambridge: Harvard University Press, 1968), pp. 10–11.
4. Poggioli, Renato, *The Theory of the Avant-Garde*, p. 10.
5. Poggioli, *The Theory of the Avant-Garde*, pp. 18–19.
6. Burwick, Frederick, *The Damnation of Newton: Goethe's Color Theory and Romantic Perception*, (New York: Walter de Gruyter. Inc. 1986), p. 8.
7. According to Robert Darnton in *The Great Cat Massacre And Other Episodes From French Cultural History*, (New York: Basic Books, 1984), p. 11.
8. Eco, "The Structure of Bad Taste," from *The Open Work*, (Cambridge: Harvard University Press), p. 186.
9. http://ec.europa.eu/eurostat/statistics-explained/index.php/Tertiary_education_statistics.
10. Eco, *The Open Work*, p. 183.
11. Clement Greenberg, "Avant-Garde and Kitsch," from *Art and Culture*, (Boston: Beacon Press, 1989), p. 10.
12. Eco, *The Open Work*, p. 189.
13. Eco, *The Open Work*, p. 189.
14. Eco, *The Open Work*, p. 194.
15. Eco, *The Open Work*, p. 197.
16. "Questions for Umberto Eco," Interview by Deborah Solomon, published November 25, 2007.
17. "3x12," *QI* (episode transcript).

18. Eco, "Postscript" to *The Name of the Rose*, p. 528.
19. Eco, "Postscript" to *The Name of the Rose*, p. 528.
20. Eco, "Postscript" to *The Name of the Rose*, pp. 528–529.
21. Eco, "Postscript" to *The Name of the Rose*, p. 529.
22. Eco, "Postscript" to *The Name of the Rose*, p. 529.
23. Eco, "Postscript" to *The Name of the Rose*, p. 532.
24. Eco, *The Aesthetics of Chaosmos*, p. 61.
25. Eco, "Postscript" to *The Name of the Rose*, p. 522.
26. Ellman, *Biography of James Joyce*, 1983, p. 608.
27. https://www.reddit.com/r/books/comments/2308lk/how_do_i_read_finnegans_wake/.
28. Jeff Israely, @Time, Milan, Sunday, June 5, 2005.

CHAPTER 7

The Aesthetics of Superman and Charlie Brown

We have seen how *The Open Work* in 1962 quickly established Eco as a leading spokesperson for postwar Italian intellectuals by becoming the manifesto and identifying slogan for the Italian Neo-avant-garde. Having explored the reaction of the Italian Neo-avant-garde to the impact of mass media consumerism, Eco turned his attention to an analysis of the content and mechanisms of the mass media with a collection of essays entitled *Apocalittici e Integrati*. As he later explained, "With *Open Work*, I studied the language of the avant-garde movements; with *Apocalittici*, I studied the language of their opposite (or, as some will say, of their fatal complement)."[1] After the broadly influential impact of *The Open Work*, Eco's focus on popular culture was published in 1964 with the full title of *Apocalittici e Integrati, Communicazioni di massa e teorie della cultura di massa* (Apocalyptics and Integrated, Mass Communication and Theories of Mass Culture). *Apocalittici e Integrati* was equally well received and further bolstered Eco's position as an emerging leader of the Italian postwar generation of artists and intellectuals. Like *The Open Work*, its title was also quickly adopted as a slogan that has since become established in the Italian lexicon to identify the opposing positions in the postwar debate on the role of the intellectual in the age of popular culture.

Apocalittici are intellectuals who see the impact of the mass media as the total degradation of culture, and *Integrati* are those who try to adapt to it as a medium of social engagement. Eco describes the apocalyptic attitude toward popular culture as follows:

> If culture is an aristocratic phenomenon – the assiduous, solitary and jealous cultivation of an inner life that tempers and opposes the vulgarity of the crowd – then even to conceive of a culture that is shared by everyone, produced to suit everyone and tailored accordingly is a monstrous contradiction. Mass culture is anti-culture.[2]

But the integrated intellectual sees the problem in a different way:

> Set against this is the optimistic response of the integrated intellectual. The combined efforts of TV, newspapers, radio, cinema, comic-strips, popular novels and the *Reader's Digest* have now brought culture within everybody's reach. They have made the absorption of ideas and the reception of information a pleasurable and easy task, with the result that we live in an age in which the cultural arena is at last expanding to include the widespread circulation of a 'popular' art and culture in which the best compete against each other. Whether the culture emerges from below or is processed and packaged from above to be offered to defenceless consumers is not a problem that concerns the integrated intellectual.[3]

The title *Apocalittici e Integrati* also reflects an historical perspective that Eco draws from his foundations as a medievalist. During the early Middle Ages, the idea of the apocalypse arose from the prophesy in the *Book of Revelation* by the apostle John of a 1,000-year period following the birth of Christ that would culminate in a final battle between God and Satan resulting in the end of earthly existence. In his study of the aesthetics of Thomas Aquinas, Eco indicated that Aquinas's attempt to unify theology and our sensory experience of the world followed "the crisis of the year 1000" when the anticipated end of times did not occur which allowed for an integration of spiritual and worldly knowledge. But Eco also discussed, in relation to the medieval conception of beauty, that, in the century preceding Aquinas, there was a contentious conflict between Saint Bernard of Clairvaux (1090–1153) and the Abbot Suger of Saint-Denis (2081–1151) concerning the proper way to communicate Christian theology to the uneducated. Bernard was strongly opposed to any decorative images in the cathedral because he believed it degraded the mystical experience of God. As a result, he was harshly critical of Suger who advocated the use of elaborate imagery as a way of teaching the illiterate.[4] Bernard was thus an apocalyptic precursor to the Italian postwar intellectuals who denounced the impact of the mass media, and Suger was a precursor of the integrated intellectuals who tried to use the mass media to communicate their ideas to a popular audience.

From Title to Slogan

In reflecting on the origins of his initial approach to popular culture and the mass media, Eco indicated that "Manners, popular culture, detective stories, [and] comic strips...had interested me greatly for a long time."[5] During his childhood, for example, Eco had collected comics and also tried to create his own. But the actual impetus for a collection of essays on popular culture and the mass media, he acknowledges, arose from a personal need to submit his earlier writings on these topics in applying for a new university chair to be called "Pedagogy and Psychology of Mass Communications." But when Eco subsequently submitted these essays for publication and suggested that title to his publisher, Valentino Bompiani, he was told that "You're mad Mr. Eco,"[6] and Bompiani flatly rejected it as unmarketable for a mass audience. So Eco suggested instead "The Problem of Mass Culture" which Bompiani also rejected. Bompiani then briefly scanned through the manuscript and seized on the title *Apocalittici e Integrati* that Eco had used to designate only the final section of the collection of essays. Although Eco tried to explain that that title would not accurately reflect the full scope of the collected essays, Bompiani insisted that *Apocalittici e Integrati* was the proper title. Eco later noted how this would have confirmed the apocalyptics' critique that "this is exactly the way that books get 'packaged' for mass consumption."[7] But, ironically, the revised title was quickly adopted by Italian academics to identify the opposing pessimistic and optimistic positions in the debate on the impact of mass media consumerism.

In *Apocalitici e Integrati*, Eco shifts from the analysis of the distinguishing character of the aesthetics of the Italian Neo-avant-garde that he explored in *The Open Work*, and thus elite or highbrow culture, to the opposite cultural pole through an analysis of the products and mechanisms of the mass media such as the comic strip worlds of Steve Canyon, Charlie Brown, and Superman, as well as the structure of "pop" songs, and the communication dynamics of radio and television. Eco's subtitle to the Italian version, *la cultura italiana e le communicazioni di massa* (Italian Culture and Mass Communication), indicates that the essays were intended to focus specifically on the Italian problem of cultural consumption that arose so quickly during the transformative postwar period of the "economic miracle" and the invasion of American pop culture.

THE POP CULTURE EPIPHANY

As indicated previously, Eco was already becoming a prominent public intellectual in Italy through his writings on various aspects of contemporary culture for Italian newspapers and magazines that were written in an accessible manner for a broad popular audience. But, at the same time, he was beginning to write on aspects of popular culture such as comic books and pop songs for an academic audience as a way of analyzing the impact of mass media consumerism on the traditional Italian cultural establishment. In 1959, Eco set out a list of potential topics for exploring aspects of popular culture that included the comic book worlds of Flash Gordon, Dick Tracy, and Peanuts; the pop songs of the Platters; and even the "aesthetics" of the "telephone" and the "football match" which, in Italy of course, is the sacred spectacle of soccer.[8] He notes, however, that, at that time, even the suitability of these topics for consideration by an elite academic audience was controversial and not readily accepted until the early sixties. Eco recalls how a "revelation came between 1961 and the beginning of 1962," when he was invited to a conference about myth involving some notable scholarly heavyweights on the classical aspects of mythology that included theologians of various orders, philosophers, and historians. He wasn't sure what to present, so he took a big leap into the scholarly unknown by deciding to talk about the mythical aspect of Superman comics.

> So I arrive in Rome and begin my paper with a pile of Superman comics on the table in front of me. What will they do, throw me out? No sirree, half the comic books disappeared; would you believe it, with all the air of wishing to examine them, those monks with their wide sleeves spirited them away... Aside from this omen, a discussion gets underway and I decide that this is a question that deserves more attention.[9]

After this epiphany in the early sixties about the potential legitimacy of academic analyses of the products and mechanisms of popular culture, Eco noted that "the first analyses of mass communication were beginning to be made in the universities" that included an "open workshop in Turin on 'mass aesthetics and communication'" organized by Eco[10] that led to the essays entitled *Apocalittici e Integrati*. In the introduction to the English translation, Robert Lumley notes that, while analyses of the mass media and popular culture are now "commonplace," at that time "Europe was struggling to come to terms with a rise of commercial culture to which the United States had become habituated."[11] While American society had adapted to the rapid rise and spread of mass media consumerism, these forces generated a hostile response on the part of European intellectuals. As Lumley points out: "There was a widespread hostility on the part of European intellectuals towards what was seen as an American-led invasion of 'mass culture' and a consequent standardization and homologization of cultural forms at the expense of rich and variegated national ones."[12] Italy was especially susceptible to the "American-led invasion" because Italy, after WWII, was just beginning to experience the full impact of mass media consumerism. These pursuits indicate how Eco's intellectual practice as an "intermediate thinker" involved not only a scholarly analysis of contemporary culture for a popular audience, but also an analysis of popular culture for an elite, academic audience that traditionally would not have considered these topics worthy of analysis.

In *Apocalittici e Integrati*, Eco's particular focus on comic books is an indicator of their importance in Italian culture in the wake of the American pop culture invasion of Italy. Italy's late development in the field of mass literacy and mass education, with a readership of only 51 percent compared to 74 percent in Britain, was further hindered by the advent of the mass media. The impact of television fostered a popular taste for visual media which caused an emerging Italian mass readership to be drawn to the literary hybrid of comic books. Called *fumetti* in Italian, comic books draw such a massive following that they can be found in great profusion not just in Italian bookstores but prominently displayed at news kiosks as a staple of Italian popular culture alongside the newspapers and periodicals for the elite such as *La Republica*. The enormous demand in postwar Italy for popular literature with a visual component even generated a curious hybrid form called the *fotoromanzo* that the analysts of Italian culture, Forgacs and Lumley, described as a series of photographs that "transferred the storytelling conventions of the cinema (sequences of shots, with long shots, close-ups, and so forth) to the panel-by-panel ones of the comic strip."[13]

SUPERMAN AND CLASSICAL MYTHOLOGY

For an understanding of Eco's early approach to the analysis of popular culture for an academic audience, we can briefly consider his essay on the myth of Superman (which is accessible in English in Eco's *The Role of the Reader*) in comparison to classical mythology. Eco looks at the myth of Superman in relation to heroes from classical mythology such as Hercules, the medieval knight Roland from the reign of Charlemagne, and Siegfried from Wagner's *Ring Cycle* operas. Placing Superman in this broader historical and cultural context was unusual at this time especially for an intellectual elite that felt threatened by the content of the mass media. It allowed Eco, however, to examine the content of Superman comics as a product meant for enjoyment by a mass popular audience in relation to the broader meaning of the hero as a cultural symbol.

In his comparative analysis of the myth of Superman, Eco draws on the concept of the hero from ancient mythology of a human who is celebrated for confronting threats to humanity by interceding with the gods, or more generally by overcoming adversity through strength, cunning, and the willingness to risk one's life. His analysis is also pursued through a "structuralist" approach which was an innovative mode of analysis that came to be broadly applied in the humanities beginning in the late fifties. "Structuralism" was derived from one of the early pioneers in the development of language theory, Ferdinand de Saussure (1857–1913), who influenced Eco's later turn to semiotics. As indications of this approach, Eco analyzes Superman comics from the perspective of "the structure of myth,"[14] "the narrative structure,"[15] and the "temporal structure"[16] of the storyline to inquire into the distinguishing character of myths marketed for popular consumption. Concerning narrative and temporal structure, Eco notes that, although there are references in the storyline of Superman to his birth and childhood, he does not age after reaching adulthood, and the events in his life do not progress in a sequence toward an eventual resolution. As Eco points out, this is in sharp contrast to the storyline of traditional myths such as Hercules whose story "had already happened" in a distant past. Eco contrasts the classical myth, in turn, with the temporal structure of the modern novel whose characters are not previously determined but unfold in unexpected ways toward the future. As Eco indicates, this structure allows the reader to identify with a character "like anyone else" whose fate "is as unforeseeable as what may happen to us."[17] Eco notes that Superman is consequently a kind of hybrid of the hero of classical myth and the modern novel because "he possesses the characteristics of timeless myth, but is accepted only because his activities take place in our human and everyday world of time."[18]

Revisiting the Familiar

Concerning the difference in aesthetic value between the products of the cultivated elite and those of the mass media, Eco focuses on what he calls the "iterative schemes" and "mechanisms"[19] of the story of Superman, and the model of the world that they reflect. Iterative schemes involve the use of repetitive scenarios that the reader comes to expect as a familiar aspect of the story. For example, the reader of Superman comics will anticipate the amusement afforded by the recurring tension between Superman's alter-ego Clark Kent and Lois Lane. According to Eco, Clark Kent "personifies fairly typically the average reader" who is secretly longing to overcome his "mediocre existence,"[20] and popular readers would enjoy the irony of Lois Lane dismissing Clark Kent for his ineptitude while professing her love for Superman. Eco notes that this "taste for redundance" can be found as well in detective fiction from writers such as Rex Stout and Agatha Christie that provide "an indulgent invitation to repose."[21] Although the storyline will vary, the reader will be drawn to these popular entertainments not for novelty and a provocation for expanding one's awareness but for the reassurance of encountering what one already knows.

> The plot must be static and must evade any development because Superman *must* make virtue consist of many little activities on a small scale, never achieving a total awareness.[22]

This "taste for redundance" can be seen in the popularity of Dan Brown's historical whodunits that feature an academic scholar drawn into a perilous situation involving historical mysteries who is assisted by a female investigator. Eco contrasts this indulgence in familiarity of the products of popular culture, with "superior" art that "proposes schemes in evolution" and "continuous alternation."[23] In other words, aesthetic works deliberately defamiliarize as a way of arousing a higher awareness.

The Ideology of Popular Culture

But what is the harm in what Eco characterizes as "escape entertainments" which he acknowledges are "healthy and indispensable" even for the "cultured person"?[24] The question that Eco considers is how escapist entertainment that may seem to be a harmless form of mental relaxation can have the effect of fostering a lack of awareness and passive acceptance of a model of the world that privileges particular class interests and values.

> The comic strip is commissioned from above, it operates according to all the mechanisms of hidden persuasion, it presupposes in the consumer an attitude of escape that immediately stimulates the paternalistic aspirations of the producers. And, as a rule, authors conform: thus the comic strip in most cases, reflects the implicit ideology of a system and acts as a hidden reinforcement of the dominant myths and values.[25]

For example, as Eco notes, the evil that is continuously thwarted by Superman only takes the form of a threat against "private property." The repetition of this familiar plot within a "static" world in which Superman engages in acts of small-scale virtue without "achieving a total awareness" would reflect, unintentionally or not, a world that, according to Eco, "pervades the cultural model in which the authors live."[26] Thus, while ostensibly serving as a harmless diversion for a mass popular audience, the authors of comic strips such as Superman would foster an unconscious acceptance of a world in which the class interests, for example, of industrial and commercial producers, are championed while broader class interests are ignored.

The strongly critical attitude by Italian intellectuals such as Eco toward the products of popular culture was thus part of a broader reaction to mass consumerism that generated the German conception of "kitsch," and the analysis of the class dynamics of mass consumerism that was taken up by American intellectuals such as Clement Greenberg (1909–1994) and Dwight MacDonald (1906–1982). Italian intellectuals, however, felt especially threatened because of the cultural invasion of Italy by American popular culture after WWII, and their response was influenced by the ideas of Antonio Gramsci (1891–1937) who was trying to reexamine the Marxist critique of industrial society and the role of the intellectual in arousing an awareness of its impact on class relations. Perhaps because of the communist witch-hunts in America in the fifties, Marxist perspectives have not been as prominently expressed in the USA in comparison to Italy where they are broadly applied in Italian critical analysis. In Eco's focus on the myth of Superman, these perspectives are indicated at the outset through his assessment of how the idea of Superman as hero can be considered from the perspective of industrial society:

> The hero equipped with powers superior to those of the common man has been a constant of the popular imagination – from Hercules to ... Peter Pan. In industrial society, however, where man becomes a number in the realm of the organization which has usurped his decision-making role, he has no means of production and is thus deprived of his power to decide. Individual strength, if not exerted in sports activities, is left abased when confronted with the strength of machines which determine man's very movements. In such a society the positive hero must embody to an unthinkable degree the power demands that the average citizen nurtures but cannot satisfy.

For understanding Eco's critical assessment of the impact of the products of mass consumption, it's also helpful to recall the concept of beauty that he derived from Thomas Aquinas that leads the individual to a higher consciousness of God. Eco's conception of the consciousness-raising role of beauty was also influenced by the idea of *forma formante*, forming form, from his intellectual mentor Luigi Pareyson. Every aspect of culture, from the products of mass consumption such as comic books to those of the "cultured" elite such as avant-garde paintings, are expressions of the human capacity for creativity. As the species that is determined through our interrelationship with the things of the world, those products, across the cultural spectrum, have a formative effect on us. From this critical perspective, it would not be overreaching for Eco to find in most comic book narratives a formative effect of creating a passive attitude toward the privileged interests of industrial and commercial producers. Eco's critique of Superman is thus useful for assessing the continuing popularity in current cinema of films featuring a proliferation of characters with super-human powers such as Supergirl, Batman, Captain America, Catwoman, Iron Man, Spiderman, X-Men, Green Lantern, and the Avengers which is the most popular superhero film of all time. More recently the super hero has even assumed an otherwise innocuous character in the persona of "The Accountant" (2016) starring Ben Affleck. These products of the mass media, like all cultural products, can be analyzed for their impact on the audience and the social interests they serve. From this perspective, we can ask what makes these characters with superhuman powers so intriguing for contemporary society? Is it a temporary fantasy relief from a broad sense of individual powerlessness and alienation by the modern forces of industrial society and mass media consumerism?

THE EXISTENTIALIST WORLDS OF JULES FEIFFER AND CHARLES M. SCHULZ

So does Eco find any redeeming value in the products of popular culture that he explored in *Apocalittici e Integrati*? Eco asserts that the representation of a model of the world that fosters passive acceptance of privileged class interests is also found in the comic strips of Dick Tracy, Dennis the Menace, Terry and the Pirates, and Little Orphan Annie. But Eco asks if, given the numerous examples previously cited, we would have to accept that all comics as a popular medium foster a "paternalism that is sometimes unconscious and sometimes deliberate" which has "a constant function of evading or concealing reality?"[27] In response, Eco offers examples of some notable exceptions in which "the artists while using the mode of expression granted to all the others, succeeded in profoundly changing the response of their consumers to develop, within their medium, a critical and liberating function."[28] The two most prominent "masters" of this use of the comic strip medium, according to Eco, are the American cartoonists Jules Feiffer (born 1929) and Charles M. Schulz (1922–2000).

Although Feiffer initially wrote comic strips for children, he went on to become a pioneer in creating comics and graphic novels for an adult audience. An example of his adult comics is the story of *Passionella* that Eco suggests is representative of Feiffer's satirical approach to contemporary society. Eco and Cathy Berberian, the American wife of the Italian avant-garde composer Luciano Berio, had collaborated on the Italian translation of Feiffer's *Passionella* in 1962 (available in English as *Passionella and other stories*, Seattle: Fantagraphics Books, 2005). *Passionella* is the story of a humble chimney sweep who watches television as her sole means of escape. But the television makes her yearn to be a glamorous movie star. One day the screen goes blank and a voice from the television of her godmother tells her that her wish will be fulfilled. But, like her fairy tale counterpart Cinderella, she will be transformed only during the evening hours. Eventually, however, Passionella tires of just being a glamorous movie star. She falls in love with a young movie actor with a taste for avant-garde theater who influences her to take up acting lessons from the "Inner Me Acting Academy." This results in her wanting to portray "one of the real people" like her original self. Feiffer's cartoons, according to Eco, reflect "precisely" and "accurately" the "ills of a modern industrial society"[29] which are portrayed through characters that represent at the same time both the bad and the good aspects of humanity. Eco notes that, while these stories may make readers laugh, including those who should be offended and alarmed, this does not diminish their impact. Once a story by Feiffer is read, Eco asserted, it cannot be "exorcised" because it will "remain in the reader's mind working on them silently."[30]

THE EVERYMAN CHARACTER OF CHARLIE BROWN

But Eco also found aesthetic value in the comic strip *Peanuts* by Charles M. Schulz that reflects the world of children while exploring, as Eco puts it, the "neuroses of a modern citizen of industrial society."[31] Eco's essay "The World of Charlie Brown," was originally published as the introduction for the "arrival" in Italy in 1963 of the comic strip *Peanuts*. It was consequently entitled *Arriva Charlie Brown!*[32] *Peanuts* is appealing to children for the lovable and sympathetic characters of Charlie Brown, Lucy, Snoopy, Schroeder, etc., but the world of *Peanuts*, according to Eco, also represents the circumstances of modern life such as "Freudian psychology, standardization, consumerism, the frustrating struggle for success, the yearning for understanding, the experience of loneliness, the problem of arrogance, and the passive acquiescence and neurotic reaction to these conditions." The appeal to adults is that these responses to modern society are expressed, as Eco puts it, "from the mouths of a group of innocents."[33] Although, as Eco points out, Schulz employs the same kind of repetitive, familiar scenarios as found in other forms of popular entertainment, there is an infinite variation at play in the relation between the characters that draws the reader into a deeper sense of affiliation with their plight. Eco describes the world of *Peanuts* as "a microcosm, a miniature human comedy."[34]

Eco describes Charlie Brown as a kind of everyman who is acutely insecure and consistently hapless in his constant quest for success and acceptance. In response to his efforts, he is treated with scorn, ridiculed as a "blockhead," accused of being stupid, and regularly subjected to minor acts of cruelty, for example, when Lucy keeps pulling the ball away before he can kick it. But, as Eco suggests, while Charlie Brown has a "pervasive inferiority complex . . . the tragedy is that he is not inferior.

What's worse is that he is absolutely normal like everyone."[35] In comparison to the acute insecurity of Charlie Brown, his nemesis Lucy is described by Eco as a "treacherous, self-confident, entrepreneur with assured profits, ready to peddle a security that is completely bogus."[36] Lucy, according to Eco, provokes the reader to admire her but also to be appalled by her arrogant self-confidence. Similarly, Charlie Brown's attempts to gain "popularity" among the "matriarchal, know-it-all girls of his group," result in being treated with "scorn, references to his round head, accusations of stupidity, all the little digs that strike home."[37] But even Lucy is subject to the unrequited love for Schroeder who represents, for Eco, the absorption in an "aesthetic religion" of "total adoration for Beethoven."[38] Linus, with his blanket and thumb in mouth, represents the yearning for the womb and the oral drive of Freudian psychology and thus the "total instability of a neurotic society."[39] Even Snoopy, in dealing with his subordinate condition as a dog, represents for Eco the "ultimate metaphysical frontier of the neurotic failure to adapt"[40] by aspiring through various fantasies to be everything that he is not. Eco concludes that, through the plight of these characters, the reader is amused while being drawn into Schulz's "poetry of childhood" concerning the "human condition."[41] According to Eco, "The world of *Peanuts* is a microcosm, a little human comedy for the innocent reader and for the sophisticated."[42]

THE PHENOMENOLOGY OF THE TELEVISION HOST

Besides critical analyses of comics, pop songs, sporting events, etc., Eco turned his attention to the content and modes of communication of television and radio. He is especially famous for an analysis of the personality and presentation style of Mike Bongiorno (1924–2009), the most popular program host in the inaugural years of Italian television. Eco's analysis, entitled "The Phenomenology of Mike Bongiorno," appeared in the magazine *Pirelli* in 1961. According to Eco chroniclers Francesca Pansa and Anna Vinci, his essay was the first analysis published in Italy by a philosopher about a television personality.[43] Mike Bongiorno's full name was Michael Nicholas Salvatore Bongiorno whose surname is nearly identical to the standard daytime greeting in Italian. He was born in the USA, but he was also an Italian citizen and ardent patriot who went to Italy during WWII to join the partisan resistance. This led to his capture by the Germans and imprisonment in a concentration camp. After the war, he returned to the USA where he started his media career. He soon left the

USA, however, to become a television celebrity in Italy after he began hosting the hugely popular quiz show "*Lascia o Raddoppia*" (Double or Nothing) which was modeled after the American quiz show "The 64,000 Dollar Question." The immense popularity of shows like *Lascia o Raddoppia* was what discouraged Eco during his time as a production assistant for educational, cultural programming, the role originally intended for the state-owned Italian television network RAI.

Eco's essay reflects his harshly disparaging attitude in the early sixties toward mass media programming modeled after American television that caters to an Italian popular audience. His analytical perspective is similar to his critique of Superman comics by considering the social values and commercial interests reflected by the quiz show through a focus on the persona of the television host who was a totally new phenomenon in Italian culture. Using an elite academic term such as "phenomenology" in the title of the essay stands out in a humorous way by being linked to the focus on a seemingly banal topic drawn from popular culture. But it is also indicative of Eco's innovative practice of bridging between elite and popular culture. Phenomenology is a mode of philosophical analysis founded by the German philosopher Edmund Husserl (1859–1938) who sought to analyze how the things of the world are perceived in our consciousness through subjective processes. Husserl set aside assessments of ideas according to their truth-value in designating the things of the world to focus instead on how they function as states of consciousness.

The role of the television host, according to Eco's "phenomenological" analysis, is to present the consumer with an image of the "average" human: "The most striking illustration of superman's being reduced to everyman is, in Italy, the figure of Mike Bongiorno and the history of his fame."[44] Eco credits his idolization by the Italian television audience to his "absolute mediocrity" along with a "spontaneous allure" because he can present his "mediocrity" without "pretense."[45] The basis of his appeal, according to Eco, is that he "cannot create in a spectator, even the most ignorant, any sense of inferiority" because he is "not particularly good-looking, not athletic, courageous, or intelligent."[46] The "hysterical love he arouses in teenage girls" can be attributed to "maternal feelings he arouses in a female adolescent," and his image of "an ideal lover, meek, and vulnerable, gentle and considerate."[47] So as not to make his viewers feel insecure about their minimal education, Mike Bongiorno, according to Eco, "is not ashamed of being ignorant and feels no need to educate himself" which appeals to the "natural tendencies" of others "to apathy and mental sloth." In an especially scathing condemnation of attitudes toward education of a popular audience, Eco notes that, while Mike Bongiorno admires the knowledge of others who engage in "reading many books," he believes that knowledge is solely "quantitative," the acquisition of a store of facts without a "critical and creative function."[48]

Eco is equally disparaging toward the "*basic* Italian" language usage of Mike Bongiorno that "achieves the maximum simplicity" by abolishing "the subjunctive, and subordinate clauses."[49] Eco concludes that Mike Bongiorno provides the perfect mass media rapport between producers and consumers because, although "he presents himself as an idol," he projects an image "that nobody has to strive for," because his audience is already at his level of "triumphant...mediocrity."[50] The harsh rhetoric of Eco's essay would seem to be an odd way for Eco to establish a rapport with a popular audience, but it should be remembered that this essay appeared in 1961, just before the formation of the Gruppo 63, when Italian intellectuals were beginning to react in an especially hostile manner toward what they perceived to be the cultural degradation by the mass media. Eco's essay was later published in *Diario Minimo* (Minimal Diary) as part of a collection of short essays on a variety of topics that Eco had contributed to Italian newspapers and magazines and thus intended for a mass popular audience.

Almost 30 years after the original publication of Eco's essay, Mike Bongiorno was interviewed about his personal response which he had never previously made public. In the interview, which is paraphrased and translated here from the Italian conducted by Eco chroniclers Francesca Pansa and Anna Vinci, Mike Bongiorno's comments provide a striking example of the stark cultural divide in Italy at that time between intellectuals and the popular icons of the emerging new medium of television. In response to the interviewer's question about Eco's unflattering portrait from 30 years ago, Mike Bongiorno said it was time to stop focusing on that particular essay. He noted that: "someone weighed the pile of news clippings over time about me which amounted to 80 kilos [176 pounds]. So why just focus on the controversy between me and Eco?" He said he never previously responded to the essay because he didn't want to give Eco the free publicity he believed he was seeking. He also offered to reveal a secret that explains everything: "in 1955 when the quiz show *Lascia o Raddoppia* was all the rage, one of the experts who wrote the questions for the competitors was a young aspiring assistant named Umberto Eco." Mike Bongiorno suggested that Eco was envious of him during that time because, while "I was in the spotlight, the experts, the so-called intellectuals, had to work behind the scenes." In response to Eco's characterization of him in the essay as "ignorant," he said that: "the so-called intellectuals at that time like Eco knew nothing about television. And even less about successful people like me. The philosopher did not understand that television was the true cultural revolution of the century."

> To him I was just the moron put there to ask the competitors ten questions. Instead everything was more complex. I already had two years of journalistic experience with 'La Stampa' in Turin and ten years at RAI. I studied television in America. At that time, someone less prejudiced than Eco wrote that with my "basic Italian" I could speak to millions of Italians. So the problem was definitely not my ignorance. I told him that Eco as a young man wanted publicity at my expense. But his attack went to my advantage. The public was all for me and against the intellectuals like him. I received hundreds of protest letters. But why talk about Eco? At that time, Montanelli [a famous Italian journalist] also attacked me. In 1963 the Corriere [the Italian newspaper *Corriere della Sera*] published a major article in which he said 'Be aware, Bongiorno, in three years you will be nobody.' But he had to think again very carefully. He really disappointed me because we spent a few weeks imprisoned together at San Vittore, in 1943 by the Nazis.

When asked if Eco ever apologized to him, he said "Not officially. But I understand that five years ago in a public meeting he confessed that he was wrong about me." Bongiorno also acknowledged that he had read *The Name of the Rose* "with great pleasure" and that he admired Eco "the writer of today." But he reiterated that Eco "never understood anything about television." He said that he had never met Eco personally because they "frequent different places." Bongiorno concluded that: "I am working sixteen hours a day. I have been doing quiz shows for thirty years, not as a moron who poses ten questions, like those pseudo-intellectuals who write them."[51]

A THEORY OF NEXT THURSDAY

Although Eco offered an innovative analysis of various aspects of popular culture and the way that they were communicated to a popular audience through the mass media, he ultimately was confronted with what he considered to be an un-resolvable problem. How can an understanding of the conditions of contemporary popular culture be pursued without becoming overwhelmed by the complex processes of mass media consumerism that are constantly changing? As Eco emphasizes in the preface to *Apocalittici e Integrati*, "the principle characteristic of mass culture is ephemerality" which applies both to the products of mass consumption as well as the ways of communicating about these products through the mass media.[52] Although academic programs in mass media analysis are now established at more than 300 colleges and universities in the USA alone and at least a few in Italy, Eco concluded that a "unitary theoretical formula" for the mass media "is impossible" because it "would be akin to a 'theory of next Thursday.'"[53] Eco didn't want to engage in analyses that he believed would quickly become obsolete because of the rapidly changing dynamics of the mass media. Consequently he decided to abandon this effort, while continuing to write essays about various aspects of popular culture and the mass media for both an academic and a popular audience, and instead to pursue what Pareyson had conceived of as the need for a "general theory of interpretation."

THE TRANSITION TO SEMIOTICS

While acknowledging the futility of a comprehensive theory of the mass media, Eco also noted that his early writings on these phenomena in *Apocalittici e Integrati* were the catalyst that "definitely opened the way to semiotic studies for me."[54] Besides his awareness of the rapidly changing character of the mass media and the passive response typically generated by the products of popular culture, the impetus for this shift can be seen to arise from two observations that he drew from his analysis of the relation between the content of the mass media and the response by a popular audience. His first observation was that the corruption of aesthetics in the mass media occurs as a result of "misunderstandings" or what he calls "misreadings." By this he meant that a mass popular audience was prone to interpret a work in a way that was not consistent with the intended meaning and formative character and content of the work. While calling upon the audience to participate in generating the meaning of the work, Eco asserted that the interpretation had to acknowledge the life experience of the author and the author's formative intentions that are embedded in the work. Because of the inherent ambiguity of language and the openness of modern aesthetic works, the audience must participate in generating their meaning, but not with total freedom according to one's individual desires. The author/artist cannot anticipate and cannot control all of the possible meanings that can be generated from the work, but, similarly, the audience cannot properly determine the meaning of the work without actively collaborating with the author's formative intentions. The value of aesthetic works is their potential for interacting with the audience in a way that is transformative. The work cannot achieve this potential if the individual interprets the work primarily from their own experience such that they overlook, ignore, misunderstand, and thus "misread" the "meaning" of the work. This is a vital issue for Eco that is equivalent to a moral principle because, drawing on Aquinas and Joyce, aesthetic works are intended as a means of communicating a shared engagement in pursuing a higher or liberatory consciousness.

Eco's second observation was that an analysis of mass culture involves an approach similar to the way in which cultural anthropology attempts to understand the differences between human societies. This involves a focus not just on so-called "undeveloped" societies from the perspective of modern industrialized societies, but also on differences between "developed" societies and between sub-cultures within societies. As Eco noted, anthropologists attempt to bridge between diverse worlds that operate according to radically different structures of meaning. This puts the anthropologist in the predicament of either analyzing other cultures from the "outside" according to the anthropologist's inherited cultural values and perspectives, or by attempting to inhabit the other's culture and explain it from the "inside" through the "natives" point of view. But in either the outside or the inside view, the anthropologist would confront difficulties in trying to straddle the cultural differences and communicate them in a way that didn't privilege one cultural perspective over the other. Consequently, according to Eco, the anthropologist attempts to find a middle way that analyzes the differences between the two cultures through a form of analysis that is "over and above" or "in between" them. This observation provides Eco with a theoretical pathway for exploring the mechanisms of mass media consumerism as an anthropologist in a foreign culture, for example, as he did in his analysis of American wax museums, from Chapter 1, and his analysis of the myth of Superman and the world of Charlie Brown above. The model of cultural anthropology is also another way of understanding Eco's practice as an intermediate thinker or public intellectual.

Since Eco recognized that the content and processes of mass media consumerism changed so dynamically that any analysis would be short-lived, he determined that an understanding of its impact could be more effectively pursued through a much broader and more fundamental focus on the common aspects across all cultures in how they generate and communicate meaning and order. The previous two observations, that the corruption of the mass media was caused by problems in interpretation, and that an understanding of the mass media should adopt the approach of cultural anthropology, were thus the impetus for Eco to explore the possibility for a general theory of interpretation that would be valid across the cultural spectrum. As a result he became a pioneering theorist in the relatively new field of "semiotics," the science of signs, or the study of the ways in which humans create and communicate meaning and order in their relationship to the world. For the humanities, this would constitute a theory of everything human as grand in scope and application as the Grand Unified Theory (GUT) of modern physics.

NOTES

1. Eco, *Apocalypse Postponed*, p. 56.
2. Eco, *Apocalypse Postponed*, (Bloomington: Indiana University Press, 1994), pp. 17–18. This is a substantially modified English version of the original edited by Robert Lumley.
3. Eco, *Apocalypse Postponed*, p. 18.
4. Eco, *The Aesthetics of Thomas Aquinas*, p. 13.
5. Eco, *Apocalypse Postponed*, p. 51.
6. Eco, *Apocalypse Postponed*, p. 53.
7. Eco, *Apocalypse Postponed*, p. 54.
8. Eco, *Apocalypse Postponed*, p. 51.
9. Eco, *Apocalypse Postponed*, p. 52.
10. Eco, *Apocalypse Postponed*, p. 53.
11. Robert Lumley, "Introduction" from *Apocalypse Postponed*, p. 1.
12. Robert Lumley, *Apocalypse Postponed*, p. 2.
13. David Forgacs and Robert Lumley, editors, *Italian Cultural Studies*, (Oxford: Oxford University Press, 1996) p. 279.
14. Eco, *The Role of the Reader*, p. 108.
15. Eco, *The Role of the Reader*, pp. 108 and 113.
16. Eco, *The Role of the Reader*, p. 117.
17. Eco, *The Role of the Reader*, p. 109.
18. Eco, *The Role of the Reader*, p. 111.
19. Eco, *The Role of the Reader*, p. 120.

20. Eco, *The Role of the Reader*, p. 108.
21. Eco, *The Role of the Reader*, p. 121.
22. Eco, *The Role of the Reader*, (Bloomington: Indiana University Press, 1984), p. 124.
23. Eco, *The Role of the Reader*, p. 121.
24. Eco, *The Role of the Reader*, p. 121.
25. Eco, *Apocalypse Postponed*, pp. 37–38.
26. Eco, *The Role of the Reader*, p. 124.
27. Eco, *Apocalittici e Integrati, Communicazione di massa e teorie della cultura di massa* (Milan: Gruppo Editoriale Fabbri, Bompiani, Sonzogno, Etas S.p. A., 1994), p. 264. The original Italian from which these translations were excerpted by me reads as follows: "Allora dovremo dire che il fumetto, chiuso nelle regole ferree del circuito industriale-commerciale della produzione e del consumo, e destinato a dare solo i prodotti standard di un paternalismo talora inconscio e talora programmato? Che se ha elaborato, come ha elaborato, moduli stilistici, tagli narrativi, proposte digusto senz'altro originali e stimolanti per la massa che ne usava, tuttavia usera sempre e comunque di queste spregiudicatezze artistiche per una costante unzione di evasione e di mascheramento della realta?"
28. Eco, *Apocalittici e Integrati*, p. 265. Translations are my own.
29. Eco, *Apocalittici e Integrati*, p. 265.
30. Eco, *Apocalittici e Integrati*, p. 265.
31. Eco, *Apocalittici e Integrati*, p. 268.
32. Eco, *Apocalittici e Integrati*, p. 44.
33. Eco, *Apocalittici e Integrati*, p. 268.
34. Eco, *Apocalittici e Integrati*, p. 269.
35. Eco, *Apocalitici e Integrati*, p. 269.
36. Eco, *Apocalittici e Integrati*, p. 42.
37. Eco, *Apocalittici e Integrati*, p. 42.
38. Eco, *Apocalittici e Integrati*, p. 271.
39. Eco, *Apocalittici e Integrati*, p. 270.
40. Eco, *Apocalittici e Integrati*, p. 271.
41. Eco, *Apocalittici e Integrati*, p. 272.
42. Eco, *Apocalypse Postponed*, p. 41.
43. Francesca Pansa and Anna Vinci, *Effetto Eco*, (Nuova Edizioni del Gallo, 1990), p. 44.
44. Eco, *Misreadings*, translation by William Weaver, (Orlando: Harcourt Brace and Company, 1993), p. 158.
45. Eco, *Misreadings*, p. 158.
46. Eco, *Misreadings*, p. 159.
47. Eco, *Misreadings*, p. 159.
48. Eco, *Misreadings*, p. 159.

49. Eco, *Misreadings*, p. 161.
50. Eco, *Misreadings*, p. 163.
51. Francesca Pansa and Anna Vinci, *Effetto Eco*, pp. 44–46. Translation is my own.
52. Eco, *Apocalypse Postponed*, p. 21.
53. Eco, *Apocalypse Postponed*, p. 33.
54. Eco, *Apocalypse Postponed*, p. 56.

CHAPTER 8

The Semiotic Species: A Grand Unified Theory of Culture

WHAT IS SEMIOTICS?

At a public book reading in Seattle of the English language version of his third novel, *The Island of the Day Before*, Eco opened up a question and answer session by saying that he and his English translator William Weaver were compiling a list of the "stupidest" questions by a public audience. Those in attendance were obviously taken aback by Eco's comment such that the first person to raise a question prefaced it by saying that he hoped it would not be considered stupid. Eco, however, responded respectfully to the questions from the audience, except in one instance when an elderly gentleman asked if Eco could explain what semiotics is. Instead of providing even a brief explanation, Eco deflected the elderly gentleman's question by informing him that, to understand semiotics, he would need to take classes at the University of Bologna, where Eco had founded the first university program in that field of study. Eco's dismissive response seemed odd given the fact that his position as an internationally recognized semiotic theorist was included in the introduction to the book reading, and semiotics is a core aspect of his novels in particular *The Name of the Rose* that features a detective monk who is a master at interpreting signs.

In contrast, for an interview with Jeff Israely for @Time, Eco explained that: "Humans communicate with language but also with everything else we do. The books you own, the way you decorate your house, whether you wear a tie or not are all signs of something else. That's semiotics in a nutshell."[1] Eco's curt response at the book reading would thus seem strange for a public intellectual with a well-established practice of mediating between an academic and a popular audience. Perhaps Eco's response can be traced to his disdainful attitude toward the invasion of American popular culture in Italy after WWII as a member of the Italian Neo-avant-garde. Since Eco had asserted, following the phenomenal success of *The Name of the Rose*, that its broad appeal indicated that a popular readership wanted to explore sophisticated topics, his response may also have reflected a resistance toward simplifying for popular consumption a complex field of study. While Eco had established himself internationally as an exemplary public intellectual, this instance is a good example of his dual role as both mediator and provocateur in relation to a popular audience.

In any case, given the impracticality for most of Eco's popular readership of taking classes at the University of Bologna, which clearly underscores the social divide between elite and popular culture, we can nonetheless explore what semiotics is by considering how it came about as a result of the longstanding and fundamental problem of language as the capacity that distinguishes humans as a species. That language is a problem, however, might not seem readily apparent outside of the longstanding concerns of academia, because we obviously use language in our everyday lives without seeming to encounter major difficulties, except, for example, between teenagers and parents. Language is absolutely central to our being as humans, but as a means of understanding our relationship to the world, it has presented a problem that goes back to our origins as a species and the foundations of Western philosophy.

The Problem of Language

In ancient Greek society, the problem of language arose over the question of whether the source of knowledge is outside or inside the sensory world which pitted Plato's upward path to pure ideas against Aristotle's downward path of our senses. Medieval philosophy tried to resolve this problem by bringing the upward path to God through faith, scripture, and contemplative thought, together with the downward path of our earthly existence which was the project of Thomas Aquinas in the thirteenth century. But the problem of language persisted during the Middle Ages because of the "nominalist controversy" between "realists" who favored the upward path, and "nominalists" who favored the downward path. The nominalist controversy was based on the question of whether the words used to refer to universal ideas such as "human" and "animal" represent something that actually exists, which was advocated by the "realists," or whether only the particular things of the sensory world, from which universal designations are derived, actually exist, which was advocated by the "nominalists." This controversy can be seen as a perpetuation of the problem of what "is" from ancient Greek philosophy, and also as a consequence of our capacity through language to think offline and thus conceive of things not physically present to our senses.

The nominalist controversy is one of the philosophical themes central to the plot of Eco's first novel *The Name of the Rose*. The detective monk William teaches his novice protegé Adso that "... the world speaks to us like a great book... and it speaks not only of the ultimate things (which it does always in an obscure fashion) but also of closer things, and then it speaks quite clearly."[2] William's position is thus an accommodation of both perspectives, but with an emphasis on the nominalist focus on the world of our senses.

In the transition from the Middle Ages to the Modern Age, the problem of language persists in a different way. Following Martin Luther's break with the Catholic Church in 1517, the medieval worldview began to shatter, and the focus of knowledge gradually shifted from the "book" of revelation, the upward path, to the "book" of nature, the downward path. The resulting rise of the scientific revolution can be seen as the triumph of the downward path and nominalism – the emphasis on the sensory world – over realism that favored preexisting abstract universals. The other response to the problem of language came from the German philosopher Immanuel Kant (1724–1804) who asserted that the conundrum of determining the true relation between the world of our senses and our concepts about it could be resolved by turning the problem upside down. Instead of trying to understand what "is" as a reflection of the world of our senses, the problem of language could be resolved by asserting that humans, through our language capacity, project our meaning on it. In other words, our language capacity does not mirror nature, but rather nature mirrors our language capacity. We will consider Kant's influence on the problem of language further in relation to one of the founders of semiotics, Charles Sanders Peirce (1839–1914).

The problem of language was confronted in particular by the scientific revolution that expanded our understanding of nature and fostered the technological revolution beginning in the eighteenth century, but also raised questions about the way that language functions to represent the things of the world. The catalyst for raising this question was the rise of nationalism in Europe that fostered the study of the historical and linguistic origins of the diverse European peoples. During the Middle Ages, although Europe was comprised of a variety of ethnic and linguistic groups, Germans, French, Italians, etc., all of Europe, before the Protestant Reformation, was unified under the Catholic Church, and all of Europe shared Latin as the specialized language of knowledge and learning. The rise of nationalism along with the advent of the printing press resulted in each nation adopting its own language as the medium of knowledge. Nationalism also led to the European competition for resources that brought about the colonization of indigenous peoples outside of Europe and the need to understand non-European languages and cultures. These historical circumstances led to an intensified focus on linguistics and cultural anthropology that confronted scholars with the problem of how to apply scientific methods that would be applicable across all languages and cultures. How could the European nations that were already discovering clear differences between each other in their way of representing the world, use the medium of their distinct language and culture toward an understanding of the indigenous cultures of non-Europeans? The rise of the scientific revolution also raised questions about the legitimacy of traditional philosophy. This led scholars such as Bertrand Russell (1872–1970) at Cambridge University to try to reform philosophy according to the logical analysis of language.

In response to the problem of language that arose from the eighteenth century, two intellectuals became the founders of what would become the field of semiotics: the Swiss linguistic scholar Ferdinand de Saussure (1857–1913), and the American scientist and philosopher Charles Sanders Peirce (pronounced "purse," 1839–1914). Saussure and Peirce were contemporaries, but they came from much different intellectual backgrounds and developed very different approaches for understanding the way that language generates meaning about our experience of the world. Saussure and Peirce, however, were both child prodigies who, in their teens, began to engage in an intensified study of advanced and complex fields of knowledge with an innovative approach. Their pioneering efforts in the development of semiotics became highly influential, but, during their lifetime, they worked in relative obscurity, and their accomplishments were not fully recognized until after their death. Saussure wrote very little and his ideas on language theory were only preserved thanks to the lecture notes of his students, while Peirce wrote voluminously yet lived in isolation and unfortunately never acquired a permanent academic appointment.

The Reluctant Linguist

Saussure's early work as a scholar was devoted primarily to classical philology which is the analysis of writings in ancient languages such as Sanskrit, Greek, and Latin. He distinguished himself from age 14 as an advanced student of classical languages, and at age 21 he had already published a study on a core aspect of Indo-European languages. Although Saussure had considered writing on general linguistics later in his career, he eventually became discouraged, and by 1894 he had become reluctant to even develop these ideas for publication. According to Jonathan Culler, a prominent writer on semiotics, Saussure had gradually withdrawn from scholarly writing and was annoyed at the task of developing a theory of general linguistics. As evidence, Culler cites a rare personal document in which Saussure complains that

> I am fed up with... the general difficulty of writing even ten lines of good sense on linguistic matters... The utter inadequacy of current terminology, the need to reform it and, in order to do that, to demonstrate what sort of object language is, continually spoil my pleasure in philology, though I have no dearer wish than not to be made to think about the nature of language in general. This will lead, against my will, to a book in which I shall explain, without enthusiasm or passion, why there is not a single term used in linguistics which has any meaning for me.[3]

Despite his reluctant attitude, Saussure was apparently the only scholar at the University of Geneva deemed sufficiently qualified in linguistics such that he was assigned by the University to offer a course on general linguistics. He only taught the course three times, however, between 1907 and 1911, and died shortly afterwards in 1913 without publishing the materials for the course. Although Saussure seems to have been an unwilling participant in the development of his course, his innovative ideas about linguistics generated such a strong following that a couple of his students decided to preserve his lectures for publication after he died. Since Saussure left few notes of his own, his *Course in General Linguistics*,[4] published in 1916, was based on lecture notes by some of his students. Thus ironically Saussure's *Course in General Linguistics*, which he did not enthusiastically pursue, subsequently became one of the foundational pillars for the development of semiotics.

So how did Saussure's ideas help to respond to the problem of language? Saussure's objective was to completely reform the study of language which he believed had previously generated a lot of misconceptions and misunderstandings because it involves so many factors such as sounds, graphic symbols, mental images, social relations of communication, cultural systems of meaning, and its own historical evolution over time. Saussure was attempting to reform linguistics through the scientific method, but he pointed out that unlike other sciences, language has no clear object of study because language is itself the medium by which we refer to objects. Consequently Saussure became discouraged about language as a field of study.

Language as Structure

To resolve the problem of how to effectively generate an understanding of language, Saussure determined that the "only" practical solution is to focus on linguistic structure: "The linguist must take the study of linguistic structure as his primary concern, and relate all other manifestations of language to it. Indeed, amid so many dualities, linguistic structure seems to be the one thing that is independently definable and provides something our minds can satisfactorily grasp."[5] The study of structure involves defining basic components and their relations to each other. The structure of a molecule is composed of atoms which are made up of protons, electrons, and neutrons in various relations that make up chemical compounds. Saussure proposed that: "a language is a system of signs expressing ideas." He thus defined the basic unit of language as the "sign," and the science of language would involve an analysis of how it functions in relation to other signs to express ideas and refer to things in the world.

The importance of Saussure's conception is that, if language is approached from a scientific perspective as a system of signs, then language can be considered as just one of many systems of meaning that constitute human culture. Saussure mentions, for example, "symbolic rites, forms of politeness, military signals, and so on." Consequently, the study of language offers a model for understanding all systems of meaning within culture because all modes of cultural expression involve signs. That insight opened up the doorway to the origins of semiotics as a general theory of culture. But Saussure didn't use the term "semiotics." Saussure proposed "a science *which studies the role of signs as part of social life*. We shall call it semiology (from the Greek semeion, 'sign'). It would investigate the nature of signs and the laws governing them." Although Saussure was not certain whether his proposed new field of study would be broadly recognized and pursued, he anticipated that it could potentially have very broad applications:

> Since it does not yet exist, one cannot say for certain that it will exist. But it has a right to exist, a place ready for it in advance. Linguistics is only one branch of this general science. The laws which semiology will discover will be laws applicable in linguistics, and linguistics will thus be assigned to a clearly defined place in the field of human knowledge.[6]

In his vision of an entirely new discipline that could encompass the full spectrum of human culture with far reaching applications, Saussure was similar to his contemporary theorist Peirce.

It's useful to note in relation to Pareyson's conception of the need for a general theory of interpretation that Saussure saw "the importance of linguistics for culture in general" and that "In the lives of individuals and societies, language is a factor of greater importance than any other." He also notes that it would be "unacceptable" for the knowledge of language to be held by "a handful of specialists" because "the study of language is...the concern of everyone."[7] Linguistics, according to Saussure, should not be restricted to elite academics because language is essential for understanding culture in general. It has a universal scope that is applicable to all in understanding our being as the linguistic species. Semiotics, however, has become a complex, technical, and highly specialized field of study with a dense vocabulary.

Without delving into the complex details of Saussure's structuralist theory of language, we can consider the most important points. Saussure considered language to be an especially difficult focus of study because it involved so many diverse aspects from the way that sounds are physically generated in the mouth, the graphic symbols that represent these sounds, the way that words are organized into statements, the mental images that they produce, the social and cultural relations in which they function, etc. He also pointed out that language does not have stable, fixed objects already established for analysis, like molecules for example, because language is the medium for referring to objects. Language is thus an odd ghostlike field of study that is difficult to approach from a scientific perspective. For this reason, Saussure believed that language could only be studied through a focus on its structural relations.

SIGN, SIGNIFIER, SIGNIFIED

Saussure attempted to clarify the way that language and culture in general generate meaning by first defining "the sign" as the basic unit of culture and how it functions within a set of structural relations. A "sign" within language refers to every functional component from individual letters as graphic symbols, the sounds that they represent (in phonetic languages), and their combinations as words that refer to ideas or states of the world. The "sign," for Saussure, functions as a "signifier," which is linked to a thing or idea, which he called the "signified." His primary focus was to explain how "signs" as "signifiers" function in language to generate meaning in relation to the "signified" which is the thing or idea that the signifier refers to.

SIGNS ARE ARBITRARY

The first principle of Saussure's theory of language is that signs are arbitrary. So what does "arbitrary" mean concerning the sign, and how does this approach help to resolve the problem of language? In order to reform linguistics according to the model of the sciences, Saussure needed to begin by clarifying the relation between signs and the things that they designate. Recall that Aristotle had begun in a similar way: "First we must settle what a name is..."[8] Saussure was annoyed with his fellow philologists for trying to find organic links between words and the things that they refer to as if the English word "tree," for example, somehow reflects the essential character of "treeness." Instead he asserted that the sign is totally arbitrary in relation to the things it designates. The arbitrary character of the sign is evident in the many diverse words across different languages that refer to the same thing such as "tree" in English, "arbre" in French, "Baum" in German, etc. He noted that the things that language refers to are also not predetermined but differ according to the arbitrary ways in which different cultures relate to the world. Similar words across different languages, for example, can refer to much different concepts about the world. Jonathan Culler notes the example of the French words "fleuve" and "riviere" in relation to the English words "river" and "stream." Not only are the words different between these languages in reference to seemingly similar things, but there are also conceptual differences in what these words refer to. As Culler points out: "The signified 'river' is opposed to 'stream' solely in terms of size, whereas a 'fleuve' differs from a 'riviere' not because it is necessarily larger but because it flows into the sea, while a 'riviere' does not."[9] Saussure's insight about the arbitrary nature of the sign was revolutionary because it indicated that language does not reflect the pre-given nature of the things of the world by simply naming them. Language actually determines not only the words that we use to refer to things, but also that human cultures make reference to particular things in the world in fundamentally diverse ways.

The Meaning of Signs Is Relational

According to Saussure, since words as "signs" are arbitrary, they are meaningful solely through their relation to other signs based on their oppositions and differences, and through their relation in a sequence to other signs. The word "boy" is different from "girl" as well as "baby" and "man," etc. These differences are what he called "paradigmatic" because words as signs function through their difference from other signs. Saussure explained the relational meaning of signs as follows: "Their most precise characteristic is that they are what the others are not."[10] The sign "girl" has meaning in relation to its opposite "boy" and not in itself alone. It is thus dependent on its opposite for generating meaning.

Signs also function to generate meaning through their relation to each other in a sequence which Saussure called "syntagmatic" relations. We can think of paradigmatic relations as functioning vertically to determine the meaning of a particular word in relation to what it is not. Because of paradigmatic relations, we can understand the meaning of a word without it being in a sentence. Syntagmatic relations function horizontally through an ordered sequence between words in a sentence. The syntagmatic structure of language is perhaps most apparent if we simply scramble the word order of a sample statement: "Case focus the is this of happens example in what that." (What happens in that case is the focus of this example.) Each of the words in the previous sentence has meaning on its own paradigmatically in relation to what they're not, but when these words are linked together in a disorderly way, they result in an unintelligible statement. The words acquire meaning as a sentence because of their relations to each other when joined in a sequence as noun, adjective, verb, subject, object, etc. Syntagmatic relations are also arbitrary because different languages vary considerably in their structural relations of word order. The word order of a number of languages like English is subject-verb-object, "The boy walked to school." The word order of Japanese, however, is topic/time-object-place-verb: "The mother after dinner the cookie to the boy in the kitchen gave."

Although Saussure's ideas about language have been displaced by later theorists, such as the American linguist Noam Chomsky, his innovative approach founded a highly influential movement called "structuralism" that applied his method more broadly to the analysis of culture in general, as Saussure had suggested. Among the most prominent figures in the structuralist movement were primarily French scholars such as the semiotician Roland Barthes (1915–1980) in the late fifties, the psychoanalyst Jacques Lacan (1901–1981) beginning in the fifties, and the French anthropologist Claude Levi-Strauss (1908–2009) in the early sixties. Barthes was famous for applying the structuralist method to contemporary French popular culture such as the world of fashion, as well as to literature through a focus on narrative structure, and Lacan became a pioneer in applying linguistic theory to psychoanalysis. Claude Levi-Strauss applied structuralism to his study of primitive or what he called "non-literate peoples." Eco was acquainted with Barthes as a friend, and Eco's early studies of popular culture phenomena such as comic books can be seen to share Barthes's focus on narrative structure, for example, in his analysis of the myth of Superman. Eco's relation to the other prominent leader of the French structuralist movement, however, was oppositional. Eco's *The Open Work* was directly attacked by Levi-Strauss as espousing "a formula that I absolutely cannot accept. What makes a work of art a work is not its being open but its being closed. A work of art is an object endowed with precise properties and... the rigidity of a crystal."[11] Eco strongly defended his conception of the open work in response to the critique by Levi-Strauss in a set of essays entitled "Series and Structure" from *La struttura assente, La ricerca semiotica e il metodo strutturale* (The absent structure, Semiotic research and the structural method) from 1968 which was his first venture as a semiotic theorist (now included in the English language version of *The Open Work*). Although Eco pursued a structuralist approach in his early analyses of popular culture, his conception of the "absent" structure was a clear break from the structuralism of Saussure as a foundation for a theory of semiotics. In an amusing reflection on that period given his earlier expulsion from the Catholic Church in 1954, Eco wrote in the preface from 1980 of the republication of *La struttura assente* about the need to "avoid being excommunicated" for "sinning" against the "reigning" theory of that time which had already caused him difficulty in getting the book published.[12]

The Solitary Scholar

Eco acknowledged the influence of Saussure in the introduction to his *A Theory of Semiotics* (1975), but he asserted that, in relation to Saussure's conception of the sign, the approach of the American co-founder of semiotics, Charles Sanders Peirce, "seems to me more comprehensive and semiotically fruitful." As a linguist, Saussure conceived of semiotics, according to Eco, "as a communicative device taking place between two human beings intentionally aiming to communicate or to express something." The key difference, for Eco, was that Peirce's conception of the sign "does not demand, as part of a sign's definition, the qualities of being intentionally emitted and artificially produced."[13] Peirce, through a dual focus on logic and science, included unintentional signs such as medical symptoms and weather indicators that are derived from natural states of the world.

While Saussure's ideas became highly influential shortly after his death, Peirce, who died a year after Saussure in 1914, was not broadly recognized until half a century later. Over the course of his career, Peirce pursued a number of advanced and innovative scholarly pursuits in philosophy and science, and he is recognized as the co-founder, along with the Harvard philosopher William James (1842–1910), of the American philosophy of pragmatism. But, despite his well-established academic credentials and his father's prominent position at Harvard, as well as the support of William James, Peirce was never able to obtain a permanent academic appointment. Unfortunately Peirce's advancement as a scholar was opposed without his knowledge by the president of Harvard University, Charles William Eliot (1834–1926), and a scientist, Simon Newcomb (1835–1909), who had studied mathematics under Peirce's father. Newcomb even secretly thwarted Peirce's attempts to obtain a Carnegie grant to support his independent efforts.[14] According to Joseph Brent's biography of Peirce, these highly influential scholars apparently took exception to Peirce for personal reasons, and Peirce was never aware of their role in obstructing his career. The historian Louis Menand suggests that the opposition to Peirce may have stemmed from a painful neurological disorder that required him to take opiates and "made him subject to violent fits of temper."[15] Even his friend and fellow pragmatist William James, who was his most loyal supporter, described Peirce as "a very smart fellow with a great deal of character, pretty independent & violent though."[16] As a result, Peirce struggled financially most of his life and died in poverty. Although Peirce, unlike Saussure, wrote voluminously, most of his vast output of writings, totaling over 100,000 pages,[17] were not published during his lifetime because of his lack of an academic appointment. According to popular science writer Keith Devlin, this may also have been the result of Peirce's ideas being far in advance of his times.[18]

After his death, the publication of the earliest anthology of Peirce's writings dates from 1923, and the first six volumes of his *Collected Papers* were not published until 1935. Although prominent intellectuals such as the English philosopher Bertrand Russell (1872–1970) and the American pragmatist John Dewey (1859–1952) acknowledged the profound influence of Peirce, the importance of his ideas for the development of semiotics and related fields did not begin to be fully recognized until the sixties through the publication of a journal by the Charles S. Peirce Society (founded in 1946), and the writings on Peirce by the American philosopher and historian Max Fisch. Consequently Peirce's impact on the development of semiotics occurred just shortly before Eco turned his attention to semiotics in 1968 which led to his founding of the first academic department in semiotic theory in Italy at the University of Bologna in 1975. In 1989, a program devoted specifically to the study of Peirce was established in Italy at the University of Milan almost a century after his death. The fairly recent recognition of Peirce's work is a testament to his unfortunate circumstances as a scholar but also to the broad scope and enduring influence of his ideas.

PEIRCE AND THE REFORMULATION OF KANT'S CATEGORIES

Peirce, like Saussure, was a child prodigy. His father was professor of mathematics and astronomy at Harvard University, and Peirce was brought up in an environment that encouraged his early interest in scientific pursuits, mathematics, and logic. Consequently Peirce's approach to language and the development of semiotics differed greatly from Saussure's approach as a linguist. Peirce's semiotic theory developed from his intensive study of the logical categories of the eighteenth-century German philosopher Immanuel Kant (1724–1804) that Peirce began at age 12. As an indicator of his advanced intellectual vision at an early age, Peirce took up the study of Kant's logical categories not just to understand them, which is an imposing challenge in itself especially at such a young age, but with the prospect of completely revising them.

Immanuel Kant reformulated the categories that Aristotle had developed more than 2,000 years previously in response to the problem of language. Aristotle attempted to resolve what he saw as Plato's misunderstanding of the meaning of the word "is" by defining the linguistic components of a statement – noun, verb, etc. – and by devising a way to evaluate the relation between statements to determine their truth-value. As part of this approach, Aristotle conceived of the most general ways in which we can make statements about the world. This resulted in his 10 categories for specifying all the ways of being that can be expressed with the word "is." In other words, all of the states of being that can be expressed through language about our relation to the world.

In the eighteenth century, Kant reformulated Aristotle's categories in a radical way through the revolutionary insight that humans are not passive receptors for predetermined states of being which are simply reflected in our use of language. Kant attempted to resolve the longstanding problem of language by turning the relation between language and the world upside down. Instead of language passively reflecting the things of the world, Kant conceived that the world reflects the way that we project our meaning on it through language. This may seem counter-intuitive because there are obviously "real" things in the world that don't seem to be affected by our perception of them. However, as indicated earlier, the French words "fleuve" and "riviere" and the English words "river" and "stream," while seeming to refer to the same things in nature, actually refer to much different ways of thinking about these things. While Aristotle conceived of his 10 categories as the broadest modes of understanding through which human perception corresponds to the reality of the world, Kant conceived of his 12 categories as the fundamental ways in which humans project their meaning on the world.

Kant revised the 10 categories of Aristotle into 12 categories divided into four groups as follows: QUANTITY: unity, plurality, totality; QUALITY: reality, negation, limitation; RELATION: inherence/subsistence, causality/dependence, community; and MODALITY: possibility, existence, necessity. Without discussing them in detail, we can use Kant's 12 categories as a reference point for understanding how philosophers after Aristotle were attempting to respond to the problem of language in relation to our sensory experience of the world. This was the challenge that Peirce first confronted in his youth a century after Kant which became the basis for his foundational theory of semiotics.

A Pioneer of American Pragmatism

Saussure's objective was to reform the field of linguistics according to the model of the sciences. In contrast, Peirce was a co-founder of the uniquely American philosophy called "pragmatism" which tries to resolve the problem of language in the domain of philosophy by asserting that the meaning of mental concepts can best be understood in relation to their practical consequences which he later refined as follows: "In order to ascertain the meaning of an intellectual conception one should consider what practical consequences might conceivably result by necessity from the truth of that conception; and the sum of these consequences will constitute the entire meaning of the conception."[19]

The pragmatic maxim is a method for clarifying the meaning of concepts by conceiving of how they would function in practice as a hypothetical belief. Peirce derived this notion of clarity from the model of the sciences that test potential theories through experimentation in the sensory world and revise them as necessary toward the determination of the truth. Peirce's pragmatic maxim can also be seen as similar to existentialism in that it focuses on the meaning of life through our actual lived experience of the world.

A Theory of First, Second, and Third

So how did Peirce use his foundations in logic and the natural sciences to develop a theory of semiotics? Without going into the extensive details of his theory of the sign, we can focus primarily on how he reformulated the 12 categories of Kant, and how Peirce's approach to the sign was different from Saussure's. Peirce reformulated the 12 categories of Kant into just three, which he called "firstness," "secondness," and "thirdness." Keep in mind that Peirce was trying to reform philosophy according to our sensory experience of the world, and to clarify the meaning of ideas according to the actions they would motivate. As a result, he conceived of the signs that allow us to orient ourselves in the world as fundamental sensory and linguistic experiences.

Peirce theorized that there are three consecutive stages or phases, what he called "gradations,"[20] in our sensory and mental experience of the world that result in a progressive extension of our meaningful relation to it. He developed the idea of a sequence of phases in our experience of the world through a kind of thought experiment like Einstein's conception of the relation between gravity, velocity, and time. Peirce considered the most fundamental ways in which our experience of the world comes about from sensory impressions which are then linked to words and ideas, according to a logical progression. That's why he called these categories "firstness," "secondness," and "thirdness."

"Firstness" is an immediate sensory impression that draws our attention before we have a sense of its relation to other things, and before it has acquired a meaning for orienting our linguistic relation to the world. Since Peirce was trying to conceptualize something through language that is the initial phase of our sensory experience but not yet fully entered into language, he refers to "firstness" as "what is present in general" through the act of "attention."[21] "Firstness" would be similar to the experience we occasionally have of our attention being drawn to something hazy or indistinct, for example, an object seen at nighttime, or at a distance, such that we can't immediately recognize it.

"Secondness" is the phase in which the pure possibility of "firstness" enters into our understanding solely based on differences and similarities: blue is different from yellow, hard is different from soft, square is different from round, a triangle is similar to a cone, a tree is similar to a bush, a wolf is similar to a dog, etc. We experience "secondness" whenever we try to initially recognize something we're not sure of by testing various guesses about its character in order to identify it in relation to other things, as indicated previously. Peirce noted that: "Empirical psychology has established the fact that we can know a quality only by means of its contrast with or similarity to another."[22] In this respect, Peirce's concept of "secondness" shares, to some extent, Saussure's idea that language generates meaning through the structural relations of difference and similarity.

"Thirdness" is explained by Peirce as the phase in which the pure possibility of "firstness" and the relational aspect of "secondness" are joined together through an interpretation that establishes a belief for orienting our understanding and practical relationship to the world. Without "thirdness," the experience of the world would be limited in meaning to relational difference or similarity. Peirce referred to "thirdness" as "habit taking"[23] or the "interpretant"[24] because it creates a bond of meaning between a state of the world and a sign that refers to it. "Thirdness" is the phase in our human experience of the world that makes us the linguistic species because it allows us to think offline through symbols that are linked to but detached from our sensory experience of the world.

Peirce considered his reformulation of the categories of Aristotle and Kant into "firstness," "secondness," and "thirdness" as "one of the births of time."[25] For Peirce, it was "the gift I make to the world" as "my child" that "shall live when oblivion has me."[26] Peirce believed that he had erected "a philosophical edifice that shall outlast the vicissitudes of time,"[27] and serve as the foundation for reconceiving all of human knowledge:

> The undertaking which this volume inaugurates is to make a philosophy like that of Aristotle, that is to say, to outline a theory so comprehensive that, for a long time to come, the entire work of human reason, in philosophy of every school and kind, in mathematics, in psychology, in physical science, in history, in sociology, and in whatever other department there may be, shall appear as the filling up of its details.[28]

Peirce's assertion of the comprehensive scope of his semiotic theory can provide an understanding of how Eco conceived of semiotics as a grand unified theory of culture.

Peirce conceived of three main types of signs in relation to the three categories, which he called "icons," "indexes," and "symbols." "Icons" are linked to "firstness" because they generate meaning in reference to themselves without being dependent on a relation to something else, for example, Madonna as a rock performer in a category of her own. An "index" is associated with "secondness" because its meaning is relationally dependent on pointing to something else, for example, smoke in relation to fire. A "symbol" connects a sensory impression, a "firstness," with a sign that points to it, a "secondness," through an interpretation, a "thirdness," that establishes a relational state of meaning. The word or symbol for "heart," for example, can signify "love." Peirce theorized that signs generate meaning in relation to other signs, and that these links between signs can continue indefinitely within language through a process he called "unlimited semiosis."

A General Theory of Culture

Eco's own theory of semiotics can be considered now in relation to the legacy of Saussure and Peirce, and how Eco was influenced by his background in the Italian humanist historicist tradition that he retained as a fundamental principle in his theoretical explorations as an intellectual. What, then, distinguishes Eco's attempt to develop semiotics as a general theory of culture? Saussure's analysis of linguistic structure had already been applied to the study of "non-literate culture" by the French anthropologist Claude Levi-Strauss and modern culture by Roland Barthes. Although the structuralist approach initially gained favor as a powerful theoretical method – which was adopted by Eco in some of his early analyses of popular culture – it was later called into question for applying a mechanistic model that functioned outside the dynamic forces of history and the aesthetics of culture. If the meaning of things generated by human language and culture is determined solely through the mechanics of arbitrary structural relations, then humans would be entirely subordinate to those structures which would effectively negate the impact of historical development and the creative role of aesthetics. Historical development and the aesthetics of human culture are core principles of the Italian humanist-historicist tradition that was a major influence on Eco's development as an intellectual and his later turn to semiotics. If humans are the species that continuously modifies the world and themselves over time, then all ideas must be understood as arising from the historical conditions that generate them as aesthetic expressions of human culture.

Besides rejecting the structuralist approach of Saussure, Eco found Peirce's ideas more useful because they included the full spectrum of our linguistic and sensory experience of the world. According to Eco, "There is a sign every time a human group decides to use and to recognize something as the vehicle of something else."[29] Eco's conception thus includes the signs intentionally communicated between humans through language that were the focus of Saussure, as well as the unintentional signs and "natural" phenomena that were included by Pierce. All signs either "artificially" created or arising from natural phenomena are determined by the way that "a human group decides to use and to recognize them." According to Eco, this approach "makes a general theory of culture out of semiotics and in the final analysis makes semiotics a substitute for cultural anthropology."[30] As we considered in Chapter 2, we are the cultural species because we alter the world and ourselves over time according to our constantly changing projection of our meaning on the world. Eco's conception of semiotics as "a general theory of culture" would thus be the basis for a grand unified theory of everything human which would encompass all aspects of our experience of the world.

For the development of a unified theory of culture, Eco found Peirce's conception of semiotics more useful than Saussure's, but he did not adopt

Peirce's categories of firstness, secondness, and thirdness and the corresponding types of signs: icons, indexes, and symbols. Like his rejection of structuralism, Eco's foundations in the Italian humanist-historicist tradition also led him to reject any conception of language and culture that was conceived as outside of the forces of history. Consequently Peirce's classification of signs, just like Saussure's structuralist approach, was rejected in the development of Eco's semiotic theory because it would fall into the same problem of asserting universal, timeless concepts that would negate the impact of history and culture.

THE INTERPRETANT AND UNLIMITED SEMIOSIS

Eco rejected Peirce's typology of signs, but he based his semiotic theory on two core concepts from Peirce: "the interpretant." and "unlimited semiosis." Peirce used the concept of "interpretant" to explain how language functions not through simple reference to things – as Saussure had suggested between "signifier" and "signified" – but rather through signs detached from things that generate meaning by being linked to other signs. Our strange ability for offline thinking functions by making reference to culturally established meanings that don't exist as physical objects in the world. Signs may refer to physical objects as points of reference but always according to a particular cultural code. Recall, again, how the English words "river" and "stream" are different in concept from the French words "fleuve" and "riviere" while pointing to what would seem to be the same objects in nature. These words actually refer to an idea that is detached from the things they refer to, and the meaning of that idea is generated through the linking function of the "interpretant."

The "interpretant" is, in turn, linked to other "interpretants" in a vast network of signs through what Peirce called "unlimited semiosis," which creates a cosmological reference library or Encyclopedia that surrounds and connects all of us through our language, culture, mass media, social class, education, family upbringing, personal experience, etc. Although this kind of cosmological Encyclopedia can be conceptualized as a necessary aspect of the way that we communicate through language, as Eco indicates, it cannot be fully described: " ... a description of the Universal Semantic System (i.e. one which shapes a cultural world vision [is] an impossible operation because that world vision, in its interconnections and its peripheral manifestations, changes constantly) ... "[31]

The "interpretant" is the link between signs that has developed historically and culturally to allow us to make sense of the world and to communicate with each other. If language were simply a mode of making reference to things in the world, then the sounds that we utter in spoken language would function solely like a finger pointing to direct our attention to an object. But, as we have seen, language instead points to an idea about things that we project on objects. Pointing to things would only have the effect of directing our shared attention to an object without generating a shared meaning in relation to it. It would be like saying "Hey, look at that" but without a meaning for the "thatness" of "that." There is also an inherent ambiguity even in the meaning of what is referred to by the pointing finger. As Eco "points out," "When the finger points with comparatively little energy, it means [[close]] and when pointing with greater energy...it means [[distance]]."[32] Instead of just pointing to things, we utter a sound that brings to mind the image of the object or an abstract idea derived from it, and then we link that image to a particular way of projecting our meaning on it. Language thus functions through a chain of interpretative links, and Eco's use of the concept of the "interpretant" indicates how semiotics serves for him as a general theory of interpretation because the act of interpretation is involved at the most fundamental level of our experience of the world.

We communicate through language by linking things or ideas through signs (words, sounds) to culturally established reference points of shared meaning. For example, the word "play" can have a number of meanings depending on how it is linked to other signs. After initially being linked as the opposite of "work," it can then have several meanings through other links, for example, as an activity of children, or the engagement in various games or sports for children or adults, or making sound from a musical instrument, or treating someone in a manipulative manner, or as a particular maneuver in a sporting activity, or as a theatrical work, or as a play on words (e.g., a pun), or the play of one's imagination, or as a euphemism for sexual activity, etc. Each one of these links functions as an "interpretant" that is made meaningful by being linked to another "interpretant" and so on. For example, if the word "play" is linked to an activity of children, that activity can, in turn, be linked to various forms of structured game playing such as "hide and go seek," or fantasy role playing, or the unstructured activity of playing with toys, etc. Each of those potential links is made meaningful, in turn, through other links, for example, in the case of structured game playing, with games governed by rules or those that are improvised, competitive or non-competitive, team or individual player, etc.

Peirce asserted that these links continue indefinitely through a process that he called "unlimited semiosis" because each link is made meaningful in relation to other links. But, according to Peirce, "... an endless series of representations, each representing the one behind it, may be conceived to have an absolute object as its limit" which he called the "final interpretant" or "habit."[33] Through the process of linking signs in the act of communication, the recipient of a particular sign will fix on the set of links that seem to best fit the shared understanding of the world between sender and recipient based on the cultural codes that apply. But because of the numerous potential interpretants involved in the communication between sender and recipient, there is also the potential for "misinterpretation" which led Eco to later become interested in the way that "misinterpretations" or "aberrant meanings" occurred especially when communicating across social classes and cultures which we will consider further in the next chapter.

A Theory of Codes and Sign Production

While rejecting Peirce's primordial types of signs, Eco draws on Peirce's concepts of the interpretant and unlimited semiosis, to develop two core approaches to his theory of semiotics: a theory of codes, and a theory of sign production. Eco's conception of a theory of codes is based on the idea that communication involves a relation between a sender and a receiver who communicate through reference to shared cultural codes. Eco's theory of sign production is based on his foundation in aesthetics. These two approaches constitute for Eco a dynamic theory of culture: If all of human culture reflects our projection of our creative capacity on the world, then our "knowledge" of the world is based on two modes of understanding: an analysis of the cultural codes of meaning at any given time historically, and the constant modifications of those patterns of meaning through the creative capacity of sign production. Human knowledge, from this perspective, involves an oscillation between the discovery of our shared codes of meaning and the creation of new possibilities through sign production. Through discovery we try to understand the ways in which we orient ourselves in the world through language and culture, and through creation we constantly modify our ways of orienting ourselves in the world by exploring our unlimited potential. Eco's semiotic theory is thus consistent with Peirce's later shift toward aesthetics. By reconceiving his original emphasis on logic as subservient to ethics, through our practical experience of the world, and both logic and ethics as subservient to aesthetics.[34]

A Theory of Lying

As part of his theory of codes, Eco conceived of the idea of "sign-function" as "an expression" that is "correlated to a content" that is actually separate from the sensory world which, according to Eco, makes semiotics "a theory of the lie":

> A sign is everything which can be taken as significantly substituting for something else. This something else does not necessarily have to exist or to actually be somewhere at the moment in which a sign stands for it. And thus semiotics is in principle the discipline studying everything which can be used to lie.[35]

A "theory of the lie" may seem like a strange way to conceptualize an understanding of our linguistic capacity, but it foregrounds in a powerful way the odd nature of the human species. What especially distinguishes humans is the language capacity that allows us to think offline separate from our sensory relation to the world. We are able to do this by substituting signs for the things that they stand for whether they are physically present or not. We are also able to substitute signs for things that don't actually exist which enables our aesthetic potential for creative imagination. This means that all signs, being separate from the things they refer to, have the potential to function as a lie. Conceptualizing how signs function in this way indicates the powerful flexibility of language and semiotics.

But since we are able to assert as "true," and to lead others to believe and act as if it were "true," something that is intentionally fabricated as a "lie," also means that it can be difficult to distinguish between these different expressions of language. Because of this strange aspect of our linguistic capacity, Eco became interested in the role of falsehoods as a cultural force which is the central theme of four of his seven novels: *Foucault's Pendulum* (1988), *Baudolino* (2000), *The Prague Cemetery* (2010), and his last novel *The Number Zero* (2015). *The Prague Cemetery*, in particular, considers the impact of a fraudulent historical text first published in 1903 entitled *The Protocols of the Elders of Zion* that purported to be the secret record of a Jewish plot for world domination. It was later widely disseminated as a true account of this fabricated conspiracy by prominent anti-Semitic figures such as Adolf Hitler and Henry Ford.

A Theory of Laughing

According to Eco, because of our dependence on cultural codes to communicate and to make sense of the world, we are also the species that "laughs" which is a central focus of his first novel *The Name of the Rose*. But what does it mean that we are the species that laughs? Other species, for example chimpanzees and orangutans, make sounds and playful gestures that seem to imitate the laughter of humans. What distinguishes human laughter is that, through our linguistic capacity, we can make reference to the world that is not a lie but rather a deliberate distortion of the truth that causes us to laugh because it violates or alters our cultural codes about the world. As Eco indicates, "...not only is semiotics the science of everything subject to the lie: it is also the science of everything subject to comic or tragic distortion." Beyond the offline capacity of language to make reference to things that are not physically present or even existent, humans can use language to engage in ridicule through distortions of our cultural codes. For example, going back to the origins of Greek philosophy, Aristophanes comedy *The Clouds* in 423 B.C. made fun of Socrates as the leader of a school called "The Thinkery" where a young man is corrupted into defying tradition by Socrates who is depicted as floating above the earth with the "Clouds" who are the goddesses of thinking. Eco indicates that "One laughs because even though one realizes that the situation is unthinkable, one understands...[its] meaning..."

For an example of a tragic distortion we could consider Orson Welles's famous radio broadcast in 1938 that included seemingly real news bulletins about a Martian invasion that caused a number of listeners – unaware that the reports were fictional – to panic. Welles's radio broadcast is an instance of tragic distortion because, even though a Martian invasion can be conceived as a possibility and was obviously perceived by some as a reality, to do so would require a major alteration of our cultural code of reality. According to Eco, "One feels fear because, even though one realizes that the situation is possible, one does not like to accept such an alarming semantic organization of one's experience."[36] But since it *can* be conceived as a possibility, Orson Welles's fictional broadcast provoked fear because listeners were not initially aware that the news bulletins were fictional. By asserting that semiotics is a theory of "the lie" as well as "the laugh," Eco is emphasizing how the cultural codes that we are dependent on are open to falsehood as well as distortion through violations of the code that can provoke ridicule as well as anxiety. Instead of generating falsehoods, laughter – or alarm in the case of tragic distortion – causes us to reflect on and question our shared understanding of reality. These distortions also point out our dependence upon complex cultural codes that determine our shared understanding of reality and enable us to communicate with each other.

BETWEEN DISCOVERY AND CREATION

Eco notes that the oddity of trying to develop a theory of language and semiotics through a theory of codes and a theory of sign production is that, "*Semiosis explains itself by itself...*"[37] Since the meaning of signs occurs through links to other signs in an unlimited and dynamic way, even theorizing about language participates in the linking process that the theory attempts to describe. As Eco has noted, however, these methodological problems are similar to the indeterminacy principle or observer effect in quantum physics that asserts that one cannot determine simultaneously both the position and the momentum of subatomic particles, and that the object of analysis is affected by the observer. According to Eco: "...to 'speak' about 'speaking', to signify signification or to communicate about communication cannot but influence the universe of speaking, signifying and communicating."[38] As Eco indicates "this condition of imbalance and apparent lack of stability puts semiotics on a par with other disciplines such as physics, governed... by such methodological criteria as the indeterminacy or complementarity [particle-wave duality of light] principles." In an interesting comparison given the historical displacement of the humanities by the natural sciences, Eco asserts the validity of semiotics as a "scientific discipline" comparable to physics, but subject to the following condition: "Only if it acquires this awareness of its own limits, and avoids aspiring to an absolute form of knowledge...,"[39] a theme that he later explores in his first novel *The Name of the Rose*.

Eco's confrontation with the limits of semiotics points out another curious aspect of our nature as the cultural, linguistic species: the world of human culture surrounds us as a species, and we can't step outside of it to see it in its entirety. This is also why Eco asserts the fallacy of aspiring to an absolute form of knowledge. We are always on the inside of a complex network or labyrinth of relations that we are constantly altering. While trying to make sense of the cultural world that we inhabit, we are always modifying it according to our limited view of its dynamic incomprehensible totality. Our experience of the world is like groping for understanding through a network of tunnels while imagining possible worlds to guide us and accommodate our aspirations.

Sign Production as Aesthetics

Eco's theory of sign production, as a theory of creation, can also be understood in relation to his conception of aesthetics. According to Eco, "... the aesthetic text represents a sort of summary and laboratory model of all the aspects of sign-function..." As Eco points out, aesthetic sign production involves "a *reassessment of the content*" through "a process of *code changing*" that "frequently produces a new type of *awareness about the world.*" Once interpretative links have become culturally encoded, they become what Peirce calls "habits" because they function automatically, and for the most part, unconsciously, to generate meaning. Consequently, according to Eco, while all cultural expressions are originally "aesthetic" in character because they involve our creative projection of meaning on the world, what distinguishes an "aesthetic" expression, as an instance of sign production, is its "*ambiguous* and *self-focusing*" character. Eco defines ambiguity as "a mode of violating the rules of the code." He cites the famous example of "green colorless ideas sleep furiously" by the American linguist Noam Chomsky that is grammatically correct but violates our commonly shared notions of meaning. Aesthetic expressions are also "self-focusing" because, by violating the rules of the code, they draw attention to the ordinarily unconscious ways in which we generate meaning, and the artificial boundaries of our cultural codes. As Eco indicates, "the aesthetic experience...focuses my attention and urges me to an interpretive effort..." And that interpretive effort "incites me toward the discovery of an unexpected flexibility in the language with which I am dealing." According to Eco, an aesthetic expression deliberately violates the codes of meaning by making the familiar appear strange in order to draw attention to the act of interpretation:

SIGN PRODUCTION AS AESTHETICS 193

A violation of norms on both the expression and the content plane obliges one to reconsider their correlation, which can no longer be the same as that foreseen by the usual code. In this way the text becomes self-focusing: it directs the attention of the addressee primarily to its own shape.

The aesthetic expression is thus especially useful for demonstrating the impact of language and culture by foregrounding our relation to cultural codes as shared norms for understanding and communicating about the world. Aesthetic expressions show how our sense of "reality" is artificially projected on the world. The aesthetic expression also provides an understanding of the disconnect that typically occurs between elite intellectuals and a popular audience because, as Eco notes, aesthetic expression often provokes a "sense of bewilderment." The experience of "bewilderment" arises from the deliberate estrangement produced by the aesthetic expression that, as Eco points out, "increases the difficulty and duration of perception." All of which explains, according to Eco, "the difficulty and obscurity of artistic creations when presented for the first time to an audience as yet unprepared for them..." The problem of ambiguity and estrangement, perhaps most radically exemplified by Joyce's *Finnegans Wake*, more generally explains the wide gulf between intellectuals, who have an awareness of the "artificial" character of human culture and the function of aesthetics in violating cultural codes, and the experience and educational background of a broad popular audience.

Besides the character of aesthetic expressions as ambiguous and self-focusing, Eco asserts that: "In the aesthetic text both the labor of the sender and the attention of the addressee are focused on the *lower levels* of the expression plane." As an explanation of the "lower levels," Eco suggests that art "conveys a *'je ne sais pas quoi'*" an "I don't know what" kind of experience. Aesthetic experience affects us subliminally through an experience that is outside of our cultural codes of expression. As Eco puts it, "...aesthetics becomes the philosophy of the unspeakable."[40] From Eco's perspective, aesthetics is not only ambiguous and self-focusing in relation to our cultural codes of meaning, but it also provokes an experience at the boundaries of our linguistic capacity as a species. Concerning "the *lower levels* of the expression plane," Eco is referring specifically to the material aspect of aesthetic expressions, for example the quality of the sound of words in poetry, or the quality of the materials used in the visual arts. As a way of understanding this experience, it can be useful to refer back to Peirce's idea of "firstness" which he described in almost mystical terms as "what is present in general" through the act of "attention."[41] Peirce's conception of firstness is reflected in Eco's suggestion that at the "lower levels" of the aesthetic expression:

> art seems to *stimulate reactions* but *not to communicate contents.* Which might seem to confirm the opinion of those who assert that in art there is something more than 'language', a sort of irreducible 'aesthetic information' radically different from 'semantic information' (Moles, 1958; or Brandi's distinction between 'semiosis' and 'astanza' or 'presence' 1968).

Aesthetics would thus function not only by provoking us to rethink our cultural codes at the upper level of cultural expression, but also by stimulating an experience at the primordial, lower level of our sensory experience of the world before it becomes culturally codified. As Eco puts it, "in aesthetic experience there exists a 'je ne sais pas quoi' that escapes 'rational' consideration" and provokes "the impression of 'unspeakability.'"[42]

THE AESTHETIC IDIOLECT

The conception of aesthetics as ambiguous and self-focusing by violating cultural codes, and by generating an experience that is "unspeakable" indicates the extent to which there is a broad gulf between an aesthetic elite of intellectuals and a broad public audience. The reasons for this gulf can also be understood in relation to Eco's conception of an "aesthetic idiolect." The "aesthetic idiolect" means that the aesthetic act of sign production reflects the unique artistic expression particular to an individual. Aesthetics involves a reformulation of our customary cultural codes of meaning which the artist generates by essentially creating what Eco calls "*a new coding possibility*" that results in an "aesthetic idolect":

> This new code is apparently spoken by only one speaker, and understood by a very restricted audience; it is a semiotic *enclave* which society cannot recognize as a social rule acceptable by everyone. Such a type of private code is usually called an 'idiolect.' The rule governing all deviations at work at every level of a work of art... is the aesthetic idiolect.

Eco explains that when the new code generated by the "aesthetic idiolect" of the artist is used in subsequent works, it becomes recognized as a "personal style," and if it is adopted by a community of artists, for example, in the case of pop art, it becomes a "movement" or "period-idolect" because it comes to represent the cultural mentality of a particular historical period. Eco asserts that, through a further development, an artistic movement can eventually become "accepted by an entire society" by altering its cultural codes, for example in the way that the pop artist Andy Warhol depicted consumerist objects such as Campbell soup cans as artistic symbols, and how these symbols became commercialized products such as images for T-shirts. According to Eco, when "the work submits to 'commercial' influence" it becomes more broadly appropriated as what Eco refers to in disparaging terms as "Kitsch art" and "philistine Beauty."[43] Pop art, as we considered in the previous chapter, indicates how an aesthetic elite responded to the proliferation of consumerism, the mass media, and popular culture by using commercial symbols as artistic images to alter the cultural code. According to Eco, art "produces further knowledge" because the aesthetic expression "compels one to reconsider the usual codes and their possibilities."

Eco's conception of the "aesthetic idiolect" is a useful way of understanding the relation between intellectuals and popular culture because it indicates how the specialized role of the intellectual has developed historically, in the case of humanistic intellectuals such as Eco, to serve as the keepers and formulators of the cultural code through both interpretive analysis, and aesthetic reformulation. The conception of the "aesthetic idiolect" suggests that critical awareness, as a form of intellectual discovery through analysis, or analysis by discovery, has become highly specialized and restricted to an elite that, apart from individuals such as Eco who attempt to communicate their ideas to a popular audience, is circulated primarily among themselves.

To conclude this exploration of Eco's semiotic theory, it will be helpful to briefly consider his analysis of how an aesthetic text functions as a mode of communication. We have already considered how the creator of the aesthetic expression engages in ambiguity and code violations to focus the reader's attention in a way that, according to Eco, "compels one to reconsider the usual codes and their possibilities." Eco asserts that the aesthetic expression also "challenges the accepted organization of the content and suggests that the semantic system could be differently ordered." Consequently " . . . to change semantic systems means to *change the way in which culture 'sees' the world.*"

Thus a text of the aesthetic type which was so frequently supposed to be absolutely extraneous to any truth conditions (and to exist at a level on which disbelief is totally 'suspended') arouses the suspicion that the correspondence between the present organization of the content and 'actual' states of the world is neither the best nor the ultimate. The world could be defined and organized (and therefore perceived and known) through other semantic (that is: conceptual) models.[44]

The aesthetic text is a form of communication that is intended to arouse an awareness of our relationship to the world. But since the aesthetic text communicates through ambiguity and violations of the cultural codes of meaning, it requires a particular labor on the part of the recipient, the reader of the aesthetic text. Since the aesthetic text is ambiguous, it requires the full interpretive engagement of the reader to generate its meaning. But because it violates the customary cultural codes of meaning, it calls for the application of a new code of possibilities that the reader must try to determine. According to Eco, this would involve

> proposing certain tentative codes in order to make the author's message understandable. The addressee does not know what the sender's rule was; he tries to extrapolate it from the disconnected data of his aesthetic experience. He may believe that he is correctly interpreting what the author meant, or he may decide to test new interpretive possibilities upon the text the author has set out before him.

Eco's conception of the aesthetic text as a particularly powerful form of communication is derived from his earliest writings on contemporary culture from 1962, on *The Open Work*, in which he emphasized the deliberate ambiguity of the aesthetic text and how it required the active participation of the reader to generate its meaning. His semiotic theory of sign production represents a further development of the relationship between, in this instance, the aesthetic text and the reader with an emphasis on the function of interpretive codes. Since meaning occurs through interpretive links that become culturally encoded, the aesthetic text is especially important in calling attention to cultural codes and how they tend to make us unaware of the possibilities for creatively reimagining the world. Eco attempts to clarify the function of aesthetic texts in proposing new possibilities for cultural interpretation, however, as a balance between interpretive freedom in response to the ambiguity of the text, and interpretive faithfulness to the text in determining its possibilities for new meanings. As Eco asserts, the reader "never wants to betray the author's intention." To avoid this, Eco suggests the establishment of "... a dialectic between *fidelity* and inventive *freedom*...":

> On the one hand the addressee seeks to draw excitement from the ambiguity of the message and to fill out an ambiguous text with suitable codes; on the other, he is induced, in an act of fidelity to the author and to the historical environment in which the message was emitted.

As a further development of his earlier conception of the "open work," Eco employs his semiotic theory of sign production to assert that "... the semiotic definition of an aesthetic text gives the structured model for an unstructured process of communicative interplay." Eco's emphasis that "a responsible collaboration is demanded of the addressee" indicates his future direction in semiotic theory with a focus on interpretation theory, the role of the reader, the limits of interpretation, and the problem of overinterpretation which will be considered in the next chapter. Eco suggests that, through the process of interpreting the "aesthetic text," the "real author remains undetermined, sometimes being the sender of the message, at others the addressee who collaborates in its development."[45] The rights of interpretation between the author, the reader, and the aesthetic text were problems that Eco took up after completing his theory of semiotics in 1975.

NOTES

1. Jeff Israely, "A Resounding Eco," @Time, June 5, 2005.
2. Eco, *The Name of the Rose*, (New York: Harcourt Brace and Company, 1983), pp. 23–24.
3. Jonathan Culler, *Ferdinand de Saussure*, (Ithaca: Cornell University Press, 1988), pp. 23–24.
4. Saussure, *Course in General Linguistics*, edited by Charles Bally and Albert Sechehaye, (La Salle: Open Court Publishing Company, 1991).
5. Saussure, *Course in General Linguistics*, p. 9
6. Saussure, *Course in General Linguistics*, pp. 15–16.
7. Saussure, *Course in General Linguistics*, pp. 6–7.
8. Aristotle, *On Interpretation* (Princeton: Princeton University Press, edited by J.L. Ackrill, 1987), p. 12.
9. Culler, *Ferdinand de Saussure*, pp. 33–34.
10. Culler, *Ferdinand de Saussure*, p. 36.

11. Cited from Peter Bondanella, *Umberto Eco and the Open Text*, p. 25.
12. Eco, *La struttura assente*, (Milan: Bompiani, 2015), p. 13.
13. Eco, *A Theory of Semiotics*, (Indiana: Indiana University Press, 1979), p. 15.
14. Brent, Joseph, *Charles Sanders Peirce*, A Life (Bloomington: Indiana University Press, 1993), p. 128.
15. Menand, Louis, *The Metaphysical Club*, (New York: Farrar, Strauss and Giroux, 2001), p. 159.
16. Louis Menand, *The Metaphysical Club*, p. 151.
17. Joseph Ransdell (1997), "Some Leading Ideas of Peirce's Semiotic" from *Semiotica* 19:157–78.
18. Devlin, Keith, *The Math Gene*, (Great Britain: Basic Books, 2000).
19. Cited from http://www.commens.org/dictionary/term/maxim-of-pragmatism.
20. Peirce, "On a New List of Categories" from *Peirce on Signs*, (Chapel Hill: The University of North Carolina Press, 1991), p. 23.
21. Peirce, "On a New List of Categories," from *Peirce on Signs*, p. 24.
22. Peirce, "On a New List of Categories," from *Peirce on Signs*, p. 27.
23. Hookway Christopher, *Peirce*, (New York: Routledge, 1992), p. 151.
24. Peirce, Charles Sanders, "A New List of Categories," from *The Essential Peirce Volume 1* (1867–1893), edited by Nathan Houser and Christian Kloesel (Bloomington: Indiana University Press, 1992), p. 6.
25. Peirce, "A Guess at the Riddle," from *Peirce on Signs*, p. 188.
26. Peirce, from the introduction to "On a New List of Categories," from *Peirce on Signs*, drawn from Max Fisch in the introduction to *Writings of Charles S. Peirce*, I, xxvi.
27. Peirce, "A Guess at the Riddle," from *The Essential Peirce*, p. 246.
28. Peirce, from *The Essential Peirce*, p. 247.
29. Eco, *A Theory of Semiotics*, p. 17.
30. Eco, *A Theory of Semiotics*, pp. 26–27.
31. Eco, *A Theory of Semiotics*, p. 83.
32. Eco, *A Theory of Semiotics*, p. 119.
33. Eco, *A Theory of Semiotics*, p. 69.
34. "Logic follows ethics and both follow aesthetics." *Collected Papers of Charles Sanders Peirce*, edited by Hartshorne C. and Weiss P., (Harvard University Press, 1931), Vol. 1, p. 311.
35. Eco, *A Theory of Semiotics*, p. 7.
36. Eco, *A Theory of Semiotics*, p. 64.
37. Eco, *A Theory of Semiotics*, p. 71.
38. Eco, *A Theory of Semiotics*, p. 29.
39. Eco, *A Theory of Semiotics*, p. 129.
40. Eco, *A Theory of Semiotics*, pp. 261–265.
41. Peirce, "On a New List of Categories," from *Peirce on Signs*, p. 24.

42. Eco *A Theory of Semiotics*, p. 267.
43. Eco, *A Theory of Semiotics*, p. 272.
44. Eco, *A Theory of Semiotics*, p. 274.
45. Eco, *A Theory of Semiotics*, p. 276.

CHAPTER 9

The Reader in the Story

In *The Open Work* from 1962 Eco had conceived of deliberate ambiguity and defamiliarization as mechanisms that characterize aesthetic or literary works and, in particular, modern avant-garde works that generate meaning by calling for the collaborative participation of the audience or reader as an interpretive "performer" of the work. But Eco later became aware that his theory of the open work had not adequately determined how the interpreter, although free to explore the infinite possibilities of the text, would at the same time be guided by the text to collaborate faithfully in fulfilling its potential. Recall that Eco's mentor Luigi Pareyson had conceived of the need for a general theory of interpretation which Eco pursued initially through his theory of semiotics. Eco's shift to the semiotics of texts can be seen as a further exploration of interpretation theory through a more specific analysis of the practical ways in which the reader, as interpretive performer of the work, responds to its formative character.

Eco's focus on interpretation theory arises initially from his study of Aquinas's conception that the truth of God could be experienced through the interpretation of one's sensory experience of the world as a reflection of the beauty of God's creativity. After becoming an exile from the Church in 1954 and after his recognition of the historical limitations of Aquinas's conception of aesthetics, Eco retained Aquinas's medieval pursuit of the interpretation of God's creativity in the sensory world by applying it to the modern pursuit of the interpretation of human creativity in the sensory world of human culture. Instead of employing interpretation as a way of transforming oneself toward the truth of God, Eco's interpretation theory is conceived as a way of transforming oneself toward one's full human potential through the interpretation of and conscious participation in human creativity. Open works encourage the pursuit of this potential by requiring the active participation of the audience. But, according to Eco, the fulfillment of this potential, like the understanding of the beauty of God's creativity, involves an attempt by the reader to be true to the formative character of the work through a focus on what could be called "interpretive ethics." Eco sought to clarify the relation between the openness of aesthetic texts, that calls for the interpretive freedom of the reader, and their closed character that guides the reader in fulfilling its potential for arousing a heightened or expanded consciousness of the world:

> In [*The Open Work*] I advocated the active role of the interpreter in the reading of texts endowed with aesthetic value. When those pages were written, my readers focused mainly on the "open" side of the whole business, underestimating the fact that the open-ended reading I supported was an activity elicited by (and aiming at interpreting) a *work*. In other words, I was studying the rights of interpreters. I have the impression that, in the course of the last few decades, the rights of interpreters have been overstressed.[1]

Eco's further elaboration of a theory of interpretation consequently involved two new paths of analysis: an understanding of how readers participate in the interpretive co-creation of the work through what came to be called "reader response theory," that emerged in Italy in the sixties,[2] and an understanding of the opposite pole of interpretive openness through an analysis of the limits of interpretation.

THE LITERARY TRINITY

As we considered in Chapter 5, Eco's conception that an aesthetic work is made meaningful through the creative engagement of the reader as an interpretive performer of its potential signaled a transition from the long historical tradition that had prescribed with varying but highly restrictive guidelines how a work was to be interpreted. In

"*Intentio Lectoris*: The State of the Art" from *The Limits of Interpretation*, Eco discusses the relation between the three focal points for literary interpretation that evolved over the course of Western history: (1) the intention of the author, (2) the intention of the text, and (3) the intention of the reader.

From ancient and medieval times, the intention of the author was the preeminent focus of interpretation which was pursued through two traditions: the synthesis of Greek rationalism and scriptural interpretation in medieval Scholasticism, and the Hermetic tradition of occult thought. Medieval scholasticism sought to determine the intention of God, the author, as the *primum causum*, the first cause in creating the order and form of the world. As Eco indicates, based on the legacy of Greek rationalism, "defining God meant defining a cause, beyond which there could be no further cause."[3] But, because God was a mysterious, otherworldly entity, and due to the inherent ambiguity of biblical scripture, the reader had to rely on a set of interpretive guidelines that had developed over time by individuals such as Saint Augustine (354–430 A.D.) who prescribed how God's intentions were reflected in the text as read from, for example, a literal or a metaphorical perspective. For example, "light" could be interpreted literally as physical brightness, or metaphorically as the illumination of spiritual faith.

Truth Is Elsewhere

The intention of God the author was determined through a much different interpretive emphasis in Hermetic thought. The Hermetic tradition runs counter to the idea that God and the world can be understood through the rational analysis of biblical scripture and the sensory world. According to the Hermetic tradition, God is a mysterious and secret entity hidden in sacred writings because human language is inadequate to express the true nature of God except in an indirect way. As Eco indicates, the sacred writings, according to the Hermetic tradition, "are saying something other than what they appear to be saying." Because the truth is hidden and therefore secret, an understanding of sacred writings can only be attained by a select group of mystics which recalls the prohibition from the gospel of Matthew that one should not "cast pearls before swine." Eco traces the occult tradition back to the Greek mystery religions and their conception of infinity as unconstrained by reason and rational causality which is identified with the Greek god Hermes and the Roman god Mercury, the messenger, who "knows no spatial limits and may, in different shapes, be in different places at the same time."[4] Thus the Hermetic tradition of interpretation is focused on the intention of the author but through a much different conception of how the author's intention can be determined.

Eco finds similarities with the Hermetic tradition in contemporary interpretation theory in the ideas of the French philosopher Jacques Derrida (1930–2004). Derrida's conception of language is difficult to concisely summarize, but perhaps it can be briefly described in relation to Peirce's idea of "unlimited semiosis." Peirce's concept, adopted by Eco, asserts that language functions through an immense Encyclopedia of signs encompassing all of human culture that are all linked together theoretically with every other sign. According to this conception, a sign generates meaning, not in itself, but through links to other signs. Since these signs are all theoretically interconnected, there could be an infinite network of links starting with a single sign. Think of Joyce's multilayered puns in *Finnegans Wake*. Peirce and Eco, however, believed that these links don't drift indefinitely because of conventional agreement on the limited links between signs in a given context. I can use the word "bark" for instance, and based on the frame of reference, you can understand whether I am referring to the exterior of a tree or the sound of a dog. Derrida's claim, in contrast, is that the meaning of signs, in the Western historical tradition, has been based on reference to a universal truth that resides outside of language, what he called the "transcendental signified." Language theory indicates that nothing has meaning except through language, and thus, according to Derrida: "There is no outside of the text" to arbitrarily constrain the relation between signs. Consequently there is an indefinite play of links between signs, which, for Eco, is similar to the Hermetic tradition of meaning as the constant drift towards elsewhere. The Hermetic tradition is thus an important reference point for Eco's interpretation theory and a central theme in *Foucault's Pendulum* that, as Eco has humorously suggested, features "Dan Brown [as] one of the characters... who start believing in occult stuff."[5]

THE FOCUS OF INTENTION

The emphasis on the author as creative genius from ancient and medieval society continued as the primary focus into the later interpretation of the novel from the eighteenth century until the advent of language theory in the fifties and what was called the "New Theory" that analyzed the text according to its structural relations of oppositions and differences following the linguistic theory of Saussure. Then, in the sixties, the focus shifted to the reader through reader response theory that acknowledged the reader's active participation in generating the meaning of the work.

Since the interpretation of a text involves a relation between three focal points: (1) an author, (2) the text, and (3) the reader, which one should be the core focus, or, in what relation of interdependence? Should the author, as the creative source, be the core focus through an analysis of the author's personal history and psychological profile following the rise of Freudian psychology? But, due to the inherent ambiguity of language (as well as the subconscious), the author cannot know or consciously control all of the possible interpretations that the work can generate. In addition, through the deliberate ambiguity of aesthetic texts, the reader is required to take an active role, and an emphasis on the intentions of the author would negate the collaborative role of the reader which prompted Eco's assertion that: "The author should die once he has finished writing. So as not to trouble the path of the text."[6]

Similarly, emphasizing the text independently of the author would negate the author's creative role and historical circumstances, as well as the creative collaboration of the reader. Therefore, since Eco has asserted that: "a novel is a machine for generating interpretations,"[7] why not defer completely to the creative freedom of the reader? But, because of the deliberate ambiguity and code violating function of aesthetic texts, the total freedom of the reader, as Eco later emphasized, would violate the rights of the text as a formative medium.

THE RIGHTS OF THE TEXT

But what does it mean to assert "the rights" of the text? Since, according to Eco, the author should step aside once the work has been created to allow for the freedom of the reader, interpretation would involve only the text and the reader. But Eco found that his earlier emphasis on the openness of texts to interpretive freedom had been "overstressed" in relation to the text. Why was it so important for Eco to insist on constraining the reader's free play of interpretation in relation to the reader's individual experience and personal desire for meaning? What would be the basis for determining what was "right" or "wrong" in the interpretation of open works, a kind of "interpretive ethics" in our relation to the world? In *The Limits of Interpretation*, Eco asserts that: "I shall claim that a theory of interpretation – even when it assumes that texts are open to multiple readings – must also assume that it is possible to reach an agreement, if not about the meanings that a text encourages, at least about those that a text discourages."[8] But, given the ambiguity of open texts, how does one determine when an interpretation is wrong?

The enjoyment of the readers of aesthetic works consists in having their imagination opened up to new possibilities in relation to their knowledge and experience of the world. But, according to Eco, unless the reader's interpretive engagement with the text responds to its transformative potential, the reader would not be engaged in an ethical interpretation. Since Eco derived from Aquinas a religious conception of interpreting the truth of God through the beauty of God's creation, we can get a sense of why, for Eco, it is so important for readers to be aware of an "interpretive ethics" in order to recognize themselves as collaborative creators of the world of human culture.

THE READER IN THE STORY

We can consider how Eco confronts the issue of interpretive ethics by initially exploring how the reader participates in an active role in generating the meaning of texts through a very powerful demonstration provided by Eco in the essay "Lector in Fabula" (The Reader in the Story) from *The Role of the Reader*, his essays on reader response theory. For this purpose, Eco uses the experience of reading a very short, literary oddity entitled *Un drame bien parisien* (*A Most Parisian Episode*) by the late nineteenth-century French humorist Alphonse Allais (1854–1905). The full text of Allais' *A Most Parisian Episode* is included here for the reader's firsthand experience. The translation is by Frederic Jameson, and, as noted in the original, "The epigraphs have not been translated because they play upon elements of slang, phonetic analogies, and so on."[9] The text of Jameson's translation of Allais' *A Most Parisian Episode* is reprinted here with permission by Indiana University Press.

A MOST PARISIAN EPISODE

Alphonse Allais

Chapter I

In which we meet a Lady and a Gentleman who might have known happiness, had it not been for their constant misunderstandings.

At the time when this story begins, Raoul and Marguerite (a splendid name for lovers) have been married for approximately five months.
Naturally, they had married for love.
One fine night Raoul, while listening to Marguerite singing Colonel Henry d'Erville's lovely ballad:

> L'averse, chère a la grenouille,
> Parfume le bois rajeuni.
> ...Le bois, il est comme Nini.
> Y sent bon quand y s'débarbouille

Raoul, as I was saying, swore to himself that the divine Marguerite (*diva Margarita*) would never belong to any man but himself.
They would have been the happiest of all couples, except for their awful personalities.
At the slightest provocation, pow! a broken plate, a slap, a kick in the ass.
At such sounds, Love fled in tears, to await, in the neighborhood of a great park, the always imminent hour of reconciliation.
O then, kisses without number, infinite caresses, tender and knowing, ardors as burning as hell itself.
You would have thought the two of them – pigs that they were! – had fights only so they could make up again.

Chapter II

A short episode which, without directly relating to the action, gives the clientele some notions of our heroes' way of life.

One day, however, it was worse than usual.
Or, rather, one night.
They were at the Théâtre d'Application, where among other things, a play by M. Porto-Riche, *The Faithless Wife*, was being given.
"Let me know," snarled Raouel, "when you're through looking at Grosclaude."
"And as for you," hissed Marguerite, "pass me the opera glasses when you've got Mademoiselle Moreno down pat."
Begun on this note, the conversation could end only in the most unfortunate reciprocal insults.

In the hansom cab that took them home, Marguerite delighted in plucking at Raoul's vanity as at an old, broken-down mandolin.

So it was that no sooner back home than the belligerents took up their respective positions.

Hand raised to strike, with a remorseless gaze, and a moustache bristling like that of a rabid cat, Raoul bore down on Marguerite, who quickly stopped showing off.

The poor thing fled, as hasty and furtive as the doe in the north woods.

Raoul was on the point of laying hands on her.

It was at that moment that the brilliant invention of the greatest anxieties flashed within her little brain.

Turning suddenly about, she threw herself in the arms of Raoul, crying, "Help, my darling Raoul, save me!"

Chapter III

In which our friends are reconciled as I would wish you also to be frequently reconciled, smart-alecks.

....
....

Chapter IV

As to how people who get involved in things that are none of their affair would do better to mind their own business.

One morning, Raoul received the following message:

> "If you would like just once to see your wife in a good mood, go on Thursday to the Bal des Incohérents at the Moulin-Rouge. She will be there, with a mask and disguised as a Congolese Dugout. A word to the wise is sufficient!
> A FRIEND"

The same morning, Marguerite received the following message:

> "If you would like just once to see your husband in a good mood, go on Thursday to the Bal des Incohérents at the Moulin-Rouge. He will be there,

with a mask and disguised as a *fin-de-siècle* Knight Templar. A word to the wise is sufficient!
A FRIEND"

These missives did not fall on deaf ears.
With their intentions admirably dissimulated, when the fatal day arrived:

"My dear," Raoul said with his innocent look, "I shall be forced to leave you until tomorrow. Business of the greatest urgency summons me to Dunkirk."
"Why that's perfect," said Marguerite with delightful candor, "I've just received a telegram from Aunt Aspasia, who, desperately ill, bids me to her bedside."

Chapter V

In which today's wild youth is observed in the whirl of the most illusory and transitory pleasures, instead of thinking on eternity.

The social column of the *Diable boiteux* was unanimous in proclaiming this year's Bal des Incohérents as having unaccustomed brilliance.

Lots of shoulders, no few legs, not to mention accessories.

Two of those present seemed not to take part in the general madness: a *fan-de-siècle* Knight Templar and a Congolese Dugout, both hermetically masked.

At the stroke of three A.M. exactly, the Knight Templar approached the Dugout and invited her to dine with him.

In reply the Dugout placed a tiny hand on the robust arm of the Templar, and the couple went off.

Chapter VI

In which the plot thickens.

"Leave us for a moment," said the Templar to the waiter, "we will make our choice and call you."

The waiter withdrew, and the Templar locked the door of the private room with care.

Then, with a sudden gesture, having set his own helmet aside, he snatched away the Dugout's mask.

Both at the same instant cried out in astonishment, neither one recognizing the other.

He was not Raoul.

She was not Marguerite.

They apologized to each other and were not long in making acquaintance on the occasion of an excellent supper, need I say more.

Chapter VII

Happy ending for everyone, except the others.

This little *mésaventure* was a lesson to Raoul and Marguerite.

From that moment on, they no longer quarreled and were utterly happy.

They don't have lots of children yet, but they will.

THE STORY UNTELLS ITSELF

After a first reading, Allais' *A Most Parisian Episode* will confront readers with a puzzling, nonsensical outcome because the conclusion of the story appears to contradict everything that led up to it. The story, in brief, "seems" to be about an easily recognizable conflict between a married couple who are jealously possessive toward each other and suspicious of each other's fidelity. They each receive a letter concerning a masquerade ball where they could presumably catch their marriage partner, disguised in a particular costume, in an affair. But when the anticipated encounter occurs, the man and woman, dressed in the specified costumes, remove their masks and exclaim "in astonishment" that they are NOT Raoul and Marguerite. They then "apologize" to each other for the mistaken expectation and become "acquainted" over dinner. For Raoul and Marguerite, who did NOT encounter each other at the ball, they nonetheless learn "a lesson" from this "misadventure" and, as a result, "no longer quarreled and were utterly happy." The story is thus deliberately contradictory in a peculiar way.

A Most Parisian Episode is one of 45 similarly very short, literary amusements by Allais that were published in 1890 in a collection called *A se tordre* (loosely translated as "Enough to make one laugh or writhe in pain"). The subtitle of *A se tordre* is *histoires chatnoiresque* (Black Cat

THE STORY UNTELLS ITSELF 211

Stories) because they originally appeared in a humorous journal entitled *Le Chat Noir* which was published by the famous French cabaret of the same name which is considered to be the origin of the modern version of the cabaret as a counter-culture entertainment venue. During its brief 16-year existence, *Le Chat Noir* was the meeting place for some of the most prominent artists of the *fin de siècle*, the end of the nineteenth century, which was also known as the *Belle Epoque* for the flourishing of the arts. It was frequented by composers such as Claude Debussy (1862–1918) and Erik Satie (1866–1925), writers such as Alphonse Allais, and the post-impressionist painter Henri de Toulouse-Lautrec (1864–1901).

The conclusion to *A Most Parisian Episode* is baffling given what first time readers would be led to expect in their interpretation of the circumstances of the two characters. But this is exactly the effect that serves for Eco and his fellow reader response theorists as an empirical demonstration of the participation of the reader in unconsciously filling in the gaps in the story to generate its meaning. As Eco indicates: "To the one-dimensional reader, Allais' *Un drame bien parisien*... may appear to be a mere literary joke, a disturbing exercise in verbal trompe-l'oeil..."[10] But, according to Eco, since the meaning that was anticipated turns out to be inconsistent with the outcome, it demonstrates how readers are always engaged in filling in the gaps created by the ambiguity of language and texts.

As Eco indicates, the first time reader of Allais' story is led to make assumptions that are not explicitly warranted by the text or that are actually contradicted by the text.

> The implicit lesson of *A Most Parisian Episode*, is, in fact, coherently contradictory: Allais is telling us that not only *A Most Parisian Episode* but every text is made of two components: the information provided by the author and that added by the Model Reader, the latter being determined by the former – with various rates of freedom and necessity. But, in order to demonstrate this textual theorem, Allais has led the reader to fill up the text with contradictory information, thus cooperating in setting up a story that cannot stand up. The failure of the apparent story of *A Most Parisian Episode* is the success of Allais' theoretical assumption and the triumph of his metatextual demonstration.[11]

A "metatextual demonstration" is a way of showing how texts function to generate meaning that is over and above the content of the text itself. The term "meta" is derived from the organization of Aristotle's works that followed after his analysis of the sensory world called the *Physics*, which was followed by the *Metaphysics*. The "meta" in the "metaphysics" thus literally means "after the Physics" but also as the knowledge that could be derived over and above the analysis of the sensory world. *A Most Parisian Episode* functions as a metatextual demonstration because its surface content is contradictory which, according to Eco, shifts the focus to a reflection on language and the readers' participation in the interpretation of the text. Allais was writing a quarter century before the development of semiotics by Saussure, and more than half a century before the emergence of reader response theory in the sixties, but his odd literary specimen has been appropriated by Eco and other semiotic theorists who see it as a "metatextual" tool for showing through direct experience how readers respond to the openness of texts.

For a better understanding of Allais' trickery, let's first consider what information is explicitly set out in the text. Raoul and Marguerite are recently married. Raoul vowed that Marguerite would belong only to him. Raoul and Marguerite regularly provoked each other and then immediately reconciled with ardent expressions of love. They were annoyed at each other at a theater performance for paying attention to someone of the opposite sex. They each received a letter informing them that their spouse would be at a masquerade ball in a specific costume. Afterwards they informed each other that they would, by necessity, be away from each other until the following day. Then the narrative shifts to the meeting of the two costumed characters who turn out not to be Raoul and Marguerite.

These narrative details would seem to be a sufficient basis for the reader's expectation of a dramatic encounter of unfaithful lovers at the masquerade ball. But, according to Eco, there are significant gaps in the text that must be filled in by the reader to reach that false conclusion. The text, for example, does not specifically state anywhere that Raoul and Marguerite have lovers. Though the text specifies that "on the fatal day" they informed each other that they would have to be away from each other until the following day, it does not specifically state that they actually attend the masquerade ball in the specified costumes. While it may seem absurdly obvious that the story sets up the expectation for the couple to catch each other in an act of marital infidelity, that outcome is not explicitly supported by the specific details set out in the actual text of the story and thus has to be provided by the reader. According to Eco, a first time, or what he calls a "naive reader," would make those assumptions as "the typical consumer of adultery stories"[12] marketed for popular consumption, that involve the suspicion of infidelity by one or both partners in a marital relationship in which the betrayal is revealed through a dramatic conclusion. As a result, Allais' *A Most Parisian Episode* demonstrates the otherwise concealed role of the reader in filling in the gaps in the story by relying on the assumption that the story reflects a popular literary genre familiar to a popular readership.

THE AUTHOR'S MASQUERADE

As Eco indicates, a second reading would reveal a number of clues that the story is about the playful seduction of the "naive reader" while being alerted against making false assumptions. For example the narrator warns that: "...*people who get involved in things that are none of their affair would do better to mind their own business.*"[13] Other clues function to undercut in an ironic way the expected plot outcome. The masquerade, for example, is called the "Bal des Incoherents" which hints at a story that is illogical or contradictory. Examples of the story's incoherence include the costume specified for identifying Marguerite as a "Congolese Dugout" which might suggest an exotic theme for a masquerade, but, since a dugout is a small boat made from a hollow log, it would be nonsensical as a costume. The costume specified for identifying Raoul as a "*fin de siècle* Knight Templar" is similarly incoherent because a Templar was a member of a religious order of medieval knights that was disbanded by the pope in 1312 almost six centuries before the *fin de siècle* of the late nineteenth century.

Another easily overlooked but crucially significant point of incoherence that would contradict the expected outcome is that, while the letters specify how Raoul and Marguerite will identify each other through the disguise of their partner, the story does NOT indicate that Raoul and Marguerite know the disguise of the supposed lover of their spouse. This means, as Eco notes, that if they had decided to attend the ball according to the information provided in the letter, "neither Raoul nor Marguerite could decide to assume the disguise of their rivals."[14] The "naive" reader has to erroneously assume that the letters contain both sets of information. Because the letters don't specify a costume to be worn by a supposed lover, they don't actually state that their spouse will be meeting a lover at all, a point which is so easily overlooked that it provides one of the strongest empirical demonstrations of the unconscious role of the reader in filling in those points of information. The conclusion of the text also indicates a "Happy ending for everyone, except the others" which can be interpreted as a sly reference to the bewildered reader.

Inferential Walks

For Eco, the lesson of Allais' story is that reading as an act of interpretation involves filling in gaps created by the ambiguity of the text based on one's knowledge and experience of the world drawn from one's cultural background. As Eco puts it: "a text is a lazy machine that appeals to the reader to do some of its work."[15] To fill in the gaps, the reader engages in what Eco calls "inferential walks"[16]:

> Every text, even though not specifically narrative, is in some way making the addressee expect (and foresee) the fulfillment of every unaccomplished sentence: /John will not arrive because.../makes one hazard forecasts about the missing information.

Inferential walks consist of guesses on the part of the reader to fill in information that doesn't exist in the text concerning the direction and outcome of the plot. Inferential walks are fundamental to our ability to communicate through everyday language as well as in response to texts. They can be seen at play in everyday conversations, for example, in the annoying habit of some people who compulsively finish the sentence of the person they are listening to by anticipating, often incorrectly, their intention. Inferential walks are also evident in misunderstandings that occur when the listener makes an incorrect assumption about the frame of reference involved. For example, when a person says that they "ran into someone yesterday" and the listener assumes a car accident while the speaker means a chance encounter. The ambiguity of texts involves a much greater reliance on inferential walks because in a conversation the listener can ask for clarification, while a text is otherwise mute.

Aesthetic texts, in particular, have intentional gaps and vague, allusive references that invite an infinity of possible interpretations. One must guess with aesthetic texts because what makes them useful and powerful for generating a critical awareness is that they don't impose a specific meaning on the reader, and they don't provide specific instructions for determining their meaning. As Eco indicates, in Allais' story, the first time, or "naive" reader guesses that the characters are involved in infidelity, and this path is followed with the expectation that the betrayal of trust between the characters will be dramatically revealed. The choice of interpretive pathways that can be explored through these guesses or "inferential walks"[17] creates what Eco calls a "ghost chapter tentatively written by the reader."[18] What Allais' story demonstrates in a powerfully empirical way is the reader's usually unconscious engagement in taking these "inferential walks" that are so fundamental to our experience of language that, in this case, only a deliberately contradictory ending can make us aware of them.

THE FICTIONAL WOODS

Eco's further development of his reader response theory can be considered through an exploration of his lectures entitled *Six Walks in the Fictional Woods*[19] (hereafter *Six Walks*) from 1995, and his lectures entitled *Interpretation and Overinterpretation*[20] (hereafter *Interpretation*) from 1992. *Six Walks* is based on Eco's invitation as the Charles Eliot Norton lecturer at Harvard University in 1993. Because the Norton lectures are intended to showcase an internationally recognized scholar or artist and are presented by Harvard University with no admission charge to a public audience, they tend to provide a forum for the lecturers to address the overall scope of their work in a broadly accessible way.

As Eco explains in the first lecture: "Woods are a metaphor for the narrative text, not only for the text of fairy tales but for any narrative text." Eco also asserts, through another metaphor, that "a wood is a garden of forking paths,"[21] which is a concept drawn from a famous short story[22] by another intellectual mentor to Eco, the Argentinean writer Jorge Luis Borges (1889–1986) who was the inspiration for one of the characters in *The Name of the Rose*. The metaphor of forking paths reflects the interpretive choices that confront the reader in fictional woods at every juncture as we considered in the response to Allais' *A Most Parisian Episode*. According to Eco, "Even when there are no well-trodden paths in a wood, everyone can trace his or her own path, deciding to go to the left or to the right of a certain tree and making a choice at every tree encountered."[23] But, as Eco points out, "readers are generally willing to make their own choices in the narrative wood on the assumption that some will be more reasonable than others."[24] Thus, while exploring the narrative woods allows the reader the freedom to make choices or to guess at possible outcomes at every turn, there are some choices that are more reasonable and appropriate than others in finding one's way through the woods which is the basis for Eco's assertion of the limits to the interpretive freedom of the reader.

Model Author and Model Reader

Besides the idea of "inferential walks," Eco offers an understanding of the relation between the reader and the text by differentiating between the following concepts: "empirical author" and "model author," "empirical reader" and "model reader," and "first level" and "second level" reader. The empirical author is the living, human entity who actually writes the text such as James Joyce, Ernest Hemingway, Charles Dickens, etc. The model author is the formative organization embedded in the text that guides the reader in responding to its interpretive potential. The empirical reader is you or I as individuals who draw on our knowledge and experience of the world in interpreting the meaning of the text. The model reader is the collaborative role that the empirical reader is called upon to fulfill by the formative pathways of the text. Eco conceives of the model reader as "a kind of ideal type whom the text not only foresees as a collaborator but also tries to create."[25] As noted previously, Eco believes that "A text is meant to be an experience of transformation for its reader"[26] which brings into play the concepts of first- and second-level reader. As Eco indicates, the transformational effect of the text would involve a first-level reader, who is focused primarily on the unfolding of the story toward its outcome through the fastest, most direct path through the fictional woods, into a second-level reader, who goes beyond the focus on story, character, and outcome, to consider how the text is organized as a way of reflecting a vision of the world.

Eco's Interpretive Ethics

The first principle of Eco's interpretive ethics is that the empirical author should not be involved in, or interfere with, the reader's engagement with the text:

> I'll tell you at once that I couldn't really care less about the empirical author of a narrative text (or, indeed, of any text). I know that I shall offend many members of my audience who perhaps spend much of their time reading biographies of Jane Austen or Proust, Dostoyevski or Salinger, and I realize only too well how wonderful and thrilling it is to peek into the private lives of real people whom we have come to love as close friends.[27]

Italy's current most popular author, Elena Ferrante, has similarly stated that: "I believe that books, once written, have no need of their authors."[28] It may seem annoyingly counter-intuitive that, as Eco specifies, the empirical author's private life as the creative source of the work should be ignored in its interpretation. But, as we have considered, due to the inherent ambiguity of language, as well as the deliberate ambiguity of what Eco calls "aesthetic" works, the empirical author cannot know and therefore should not control the interpretive pathways of the work. While empirical authors have a copyright to their text which allows them to control its reproduction and sale, they must relinquish control, according to Eco, over its interpretive ownership. This principle of interpretive ethics also means that the reader should not rely on or be limited by the empirical author's personal life in exploring the meaning of the text, but rather they must do their own work as collaborators in the interpretation of the work.

But because of his background in the Italian humanist-historicist tradition, Eco does take into consideration the historical horizon of the empirical author. In *A Theory of Semiotics*, Eco asserts that:

> in the interpretive reading a dialectic between fidelity and inventive freedom is established. On the one hand the addressee seeks to draw excitement from the ambiguity of the message and to fill out an ambiguous text with suitable codes; on the other, he is induced by contextual relationships to see the message exactly as it was intended, in an act of fidelity to the author and to the historical environment in which the message was emitted.

But, according to Eco, this does not extend to the author's personal circumstances, family life, neuroses, intimate correspondence, etc., all of which are typically explored in biographies. As Eco indicates, apart from an understanding of the author's historical background, the intention of the empirical author is "very difficult to find out and frequently irrelevant for the interpretation of a text..."[29]

The emphasis on not involving the author's personal circumstances in interpreting a text may seem, however, to be directly contradictory in relation to this exploration of Eco's intellectual practice because we are obviously considering aspects of his historical background and personal life toward an understanding of his theoretical and fictional writings. In response to Eco's assertion about putting aside the influence of the empirical author, Rocco Capozzi, Professor of Italian Literature at Toronto University suggests that: "In the process of interpretation, we all agree, it should never be a question of having to get the author's approval, but this does not imply that we should not be concerned with the author's encyclopedic competence, his historical consciousness, his coherence, and his possible intentions in using specific textual strategies."[30] It may be difficult to know, however, how to make a clear distinction between the personal circumstances and historical context of empirical authors in interpreting their work. The complex symbolism of the novels of James Joyce, for example, includes numerous references to his life in Dublin which is an essential historical and cultural context for his work. But a concentrated focus on an author's family relations, psychological profile, or personal idiosyncracies is not necessary, according to Eco, for understanding the text:

> ...we all know that there are people who go looking for Sherlock Holmes in Baker Street, and I happen to be one of those who has gone looking for the house in Eccles Street in Dublin where Leopold Bloom is supposed to have lived. But these are episodes of literary fanship – which is a pleasant activity, and moving at times, but different from the reading of texts. To be a good reader of Joyce, it's not necessary to celebrate Bloomsday on the banks of the Liffey.[31]

In the "Postscript" to *The Name of the Rose*, Eco attempts to clarify the relation between author and text by asserting that: "The author must not interpret. But he may tell how and why he wrote his book."[32] The "Postscript" allowed Eco to provide a revealing demonstration of how the empirical author cannot know all of the interpretive pathways of the text and thus should not interfere with the engagement of the reader. Eco notes, for example, that some readers pointed out connections in *The Name of the Rose* that he was not aware of and did not consciously intend. In one instance, for example, a reader noted that, on the same page of *The Name of the Rose*, two different characters express a concern about "haste" in judgment, but with opposing viewpoints which prompted the reader to ask Eco what connection he had intended between them. But Eco acknowledged that he was totally unaware of this connection because it happened by accident when he added the reference to "haste" by the second character through a minor editing revision just before publication.[33] Although not consciously intended by Eco, the connection pointed out by the reader, according to Eco, is fully warranted by the text.

In one of his Tanner lectures (published in 1992 as *Interpretation and Overinterpretation*), Eco goes a bit further. Through what he describes as a "risky" "laboratory experiment," Eco temporarily bends his own rules about the relation of the empirical author to the reader by allowing himself, as both empirical author and "textual theorist," to respond to some of his readers' interpretations of his novels.[34] For example, readers pointed out signs in the text of literary influences that Eco admits that he was not aware of but that he recalled reading in his youth. Those interpretive links, Eco acknowledges, are warranted by the text even though he was not consciously aware of them which is another indication that the empirical author cannot be aware of all of the interpretive possibilities that become embedded in the text. Eco, however, also notes some instances when readers made interpretive connections that were not warranted, for example, when they believed that they had found allusions in the text to particular historical figures that were not consistent with the narrative. This was the case not because he, as the empirical author, had not consciously intended them, but instead because they were not supported by the textual strategy of the work as a whole. Consequently they were examples of overinterpretation.

Concerning the role of the empirical author in relation to the reader, it's interesting to note that Eco also acknowledges that in *The Name of the Rose* he "cunningly concealed" some sources and was pleased that some readers had "cunningly discovered" them.[35] In reference to *Foucault's Pendulum*, Eco similarly noted that: "many authors like to put in their texts certain shibboleths for a few smart readers."[36] Concerning an erotic passage in *The Name of the Rose*, Eco identifies his model readers by suggesting that "This episode, as the dullest of my readers can easily guess, is entirely made up of quotations from the *Song of Songs* and from medieval mystics."[37] These examples indicate the kind of interpretive game of concealment and discovery involved in the relation between author and reader that rewards certain readers who possess a particular cultural competence and completely eludes a more general popular readership for whom these references would be completely opaque. Presumably the initially uninformed reader would eventually be led to learn about those sources by becoming a model reader, but there are, however, practical limitations involved in his conception of the potential for the text to be a transformative experience for the reader.

The Author Inside the Story

The second principle of Eco's interpretive ethics is that, besides setting aside the personal life of the "empirical author," the reader should be guided by the model author embedded in the text as a kind of organizational map of a possible world. According to Eco's interpretive ethics, the author must step aside and let the text do its own work in relation to the reader. But there is a formative entity found in the work itself that Eco calls the "model author" that guides the reader in fulfilling its interpretive potential. The model author, according to Eco, is expressed through the ways in which the text "is manifested as a narrative strategy, as a set of instructions which is given to us step by step and which we have to follow when we decide to act as the model reader."[38] Aesthetic texts are thus open to infinite interpretations, but the model author in the text guides the reader in pursuing these interpretive pathways through what Eco calls a formative "textual strategy."[39]

The Reader Inside the Story

The third principle of Eco's interpretive ethics is that empirical readers should not impose their personal meaning on the text but should instead strive to become model readers who are the counterparts or interpretive partners to the model authors. Like the separation between empirical author and model author, the model reader is a distinct entity in relation to the empirical reader that is called upon by the text to fulfill its interpretive potential:

> To make his text communicative, the author has to assume that the ensemble of codes he relies upon is the same as that shared by his possible reader. The author has thus to foresee a model of the possible reader (hereafter Model Reader) supposedly able to deal interpretively with the expressions in the same way as the author deals generatively with them.[40]

In the act of reading, we are all empirical readers who look for meaning in texts and refer, as indicated earlier, to our knowledge and experience of the world by taking inferential walks as guesses about the paths to pursue in making sense of the work. But, just like the prohibition against the empirical author's interpretive interference, the empirical reader, according to Eco, must also avoid making the text conform solely to one's personal experience. To reiterate, however, if reading is a mode of individual cultural engagement, what is the problem with interpreting the text in a way that speaks to me personally? The problem, according to Eco, is that, like the intrusion of the empirical author's persona, this would obstruct and undercut the interpretive potential of the work:

> It is right for me while walking in the wood to use every experience and every discovery to learn about life, about the past and future. But since a wood is created for everybody, I must not look there for facts and sentiments which concern only myself. Otherwise (as I have written in two recent books, *The Limits of Interpretation* and *Interpretation and Overinterpretation*), I am not interpreting a text but rather using it. It is not at all forbidden to use a text for daydreaming, and we do this frequently, but daydreaming is not a public affair; it leads us to move within the narrative wood as if it were our own private garden.[41]

Similar to Eco's prohibition on being influenced by the empirical author, the prohibition against empirical readers making the text conform to their personal experience may also seem like an annoyingly unrealistic principle to maintain. Reading is such an intimate, private experience of personal discovery that can seem like a direct communication between the empirical author and the empirical reader. Avoiding such private appropriations of the meaning of the text is an important aspect of Eco's interpretive ethics, however, because otherwise it would negate the cultural function of aesthetic works which are intended to be a transformative experience for the reader rather than a mirror of the reader's identity:

> You cannot use the text as you want, but only as the text wants you to use it. An open text, however 'open' it be, cannot afford whatever interpretation.[42]

Admittedly the intimate connections between the empirical reader and the text may be emotionally and intellectually powerful, but, according to Eco, the transformative potential of the text goes beyond these experiences. The aesthetic function of the text "creates the competence of its Model Reader"[43] as a transformative process, for example, the way the reader of Joyce's *Finnegans Wake* would be provoked to acquire the competence to reflect on the multiple pathways of language as a formative medium.

First- and Second-Level Readers

The transformation of the empirical reader into the model reader through the guidance of the model author involves Eco's concepts of "first level" or "naive" reader, into "second level" or what he calls a "smart," "semiotic," or "ideal reader." As Eco indicates, there are two ways of exploring the woods, either to go directly to the end of the woods to see what is there, or instead to see why, as Eco indicates, "some paths are accessible and others are not."[44] In a narrative text, readers are typically drawn by the unfolding of the plot and the relationship between the characters toward a meaningful conclusion which is what Eco calls a model reader of the "first level" or "naive" reader. But, according to Eco, "every text is also addressed to a model reader of the second level, who wonders what sort of reader that story would like him or her to become and who wants to discover precisely how the model author goes about serving as a guide for the reader."[45] The full aesthetic value of the text is thus achieved by transforming the first-level reader into a second-level reader who reflects on the text as a whole and its textual strategy as a vision of a possible world.

According to Eco, "Only when empirical readers have discovered the model author, and have understood (or merely begun to understand) what it wanted from them, will they become full-fledged model readers." This principle of interpretive ethics obviously sets a very high standard for the reader's engagement which indicates the stark divide between elite and popular culture. Eco asserts that: "In order to know how a story ends, it is usually enough to read it once. In contrast, to identify the model author the text has to be read many times, and certain stories endlessly."[46] The second-level reading suggested by Eco would involve an intensive textual engagement which would call upon a previous awareness of narrative structure, etc. Eco's analysis of Allais' *A Most Parisian Episode* is highly instructive, in particular in relation to his novels, because it shows how first-level readers are unconsciously drawn into following particular pathways based on assumptions drawn from popular literature, while ignoring a variety of fairly elusive suggestions, which leads them to a narrative breakdown through a contradictory conclusion. But without Eco's detailed analysis, would a first-level reader be inclined to engage in a second-level exploration of its meaning? How would this transformation of a "naive" reader into a "smart" or "semiotic" reader occur outside of an academic focus on textual analysis, language theory, and semiotics?

Interpretation as Formativity

Eco's emphasis on a model reader of the second level can be understood in relation to his mentor Luigi Pareyson's idea of formativity, or forming form. Formativity is the way in which the text is organized to set up interpretive pathways to challenge the reader to go beyond a first-level engagement in the plot and outcome. The formativity of the text is what potentially transforms the reader through the consciousness raising character of works that Eco describes as having "aesthetic value" by provoking a reflection on the formative boundaries of our experience. Eco's emphasis on a second-level reading also arises from his experience with the Gruppo 63 whose response to the encroachment of mass media consumerism involved a reflection on language rather than content, or on language *as* the *formative content*. Frustrating or defying the expectations of first-level readers was central to the militant campaign of the Italian Neo-avant-garde in order to assert and preserve the cultural function of aesthetics in relation to first-level readers of the products of mass consumption whom Eco described as "lobotomized mass media illiterates."[47] But how would it be possible for these first-level readers, critically incapacitated by the mass media, to become second-level, model readers?

Open and Closed Texts

The concepts of model author and model reader, and first- and second-level reader, are, in turn, linked to Eco's distinction between "open" and "closed" texts. These concepts can be a bit confusing because, for Eco, "open" texts are open to infinite interpretations, but they contain a "closed" textual strategy that guides a second-level reading. In contrast, "closed" texts attempt to lead the reader along a single, fixed path of interpretation. But, because they are written in a generic way for a mass audience, they are "open" to any kind of misinterpretation because they lack a model author. As Eco indicates: "An open text outlines a 'closed' project of its Model Reader as a component of its structural strategy."[48] But a closed text, in contrast, is intended by its author for "an average addressee referred to a given social context."

> Those texts that obsessively aim at arousing a precise response on the part of more or less precise empirical readers (be they children, soap-opera addicts, doctors, law-abiding citizens, swingers, Presbyterians, farmers,

middle-class women, scuba divers, effete snobs, or any other imaginable sociopsychological catetgory) are in fact open to any possible 'aberrant' decoding. A text so immoderately 'open' to every possible interpretation will be called a *closed* one.[49]

Eco's conception of a closed text is indicative of his association with the Italian Neo-avant-garde's confrontation with the impact of mass media consumerism. As examples of closed texts, Eco specifies prominent products of popular culture such as *Superman* comic strips and James Bond spy novels by Ian Fleming. But he also cites *Les Mysteres de Paris* (1843) from the nineteenth-century French novelist Eugene Sue (1804–1857), a pioneer in publishing his novels in serial form for a popular newspaper audience, because it serves for him as a historically documented instance of "aberrant decoding" or misinterpretation in relation to the intentions of the author. As Eco notes, the author intended the work to motivate the Parisian underclass, during a period of ongoing class tensions, toward "a moderate vision of social harmony," but instead "it produced as a side effect a revolutionary uprising."[50] Eugene Sue's novel thus indicates through an historical example how texts aimed at a broad popular audience intending to arouse a specific response are subject to misinterpretation and are thus closed in creating a model reader.

The Da Vinci Code *as Closed Text?*

According to Eco's definition of closed text, would it be applicable to Dan Brown's *The Da Vinci Code*? While Dan Brown has indicated that he wanted to explore his interest in intellectual puzzles, he specifically chose the model of a commercially successful bestseller with an emphasis on dynamic plot development to reach the broadest possible popular audience. But is there any evidence that the phenomenal popular audience of *The Da Vinci Code* as both a novel and a movie version of an historical whodunit engaged in aberrant interpretations? *The Da Vinci Code*, by all accounts, did not, for instance, arouse a massive conversion to Catholicism which clearly would have been counter to the novel's intended theme of questioning the traditional paternalism of the Church. Eco, however, later clarified his conception about the value of works marketed specifically for a broad popular audience:

If there is a difference, it lies between the text that seeks to produce a new reader and the text that tries to fulfill the wishes of the readers already to be found in the street. In the latter case we have the book written, constructed, according to an effective, mass-production formula; the author carries out a kind of market analysis and adapts his work to its results. Even from a distance, it is clear that he is working by a formula; you have only to analyze the various novels he has written and you note that in all of them, after changing names, places, distinguishing features, he has told the same story – the one that the public was already asking of him.[51]

Eco acknowledges that, in relation to Eugene Sue's *Les Mysteres de Paris*, "we lack comparable sociopsychological evidence"[52] for aberrant readings of contemporary popular culture products. *The Da Vinci Code* and the related series of mystery novels featuring the detective Robert Langdon would seem to clearly specify the extent of their interpretive potential for an audience drawn to detective thrillers, but, because they are marketed for popular consumption according to a proven formula, they don't attempt to go beyond a first-level reading and therefore could be considered "closed" as vehicles of aesthetic transformation in contrast, for example, to open works such as James Joyce's *Finnegans Wake*: "one can extrapolate the profile of a 'good *Ulysses* reader' from the text itself, because the pragmatic process of interpretation is not an empirical accident independent of the text *qua* text, but is a structural element of its generative process."[53] According to Eco, *Superman* comics and James Bond novels, as well as *The Da Vinci Code*, are closed texts because they don't provide the formative structure to guide the reader toward a second level or model reading.

But, while the Robert Langdon novels clearly follow a narrative and thematic formula, don't they have educational value for a popular audience by exposing them to questions about art, religion, and history that otherwise would be the province of the cultivated elite? In this way, they would appeal to what Dwight MacDonald calls the "midcult" aspiration for elite culture. The question would be whether the focus on these topics through the medium of a plot engine drawn from proven bestsellers would tend to undercut the engagement of a popular readership with the world of "high brow" culture as an example of "kitsch": "Midcult... aspires to appropriate the status symbols and sophistication of the aesthetic 'high' cult without acquiring the sophistication to appreciate it."[54] The tendency of popular culture entertainment intended for a mass audience is to draw the audience through the lure of a dynamic plot engine with the promise of an unambiguous conclusion. Once the conclusion has been reached, its entertainment value would supposedly be exhausted. The other question is whether this type of escapist entertainment, that tends to have the effect of closing off a more strenuous engagement in critical reflection, at the same time reaffirms the uncritical acceptance of the status quo.

A Vehicle of Escape

For Eco, the problem with closed texts is that, by being marketed for a broad popular audience, they lack a textual strategy that would generate their model, second-level reader. They consequently consist of a marketing formula for generating first-level effects that creates a passive experience for the reader. As Eco indicates, "They apparently aim at pulling the reader along a predetermined path, carefully displaying their effects so as to arouse pity or fear, excitement or depression at the due place and at the right moment. Every step of the 'story' elicits just the expectation that its further course will satisfy."[55] Consequently, these texts are "closed" because they contain a narrative structure that traps the reader at a first-level reading by fostering a passive response to the text. In this way, they support an underlying ideology of consumerism that undercuts the consciousness raising function of aesthetics through escapist entertainment.

Eco, however, has asserted that: "I'm one of those who still (or again) maintain that enjoyment is reason enough to read a story."[56] The question to consider is what kind of enjoyment in relation to what kind of story? Eco suggested that *Superman* comic books reflect the privileging of property values in capitalistic society, and the James Bond novels reflect a narrative formula of escapist entertainment while legitimizing elitist power struggles. In contrast, Eco found that the *Peanuts* comic strips by Charles M. Shulz and the graphic novels of Jules Feiffer provoked a reflection on the identity struggles of contemporary society. Concerning Eco's basis for evaluating these popular culture products, Norma Bouchard suggests in her essay on "Eco and Popular Culture," that "Eco rarely admits that his critique of popular American culture reflects his own leftist ideology, one colored (if not dominated) by Marxist values and a common disrespect for American popular culture often found among European intellectuals."[57] Eco's critiques reflect the influence of Pareyson and Gramsci on an assessment of the impact of cultural products according to whether they promote a passive response or an active critical consciousness. But are works of escapist entertainment inherently invalid as cultural products?

SNOBBY AESTHETICS

If, according to Eco, we are surrounded by powerful messages generated by mass media consumerism, how do we assess their aesthetic value? How do we rise above kitsch and the underlying ideological bias of cultural products? On the other end of the cultural spectrum, if the intended effect of aesthetic works is to create a second-level model reader with a critical consciousness, how would such works transform first-level readers into second-level readers outside of an academic setting? In *The Limits of Interpretation*, Eco confronts this problem of the interface between elite and popular culture through a consideration of the possibility of "a new aesthetics of the 'abstract' applied to the products of mass communication."

> ... this requires that the naive addressee of the first level disappear, by giving place only to the critical reader of the second level. In fact, there is no conceivable naive addressee of an abstract painting or sculpture.... Of abstract works there is only a critical "reading": what is formed is of no interest; only the way it is formed is interesting.

Abstract paintings consist solely of a relationship between particular forms or shapes that have no meaning in themselves. What is interesting for the elite audience of abstract painting is just the formative arrangement of those shapes. As a result, according to Eco, there is no first-level reading. But where does this leave the vast audience of mass media products that are aimed at a first-level reading? Eco asks if the critical awareness engaged in by the elite audience of abstract works can be communicated through the mass media: "Can we expect the same [critical reading] for the serial products of television?"

> If it should not happen that way, the radical proposal of the postmodern aesthetics would appear singularly snobby: as in a sort of neo-Orwellian world, the pleasures of the smart reading would be reserved for the members of the Party; and the pleasures of the naive reading, reserved for the proletarians.

Eco concludes that this would result in bringing "pleasure to the happy few, reserving pity and fear to the unhappy many who remain."[58]

THE ENCYCLOPEDIA AND ME

To avoid the Orwellian scenario indicated above, it would be necessary to find a way to intersect the two worlds of elite aesthetics and mass media consumerism, and Eco has become one of the foremost proponents of that possibility. But the problem of the relationship between elite and popular culture can be understood in relation to Eco's concept of the "Encyclopedia":

> By "Encyclopedia" I mean the totality of knowledge with which I'm only partly acquainted but to which I can refer because it is like an enormous library composed of all books and encyclopedias – all the papers and manuscript documents of all centuries, including the hieroglyphics of the ancient Egyptians and inscriptions in cuneiform.[59]

The "Encyclopedia" represents the entire cultural inheritance of the world that each of us is acquainted with in a limited way depending on our ethnicity, gender, nationality, education, socioeconomic status, personal circumstances, etc. We draw upon our acquaintance with the Encyclopedia to make sense of our existence and direct our actions in the "real" world of human society, work relations, family, etc. In a similar way, we use our knowledge and experience of the Encyclopedia to derive meaning from the diverse expressions of popular and elite culture through television, movies, art, literature, etc.

Our relation to the Encyclopedia allows us to take what Eco calls "inferential walks" to make sense of our experience and to interpret, as Eco has indicated, the cultural "messages" that surround us. But what about first level or naive readers of *A Most Parisian Episode* who get stuck at a first-level reading because of the limitations of their knowledge of the cultural Encyclopedia? Won't they just be perplexed and put off by the snobbery of the elite? On the other side of the cultural spectrum, Eco's characterization of the James Bond novels as a cynical exploitation of a popular audience is an indicator of how popular culture products tend to maintain a limited understanding of the cultural Encyclopedia through the broad impact of mass media consumerism. From a popular consumer's perspective, the mass media have greatly expanded the access to cultural products in all forms, visual, literary, musical, etc., which has democratized the engagement in culture in a fundamental way. From an elite cultural perspective, however, the mass media, while greatly expanding the access to cultural products, have undermined the potential of culture to arouse a critical awareness because mass media consumerism has displaced the role of the intellectual and artist. Popular culture is determined instead by producers to accommodate the variable taste of a mass audience.

But since the advent of mass media consumerism, there has been a cross-pollination between the traditional arts and popular culture with the potential for expanding what Eco would call an "aesthetic" awareness of our collaborative role in human culture. Andy Warhol's images of Elvis Presley and Campbell Soup Cans are prominent examples of elite culture appropriating the symbols of popular culture to provoke a reflection on art in relation to mass consumerism. The Robert Langdon novels of Dan Brown such as *The Da Vinci Code* are an example of popular culture appropriating the symbols of elite culture to arouse a curiosity, according to the author, about intellectual mysteries.

The Interdependence of Fiction and Reality

Eco has been both an analytical critic of the products of mass media consumerism for a mass audience through his articles in magazines and newspapers, as well as an experimenter in using mass media consumerism to communicate his ideas through his magazine articles and novels. But why does any of this matter when we are dealing with fictional products of the imagination disseminated through mass media consumerism? Aren't fictional works at both the elite and popular level primarily an indulgence in leisure entertainment or, for elite culture, a stimulation of the intellect as a way of distinguishing one's class status through the ability to converse about one's appropriation of the cultural Encyclopedia? For Eco, however, fiction is the fundamental way in which we create the "real" world and make sense of it. Fictional worlds are attractive and powerful because they help us to understand our existence as humans and give us reassurance about the "meaning" of the "real" world when it can otherwise seem chaotic, uncertain, and meaningless. The real world is constantly changing, and its complexity is difficult to encompass with a unified sense of meaning. Fictional worlds, in contrast, can provide a totalized sense of meaning and order. According to Eco:

> ...any walk within fictional worlds has the same function as a child's play. Children play with puppets, toy horses, or kites in order to get acquainted

with the physical laws of the universe and with the actions that someday they will perform. Likewise, to read fiction means to play a game by which we give sense to the immensity of things that happened, are happening, or will happen in the actual world. By reading narrative, we escape the anxiety that attacks us when we try to say something true about the world. This is the consoling function of narrative – the reason people tell stories, and have told stories from the beginning of time. And it has always been the paramount function of myth: to find a shape, a form, in the turmoil of human experience.

Truth as a Fiction

The understanding of the truth is also easy to determine in a fictional text because, according to Eco, "fictional statements are true within the framework of the possible world of a given story."[60] That Superman can fly faster than a speeding bullet is true because, in the world of the story, it is accepted as normal for a being with super powers. As a point of comparison, Eco asks us to consider whether "our notion of truth in the actual world is equally strong and clear cut?"[61] Eco notes that "truth" in the "real" world is actually similar to "truth" in a fictional world because they are both based on "trust." We trust in a fictional world by deferring to the text as representing a possible world according to the author's imagination through what is called "suspension of disbelief." If we didn't accept at least provisionally the truth of the fictional world, we could not experience its meaning. We can feel reassured, however, about our ability to visit that world and leave it at will. This is not the case with the "real" world which we enter and leave, in normal circumstances, outside our will.

In the "real" world we may think that we orient ourselves according to our direct experience, but, according to Eco, citing the American philosopher Hilary Putnam (1926–2016), we "delegate to others the knowledge of nine-tenths of the real world, keeping for [ourselves] the knowledge of the other tenth."[62] The "truth" of the "real" world is based on our "trust" in others who have produced the knowledge that makes up the Encyclopedia. Because we rely on others for the truth of the real world, facts can be disputed as they often are based on different interests and perspectives. As a result, Eco asserts that: "we read novels because they give us the comfortable sensation of living in worlds where the notion of truth is indisputable, while the actual world seems to be a more treacherous place."[63]

To respond to the question about what really matters concerning the uses of fiction, we can say that it serves as a fundamental way of making sense of the world, and that fictional truths are more reliable than actual truths. Eco points out that "in order to decide what is true or false in the actual world... I must decide which portions of the Total Encyclopedia are to be trusted, while rejecting others as unreliable."[64] From this perspective, the real world is dependent upon, or as Eco puts it, "parasitic" on the fictional knowledge of the world. We are expected to accept the truth of the real world on the basis of trust similar to the way that fictional worlds are accepted through the "suspension of disbelief." As Eco notes: "Our perceptual relationship with the world works because we trust prior stories."[65] But in order for readers to make sense of a fictional world, they must make reference to aspects of the real world or it could not be understood. We can marvel at the world of Superman's fantastic powers, but they are extraordinary due to their relation to what we understand as the normal capacities of humans. According to Eco: "This means that fictional worlds are parasites of the real world."

Thus fiction and the real world are closely interconnected and dependent on each other. Our understanding of the real world is dependent on the stories told over time by others that become part of the Encyclopedia. According to Eco, "fiction fascinates us" as a way of "perceiving the world and reconstructing the past."

> Fiction has the same function that games have. In playing, children learn to live, because they simulate situations in which they may find themselves as adults. And it is through fiction that we adults train our ability to structure our past and present experience.[66]

The power of fiction as a way of making sense of the world as well as a means for exploring the role of interpretation was what Eco took up in his turn to the novel in 1978 which we will consider in the next chapter.

Notes

1. Eco, from the introduction to *The Limits of Interpretation*, (Bloomington: Indiana University Press, 1990), p. 3.
2. Eco, *The Limits of Interpretation*, p. 48.
3. Eco, *Interpretation and Overinterpretation*, p. 27.
4. Eco, *Interpretation and Overinterpretation*, p. 29.

5. Sullivan, Jane (2004-12-24). "Religious Conspiracy? Do Me a Fervour," http://www.theage.com.au/articles/2004/12/23/1103391886435.html.
6. Eco, *The Name of the Rose*, (New York: Harcourt Brace and Company, 1994), p. 508.
7. Eco, *The Name of the Rose*, p. 505.
8. Eco, *The Limits of Interpretation*, p. 45.
9. Eco, *The Role of the Reader*, (Bloomington: Indiana University Press, 1984), pp. 263–266.
10. Eco, *The Role of the Reader*, p. 204.
11. Eco, *The Role of the Reader*, p. 206.
12. Eco, *The Role of the Reader*, p. 207.
13. Eco, *The Role of the Reader*, p. 264.
14. Eco, *The Role of the Reader*, p. 205.
15. Eco, *Six Walks in the Fictional Woods*, p. 49.
16. Eco, *The Role of the Reader*, p. 214.
17. Eco, *The Role of the Reader*, p. 209.
18. Eco, *The Role of the Reader*, p. 214.
19. Eco, *Six Walks in the Fictional Woods*, (Cambridge: Harvard University Press, 1995).
20. Eco, *Interpretation and Overinterpretation*, (Cambridge: Cambridge University Press, 1992).
21. Eco, *Six Walks in the Fictional Woods*, p. 6.
22. Jorge Luis Borges, from *Collected Fictions*, translated by Andrew Hurley (New York: Penguin Books, 1998), pp. 119–128.
23. Eco, *Six Walks in the Fictional Woods*, p. 6.
24. Eco, *Six Walks in the Fictional Woods*, p. 8.
25. Eco, *Six Walks in the Fictional Woods*, p. 9.
26. Eco, *The Name of the Rose*, (New York: Harcourt Brace and Company, 1994), p. 524.
27. Eco, *Six Walks in the Fictional Woods*, p. 11.
28. *The Guardian*, November 6, 2016.
29. Eco, *Interpretation and Overinterpretation*, p. 25.
30. Rocco Capozzi, "Interpretation and Overinterpretation," from *Reading Eco*, (Bloomington: Indiana University Press, 1997), p. 226.
31. Eco, *Six Walks in the Fictional Woods*, p. 84. Joyce's novel Ulysses, as mentioned in Chapter 4, is about the experience of a single day in the life of the main character Leopold Bloom, and Bloomsday is an annual celebration in Dublin and other cities of Joyce's life through the reenactment of the events of the novel.
32. Eco, *The Name of the Rose*, p. 508.
33. Eco, *The Name of the Rose*, p. 507.

34. Eco, *Interpretation and Overinterpretation*, p. 73.
35. Eco, *Interpretation and Overinterpretation*, p. 75.
36. Eco, *Interpretation and Overinterpretation*, p. 82.
37. Eco, *Interpretation and Overinterpretation*, p. 78.
38. Eco, *Six Walks in the Fictional Woods*, p. 15.
39. Eco, *Six Walks in the Fictional Woods*, p.25.
40. Eco *The Role of the Reader*, p. 17.
41. Eco, *Six Walks in the Fictional Woods*, p. 9.Eco refers to his publications on interpretive boundaries: *The Limits of Interpretation*, (Bloomington: Indiana University Press, 1990), and *Interpretation and Overinterpretation*, (Cambridge: Cambridge University Press, 1992) which was drawn from Eco's Tanner lectures at Cambridge and an accompanying seminar that included the participation of Richard Rorty, Jonathan Culler, Christine Brooke-Rose, and Stefan Collini.
42. Eco, *The Role of the Reader*, p. 9.
43. Eco *The Role of the Reader*, p. 7.
44. Eco, *Six Walks in the Fictional Woods*, p. 27.
45. Eco, *Six Walks in the Fictional Woods*, p. 27.
46. Eco, *Six Walks in the Fictional Woods*, p. 27.
47. Eco, "Postscript" from *The Name of the Rose*, p. 532.
48. Eco, *The Role of the Reader*, p. 9.
49. Eco, *The Role of the Reader*, p. 8.
50. Eco, *The Role of the Reader*, p. 8.
51. Eco, "Postscript" to *The Name of the Rose*, p. 523.
52. Eco, *The Role of the Reader*, p. 8.
53. Eco, *The Role of the Reader*, p. 8.
54. Eco, *The Open Work*, p. 189.
55. Eco, *The Role of the Reader*, p. 8.
56. Eco, *The Limits of Interpretation*, p. 156.
57. Bouchard, Norma, "Eco and Popular Culture," from *New Essays on Umberto Eco*, edited by Peter Bondanella (New York: Cambridge University Press, 2009), p. 6.
58. Eco, *The Limits of Interpretation*, pp. 98–99.
59. Eco, *Six Walks in the Fictional Woods*, p. 90.
60. Eco, *Six Walks in the Fictional Woods*, p. 88.
61. Eco, *Six Walks in the Fictional Woods*, p. 88.
62. Eco, *Six Walks in the Fictional Woods*, p. 89.
63. Eco, *Six Walks in the Fictional Woods*, p. 91.
64. Eco, *Six Walks in the Fictional Woods*, pp. 92–93.
65. Eco, *Six Walks in the Fictional Woods*, p. 130.
66. Eco, *Six Walks in the Fictional Woods*, p. 131.

CHAPTER 10

The Literary Provocateur

After nearly 30 years as an academic theorist and writer of popular articles on contemporary culture for Italian magazines and newspapers, Eco published his first novel, *The Name of the Rose*, in 1980. Since he had already been successful in linking his scholarly pursuits with a prominent position in the public media long before his advent as a novelist, what were the circumstances that would have prompted him at age 46 to turn to narrative fiction in the late seventies? On the back cover of the original Italian version of *The Name of the Rose*, Eco asserted that "those things about which we cannot theorize, we must narrate"[1] which is a playful allusion to Ludwig Wittgenstein's famous assertion that "Whereof one cannot speak, thereof one must be silent" from the *Tractatus Logico-Philosophicus* (1922). This would indicate an awareness that he needed to shift his approach to a popular audience through fiction, but he indicated elsewhere that he was also attracted to the great potential of the medium of literature:

> We are surrounded by intangible powers, and not just those spiritual values explored by the world's great religions.... And among these powers I would include that of the literary tradition; that is to say, the power of that network of texts which humanity has produced and still produces not for practical ends (such as records, commentaries on laws and scientific formulae, minutes of meetings or train schedules) but, rather, for its own sake, for humanity's own enjoyment—and which are read for pleasure, spiritual edification, broadening of knowledge, or maybe just to pass the

time, without anyone forcing us to read them (apart from when we are obliged to do so at school or in the university).[2]

THE MORO AFFAIR

As an academic theorist for 30 years, however, Eco's venture into the literary domain was also motivated by a horrendous political tragedy in the late seventies called "The Moro Affair" that had a major impact on how Italian intellectuals reflected on their role in relation to a public audience. Aldo Moro (1916–1978) was Prime Minister of Italy during the sixties and late seventies when Italy was experiencing the phenomenal growth in prosperity arising from the "economic miracle" of 1959–1963 but also volatile social tensions which resulted in a political crisis in 1978. In that year, Moro was just about to finalize what was called the *compromesso storico*, a long anticipated historical compromise to bring the Communist Party into an unprecedented alliance with the centrist Christian Democrats through negotiations led by Moro as its principal architect. The impending success of this effort, however, precipitated a violent response by leftist radicals against what they perceived to be a betrayal by the Communist Party of efforts to respond to the widespread social inequities that were afflicting Italian society since the end of WWII. Before the war, Italy was a comparatively underdeveloped, mostly agricultural society that was dramatically transformed into a modern industrial economy, primarily in northern Italy, in the span of two decades. The resulting rise in personal income created the conditions for an Italian middle class and the advent of mass media consumerism which prompted Eco and the Gruppo 63 to confront what they perceived as the degradation of Italian culture. But the economic miracle also caused large-scale migrations of jobless southern Italians to the north such that, according to historian Paul Ginsborg, "By the end of the sixties, Turin had become the third largest 'southern' city in Italy, after Naples and Palermo."[3]

The mass migration of southerners to the north led to a legacy of ethnic conflicts because southerners were discriminated against as *terroni* by northern Italians for what they perceived to be their peasant origins. They were regarded as "backward" and "practically African or Arabs," as well as "thieves, lazy, inefficient, intolerant," and morally degenerate because they "beat their women, prostitute their wives and daughters and are insanely jealous."[4] Southern Italians were consequently blamed for "crime, illiteracy, sponging on welfare, and overloading the available public services—transport, public housing, schools, etc."[5] As a result, southern Italians encountered great difficulty in adapting to the culture of the north especially from blatant discrimination in housing. In addition to these social tensions, university students were engaged in what were called the years of *contestazione*,[6] 1968 and 1969, through protests against a lack of university funding[7] which was linked to the international student protest movement and militant resistance by Italian workers against both international corporations and union officials. The broad expansion of these movements resulted in a prolonged period of mass demonstrations and crippling labor strikes which were reflected in Eco's second novel *Foucault's Pendulum* (1988).

THE STRATEGY OF TENSION

At the end of 1969, mass public protests were displaced by a campaign of covert terrorist attacks, called the *strategia della tensione*, involving a series of terrorist bombings later determined to be perpetrated by the extreme right to discredit the political agenda of the left. But, beginning in 1974, autonomous elements of the left also began a terrorist campaign of armed assaults, kidnappings, and assassinations against corporate managers, union leaders, and journalists, but, in particular, public officials suspected of collaborating with the reformist tendencies of the Italian Communist Party (PCI) in alliance with the centrist Christian Democrats.

After prolonged and painstaking negotiations by Moro, a parliamentary coalition in favor of the historical compromise was finally achieved on March 16, 1978. But that same day Moro was kidnapped in Rome by the Red Brigades, an extremist leftwing revolutionary group, who killed five members of Moro's entourage and took him into hiding. After a secret trial and conviction for "political crimes," he was held for ransom to secure the release of political prisoners affiliated with the terrorist underground. During his captivity, Italian newspapers published a series of letters by Moro in which he pleaded for his release and criticized government officials, including close allies, for not interceding on his behalf. The newspapers also published communiques from the Red Brigades, as well as letters by various civic and religious leaders, including the Pope, who appealed to the Red Brigades for Moro's release. After losing faith in his former allies, and anticipating his inevitable execution by his captors, he wrote to his family requesting that both government and party officials be excluded from his funeral. After 55 days in captivity, his captors carried out their threatened execution and notified the police on May 9, 1978 that Moro's body had been left in the trunk of an abandoned car in Rome.

Although Moro's political motives had been unfavorably criticized by prominent Italian intellectuals (his efforts were also strongly opposed by both the USA and Russia), his assassination shocked the conscience of Italian society and served to discredit not only the extremists but also the centrist politicians who were denounced for betraying Moro by exploiting his kidnapping for political purposes. The Moro Affair, for many Italian intellectuals, was thus a defining moment that caused a total disillusionment with the Italian political process.

Eco notes in the "Postscript" to *The Name of the Rose* that he began working on his first novel in March 1978 which was when the Moro Affair began to unfold in the Italian media.[8] The impact on him is reflected in his journalistic writings from 1978 entitled "Striking at the Heart of the State,"[9] that criticized the Red Brigades for targeting a high-ranking figure such as Moro even though they had acknowledged that their enemy was the complex system of multinational capitalism that was beyond the control of any particular individual. In another column from 1978, Eco referred to the Red Brigades as "those last, incurable romantics of Catholic-papist origin, [who] still think the state has a heart and that this heart can be wounded..."[10]

As further evidence of the profound impact of the Moro Affair, Eco wrote a column about the trial of the suspects in 1982, after the publication of *The Name of the Rose* in Italy in 1980, that indicates the importance of that episode for Eco and how it influenced his practice as an intellectual. He saw the assassination of Moro as symptomatic of an underlying propensity toward violence that found its contemporary outlet in the corrupting effects of ideology: "If we don't accept and recognize, bravely, the inevitability of this behavior (studying techniques to confine it, prevent it, offering other, less bloody safety valves), we run the risk of being idealists and moralists as much as those whose bloodthirsty madness we so reprove."[11]

Becoming *Imbestialito*

The demoralizing impact of the Moro Affair made Eco aware of the limitations of his project as a theorist and public intellectual which motivated his turn to the novel. In an interview in 1980 following the publication of *The Name of the Rose*, Eco acknowledged that the Moro

Affair had caused Italian intellectuals to question their ability to influence public opinion through the usual means of communication. When asked about the origins of his first novel, Eco pointed to the Moro Affair as well as his longstanding interest in the Middle Ages as a lens for understanding the present. He said that he had acquired voluminous notes over time from his medieval studies that he wanted to use for this purpose: "I thought seriously about retrieving these notes to write a novel, set in this epoch, about the Moro Affair." When asked whether direct links therefore existed between the Moro Affair and the Middle Ages, Eco replied that:

> No they don't exist. But the fact was that, before the Moro Affair, an intellectual had the impression of being able to influence current events by writing an article, or a manifesto, or by participating in a conference. But afterwards a sense of impotence was born.[12]

The problem for intellectuals at this time, according to Eco, was that their ideas were interpreted "elsewhere" in a "*buco oscuro*," a dark hole, in ways that the intellectual could not "describe or determine." Eco suggested that: "The way out of this situation was to write a story about the experience of this 'dark hole' which, in effect, would be the encounter of the intellect with a labyrinth." As he points out in the interview, "The intellect tends to simplify, while a labyrinth tends to complicate, the paths of inquiry." Eco also indicated that the reason for not previously engaging in narrative fiction was the result of his origins as a medievalist and his unconscious adherence to the medieval division between "*arti liberali e arti meccaniche*," the liberal and mechanical arts:

> Theory was dedicated to the liberal arts, while narrative, painting, and the cinema were considered mechanical arts, and thus more worldly. My relation to artists was always like the relation between a zoologist and his animals. I never thought that I would succumb to this bestiality.
>
> When asked why he finally became "*imbestialito*," Eco replied:
>
> I was in a hurry to write this novel like someone who has to go to the bathroom [in Italian, "*far pipi*"]. I felt compelled to do it even though I had neither the time nor the intention, so evidently a situation emerged that could not be addressed in an essay, and was worth writing as a narrative.[13]

Poetic Acne

In his recollections on his childhood, however, Eco had acknowledged some early aspirations as a writer of fiction. Eco recalled that "I began writing short stories and novels between the age of eight and fifteen, then I stopped, only to resume as I approached fifty." His way of writing as a young boy was to start with a title page in a blank notebook and then, "every ten pages or so," place an illustration taken from adventure tales he found in his basement. "The choice of illustration determined the story that I was going to create, of which I used to write only the first few pages of the first chapter." As he recalls, "...back then, I was only an author of great unfinished novels."[14] He notes that "After those attempts, I had decided to focus on comic strips, and I completed a few." But he became discouraged when confronted with the tedious process of trying to make copies by hand [before the advent of photocopiers] for distribution to his friends. In middle school, as an alternative to a personal journal, he was able to write fictional compositions which he described as "humorous sketches" on the model of P.G. Wodehouse.[15] Afterwards, he became enamored with poetry of various sorts but finally concluded that: "my poetry had the same functional origin and formal configuration of adolescent acne" which led him to "abandon all so-called creative writing and to confine myself to philosophical reflections and essayistic prose."[16]

The Experience of the Labyrinth

Eco's belated return to "creative writing" was thus motivated by the need to adapt his way of communicating as a public intellectual with a popular mass audience in the aftermath of the Moro Affair. Because of his foundations as a scholar, he chose the setting of the Middle Ages, and he chose the genre of the "crime novel" because, as Eco indicates, it "represents a kind of conjecture, pure and simple." He noted that, conjecture is similar to what happens with "medical diagnosis, scientific research" and philosophy, whose "fundamental question," according to Eco, "is the same as the detective novel: who is guilty?"[17] The confrontation of the intellectual with the labyrinth thus served for Eco as "an abstract model of conjecture" which is similar to what he did in his theoretical writings:

> When I presented my doctoral dissertation on the aesthetics of Thomas Aquinas... one of my examiners charged me with a sort of "narrative fallacy."

He said that a mature scholar, when setting out to do some research, inevitably proceeds by trial and error, making and rejecting different hypotheses; but at the end of the inquiry, all those attempts should have been digested and the scholar should present only the conclusions. In contrast, he said, I told the story of my research as if it were a detective novel.[18]

Similarly our contemporary experience of searching for the "truth" is, for Eco, a labyrinth like a "rhizome" which is a tangle of roots where "every path can be connected with every other one. [It] has no center, no periphery, no exit, because it is potentially infinite."[19] It can be compared to Borges' garden of "forking paths" and Peirce's "unlimited semiosis" which require one to take inferential walks based on conjecture with uncertain outcomes. Through the detective novel, Eco could go beyond analyses about language, semiotics, and interpretation theory from the outside, and take the reader inside these concepts to experience firsthand the problem of finding one's way through the labyrinth of the world.

THE ITALIAN POPULAR READERSHIP

Besides being a model of conjecture, there were other reasons why the detective genre would have been a useful vehicle for Eco's first novel that involved practical considerations involving the Italian book publishing market. Although Eco had a longstanding association with Bompiani, a prominent Italian publishing firm, he was confronted with a well-established reluctance among Italian publishers to fund the publication of contemporary Italian novelists because the broad readership necessary for such ventures had yet to develop. As Lino Pertile notes in the introduction to *The New Italian Novel*, "Traditionally, new writers have not been viewed in Italy as a sound commercial investment."[20] Before the unprecedented success of *The Name of the Rose* it was difficult for Italian writers of fiction to get their work published because "the reading public" in Italy from the early fifties was still a comparatively small audience comprised of "the cultivated middle classes, intellectuals, and students." In 1957, for example, the student population was still only 212,000, and "40.8% of Italian families... did not habitually read printed matter of any kind."[21] Eco has been quoted as saying that "Italy is not an intellectual country. On the subway in Tokyo everybody reads. In Italy they don't. Don't evaluate Italy from the fact that it produced Michelangelo and Raphael."[22]

The advent of mass consumerism in the sixties caused sweeping changes in cultural consumption in Italy, but the Italian publishing industry was still confronting the impact of Italy's longstanding regional and linguistic fragmentation that had slowed the development of a national literary culture. During the fifties, only 18 percent of the population spoke Italian regularly (but not all the time), 20 percent spoke only dialect, and 12.9 percent (24 percent in the south) were still illiterate. The expansion of the Italian reading public during the sixties and seventies was due to the economic miracle that caused a massive migration from the farms to the cities, the advent of consumerism that generated for the first time a mass market for a variety of cultural products, and the educational reform in 1964 that led to increased enrollments in higher education from 212,000 in 1957 to 800,000 in 1973.[23] The shift in population from agriculture to urban life and the exposure to the mass media, especially television, slowly displaced the use of dialect toward an identity with a national language. But Italian publishers tended to restrict their mass-marketing efforts to a limited number of established authors, which excluded the postwar generation of writers, such as Eco, whose appeal to a broad popular audience was, at that point, still uncertain.

The *Giallo*

While choosing the detective story as a model of conjecture, Eco could also have seen it as an effective genre for reaching a broad Italian popular readership because of the longstanding popularity after the war of the *giallo*, a cheaply produced, magazine-style booklet of detective fiction that was named after its characteristic yellow cover. The widespread popularity of the detective novel for the emerging Italian popular readership can be seen to arise from its predictable narrative structure involving a crime with disturbing and elusive circumstances which is investigated by a detective as a kind of intellectual hero who provides a full explanation of the mysteries at the conclusion. The mystery novel thus incorporates its own interpretive guide through the role of the detective. This would explain as well the phenomenal popularity of the historical whodunit that offers an exploration of the exotic mysteries of the past and a window into elite culture while providing the reader with an interpretive guide who explains its meaning along the way.

A Reader's Guide and Companion

In the case of *The Name of the Rose*, a popular readership could feel reassured in confronting the dense historical references and untranslated passages in other languages through the guidance of the detective monk William as an exemplary interpreter guide. In addition, readers could identify with the naiveté of the novice monk Adso who, according to Eco, tells the story with "the voice of someone who records the events with the photographic fidelity of an adolescent, but does not understand them." The reader can thus feel reassured about exploring an unfamiliar historical environment and mysterious circumstances alongside the narrator who, as Eco indicates, "understands nothing,"[24] while being guided by an expert in deciphering signs who seems to understand everything. Adso, the narrator, can be seen as a first level, or naive reader, and William as a second level or model reader.

Poverty, Laughter, the Simple, and Heresy

The Name of the Rose follows William and Adso as they investigate a series of mysterious deaths at a monastery while awaiting the convening of a council between emissaries of the Pope and the secular Holy Roman Emperor concerning a conflict over the poverty of Christ. The investigation of the series of deaths leads to an exploration of the labyrinth of the monastery library and to link the deaths of the monks to the seven trumpets of the Apocalypse and a forbidden treatise by Aristotle on laughter. The controversy concerning the poverty of Christ also involves a conflict between the poor and uneducated, who are referred to by William as "the simple," and the elite members of the clergy. The conflict over poverty leads to a charge of heresy against two of the monastery's monks. While the central focus of the novel concerns the search for the forbidden book linked to the deaths of the monks, the investigation thus brings together the intertwined themes of poverty, laughter, the simple, and heresy.

Did Christ Laugh?

The question of laughter and comedy is taken up through the encounters between William and the elderly, blind monk Jorge, "the library's memory and the soul of the scriptorium"[25] who was inspired by the Argentinian writer Jorge Luis Borges (1899–1986) from his writings about labyrinths, forking paths, and the global encyclopedia of world knowledge. As justification for the laughter of Christ, William cites numerous authorities going back to antiquity that "laughter is proper to man" as a "sign of his rationality"[26] which prompts Jorge's response that: "Christ did not laugh" because "Laughter foments doubt." To which William to replies that: "sometimes it is right to doubt."[27] In their confrontation at the conclusion of the novel, Jorge reveals the existence of the forbidden book in which Aristotle argues that "alone among the animals—man is capable of laughter."[28] According to Jorge, this idea would undermine Church authority by "freeing oneself of the fear of the Devil," and by fomenting the threat of heresy by the poor and uneducated: "...the church can deal with the heresy of the simple, who condemn themselves on their own, destroyed by their ignorance." But, for Jorge, Aristotle's book on laughter "could teach that freeing oneself of the fear of the Devil is wisdom."[29] Jorge insists that: "The simple must not speak. This book would have justified the idea that the tongue of the simple is the vehicle of wisdom."[30] For Jorge, laughter, the poverty and ignorance of the simple, and heresy are closely linked.

The novel's central focus on Aristotle's lost book on comedy is linked to a key component of Eco's semiotic theory that demonstrates how he uses the novel as a way of communicating his academic theory through his practice as a public intellectual. Recall that, besides being a theory of the lie, Eco's semiotic theory is also a theory of laughter: "...not only is semiotics the science of everything subject to the lie: it is also the science of everything subject to comic or tragic distortion."[31] Language can be used to lie, but also to laugh through a deliberate distortion of the truth that causes us to laugh because it violates our conventional cultural codes and allows us to see the "truth" in a different light. Comedy and laughter are thus an aspect of human rationality that aid us against "the insane passion for the truth," that was afflicting Italian society in the late seventies when Eco wrote the novel.

The Poverty of Christ

A central theme in the novel is also the poverty of Christ which is the source of the historical tension at play at the monastery. The question of the poverty of Christ is discussed through extensive exchanges between the characters, and it is intertwined with the other themes of the novel which are indications of Eco's practice as a public intellectual, and how his first novel reflects the circumstances of the Moro Affair. The poverty of

Christ is linked, for example, to the economic exclusion and revolt of the poor, the threat of heresy, the specter of the Apocalypse, and the elite monopoly of knowledge in relation to the poor and illiterate who are referred to in the novel as "the simple."

The visit to the monastery by William and Adso is initially motivated by the convening of a council between emissaries of the Pope and the secular Holy Roman Emperor in alliance with the Franciscan Order concerning the Franciscan Spirituals' principle of the poverty of Christ. The Spiritual wing of the Franciscans wanted to return to the founding principles of St. Francis (1181–1226) who was from a wealthy merchant family but renounced his worldly possessions in order to emulate Christ's humble origins and close affiliation with the poor. The assertion by the Franciscan Spirituals of the poverty of Christ was also motivated by the perception that the Franciscan order, like the papacy, had become corrupted by wealth and power. As Adso notes in the narrative, after St. Francis received the blessing of the papacy to establish the order, it gradually became "too powerful, too bound to earthly matters, and many Franciscans wanted to restore it to its early purity."[32]

The principle of the poverty of Christ linked the Fransiscan Spirituals with the revolt of the poor against the wealth of the Church which caused them to be denounced as heretics. The Franciscan Spirituals were also Apocalyptics who anticipated the imminent triumph of good over evil followed by the reign of Christ which motivated their efforts to purify their order. In relation to the circumstances of Italy in the late seventies, the Franciscan Spirituals' assertion of the poverty of Christ can be compared to radical reform movements within the Italian Communist Party who were attempting to reassert the original call for a more equitable distribution of the wealth in response to the perceived corruption of the Party by corporate power. These were the circumstances that motivated them to engage in violent revolutionary practices like the Red Brigades.

THE REVOLT OF THE POOR

In the early fourteenth century depicted in the novel, the poor were associated with the subsistence economy and the bartering of goods which was being displaced by the rise of the cities and the new economy of money and trade. The poverty of Christ thus concerns more broadly the plight of the poor in relation not only to spiritual purity, but also in response to what they perceived to be the corruption of the Church by the new merchant class. The resulting tension between social classes and religious doctrines created the potential for uprisings by the poor. William explains to Adso that, in the cities, power is held by "the merchants" whose "weapon is money." As a result, "money circulates everywhere" thus displacing "the bartering of goods" by the peasants, and "even priests, bishops, and religious orders have to take money into account." William concludes that: "This is why, naturally, rebellion against power takes the form of a call to poverty." According to William, "The rebels against power are those denied any connection to money."[33] The spiritual reform movements of various kinds within the Franciscan order thus developed in response to the problem of the new money economy and they tended to attract the poor for both spiritual and economic reasons. As William explains to Adso: "The movements grow, gathering simple people who have been aroused by other movements and who believe all have the same impulse of revolt and hope..."[34]

The medieval revolt of the poor can be compared to the circumstances of Italy during the late seventies when the agricultural economy of the south was being displaced by industrial production in the north and students felt exploited by corporate power which led them to openly resist what they perceived as a corrupt corporate elite allied with the political parties and the Church. The rebellion of the poor took various forms in the Middle Ages through the different religious orders, and the revolt of workers and students in the seventies similarly involved peaceful protests, political action, labor movements, etc. as well as the violent tactics of the Red Brigades who can be compared to the medieval Dolcinians, followers of Fra Dolcino, who are mentioned repeatedly in the novel as radical heretics for linking religious purity with the revolt of the poor and the need for violent resistance against the corruption of the wealthy.

Apocalyptics and Poverty

The revolt of the poor was also linked to the end times of the Apocalypse since the corruption of the Church was perceived by some elements of the Spiritual Franciscans as evidence of the Anti-Christ foretold in the Book of Revelation. The plight of the poor against the corruption of the Church was thus seen as a justified form of religious fervor that called for the violent overthrow of the wealthy and powerful to bring about a new age of religious purity. Similar to the Dolcinians, the Red Brigades were motivated in opposition to the corruption of government by corporate wealth and power, and they believed in a moral rebellion and revolutionary overthrow of the evils of capitalism that was supposed to bring about a Communist utopia similar to the Apocalyptics anticipation of an end to the evil of moral corruption followed by the reign of Christ.

POVERTY AND HERESY

The radical Dolcinians were considered heretical by the moderate wing of the Franciscan order because they took the principle of poverty to extremes and engaged in violence. More broadly, heresy was officially the condemnation by the papacy of any doctrine or practice that was seen as inconsistent with or counter to the beliefs and ideals of Christianity. The militant defense against heresy gave rise to the Inquisition practices of interrogation, torture, and execution. The assertion by the Franciscan Spirituals of the poverty of Christ was condemned by the Pope as heretical because it would undermine the papacy's attempts to maintain its power by adapting to the new money economy, as well as providing justification for uprisings by the poor. For the importance of these issues in Eco's first novel, it's useful to recall that Eco and his fellow leaders of the Catholic youth group at the University of Turin in the late fifties were expelled from the Church by the Pope as Communists and heretics for pursuing liberal reforms.

THE ELITE AND THE SIMPLE

The relation between elite intellectuals and popular culture, and Eco's practice as a public intellectual is also reflected in *The Name of the Rose*. There are numerous references to the role of visual images for the uncultivated who are referred to as "the simple." In William's discussion with the Abbot, he indicates that: "The life of the simple, Abo, is not illuminated by learning and by the lively sense of distinctions that makes us wise."[35]

Concerning the simple, Adso notes that:

> Often during our journey I heard William mention "the simple," a term by which some of his brothers denoted not only the populace but, at the same time, the unlearned. This expression always seemed to me generic, because in the Italian cities I had met men of trade and artisans who were not clerics but were not unlearned, even if their knowledge was revealed through the use of the vernacular."[36]

Adso acknowledges, however, that "images are the literature of the layman," and even he, as a novice monk, was completely enthralled by the images of the Apocalypse at the entrance to the church as the "silent speech of the carved stone" that "dazzled my eyes and plunged me into a vision that even today my tongue can hardly describe."[37] In reference to the doorway of the church that was so captivating for Adso, Jorge's fellow Apocalyptic Ubertino condemns the lavish decoration of the church as signs of the Anti-Christ: "There is no escaping the pride of images."[38] In this way, Eco also reflects in the novel on the problem that Italian postwar intellectuals saw in the degradation of knowledge and culture through the rise of the mass media and the problem of communicating between the knowledge of the elite and a popular audience. For example, in opposition to the Apocalyptics such as Jorge and Umbertino, who denounced the use of images to communicate with the illiterate, William, as a progressive Franciscan and follower of Roger Bacon, held a different view of the simple:

> Bacon believed in the strength, the needs, the spiritual inventions of the simple. He wouldn't have been a good Franciscan if he hadn't thought that the poor, the outcast, idiots and illiterate, often speak with the mouth of our Lord. The simple have something more than do learned doctors, who often become lost in their search for broad, general laws. The simple have a sense of the individual, but this sense, by itself, is not enough. The simple grasp a truth of their own, perhaps truer than that of the doctors of the Church, but then they destroy it in unthinking actions. What must be done? Give learning to the simple? Too easy, or too difficult. The Franciscan teachers considered this problem. The great Bonaventure said that the wise must enhance conceptual clarity with the truth implicit in the actions of the simple...[39]

The question of the role of intellectuals in relation to a popular audience is thus another aspect that made its way into Eco's first novel that allowed him to reflect on the scholarly elite who possess a knowledge of abstract generalities and the experience of the individual as part of a broad popular audience whose understanding of the world is increasingly communicated through visual media.

THE FAILED DETECTIVE

Consistent with a popular readership's conventional expectations for a detective story, the conclusion of *The Name of the Rose* features a dramatic confrontation between the detective and the perpetrator that includes a recounting of the detective's reasoning about the pattern of clues that uncovered the mystery, and the perpetrator's confession of his motives. The detective story is especially accessible to a popular readership just because of this expectation of an interpretive summary of the mysterious circumstances that provides closure to the questions that are raised by the plot. But while resolving the mystery of the murders, Eco's detective novel breaks with convention through the acknowledgment of failure on the part of the detective. Instead of the triumph of reason in resolving the mystery, William admits in the end that "There was no plot and I discovered it by mistake." He explains to Adso that: "I arrived at Jorge through an apocalyptic pattern that seemed to underlie all the crimes and yet it was accidental." And he dejectedly asks: "Where is all my wisdom then? I behaved stubbornly, pursuing a semblance of order, when I should have known well that there is no order in the universe." In his defense, Adso lists all of William's interpretive accomplishments beginning with the evidence for the runaway horse at their arrival, the suicide of the first dead monk, the layout of the labyrinth, the book by Aristotle on laughter, etc. Adso insists that: "... in imagining an erroneous order you still found something..." While gratefully accepting Ado's encouragement, William offers his assessment of the resolution of the mystery:

> Perhaps the mission of those who love mankind is to make people laugh at the truth, *to make truth laugh*, because the only truth lies in learning to free ourselves from insane passion for the truth.
>
> "The only truths that are useful are instruments to be thrown away."[40]

This conclusion is especially significant in relation to the circumstances of the Aldo Moro affair that involved the clash of conflicting ideologies that implicated and demoralized everyone.

Eco's "Postscript" to *The Name of the Rose* provides some useful hints for understanding more generally the conclusion of the novel. Eco notes that: "A text is meant to be an experience of transformation for its reader," and that: "The reader should learn something either about the world or about language." About *The Name of the Rose*, Eco suggests that:

> It is no accident that the book starts out as a mystery (and continues to deceive the ingenuous reader until the end, so the ingenuous reader may not even realize that this is a mystery in which very little is discovered and the detective is defeated).

Eco also addresses the reader directly:

> And then, if you are good, you will realize how I lured you into this trap, because I was really telling you about it at every step, I was carefully warning you that I was dragging you to your damnation...[41]

At the conclusion of the "Postscript" Eco adds that:

> It seems that the Parisian Oulipo group has recently constructed a matrix of all possible murder-story situations and has found that there is still to be written a book in which the murderer is the reader. Moral: there exist obsessive ideas, they are never personal; books talk amongst themselves, and any true detection should prove that we are the guilty party.[42]

The phenomenal popular readership of *The Name of the Rose* obviously found the novel immensely entertaining, and Eco indicates in the "Postscript" that: "I wanted the reader to enjoy himself, as least as much as I was enjoying myself." But Eco also asserted that: "The reader was to be diverted but not di-verted, distracted from problems." A popular readership was clearly motivated to learn more about the medieval world of the novel and to resolve some of its ambiguities which generated the "Postscript" as well as *The Key to "The Name of the Rose."* But beyond the possibility of learning useful comparisons between the Middle Ages and the contemporary world, Eco's narrative strategy was intended to overturn the reader's expectations for the conventional detective novel—which promises an unambiguous resolution attributable to a single cause—in order to make the reader aware of the problem of language and interpretation. Although the novel is set in the Middle Ages, the experience that confronts readers of *The Name of the Rose* is the contemporary labyrinth that has no single cause and no universal order because all paths intersect without a center or definable boundaries. William was successful in solving the plan of the library's labyrinth that was intended to disorient and conceal its mysteries, but he acknowledges that he "stubbornly" pursued an "erroneous" order, and thus was "defeated" in relation to the actual world where "there is no order," and conjectures about a single cause are mistaken. As Eco notes in the "Postscript," the "world in which William realizes he is living...can be structured but is never structured definitively."[43] Consequently the reader, along with

William, is implicated in pursuing the erroneous interpretation of a single truth that collapses at the conclusion similar to the effect of Allais' *A Most Parisian Episode*.

But given what seems to be the apparent success of the investigation based on William's summary of his interpretive path at the conclusion of the novel, Eco's assertion that "very little is discovered" and "the detective is defeated" may consequently seem unjustified. Like the typical detective story, the conclusion seems to provide the reader with a full explanation of the mysteries, and the detective defeats his adversary although with disastrous consequences. But, another look at the actual course of the investigation can allow us to consider Eco's hints about the failed detective.

A Confusion of Causes

In retrospect, we can see that the linking of the "seven trumpets"[44] of the Apocalypse to the circumstances of the deaths, as well as the focus on the labyrinth of the library, was not "discovered" by William at all. These investigative paths were acquired inadvertently by William from a potentially unreliable source, the elderly monk Alinardo. As the oldest of the monks—who considers even Jorge "young" by comparison—Alinardo is described by Adso as "ancient" and "addled,"[45] and by William and the other monks as "raving"[46] and "mad."[47] Although the connections between the deaths and the apocalypse seem to fit that pattern, they turn out to be accidental. And, ironically, when Jorge learns that William is pursuing a connection between the deaths and the apocalypse, he becomes convinced that "a divine plan was directing these deaths for which I was not responsible." William thus realizes in his final confrontation with Jorge in the library that: "I conceived a false pattern to interpret the moves of the guilty man, and the guilty man fell in with it. And it was this same false pattern that put me on your trail."[48] Thus, ironically, the murders were only accidentally linked to the apocalypse, but, because of William, Jorge took them to be actual links ordained by God. And William, by following the false lead of the apocalypse, accidentally happened upon the true lead to Jorge because of Jorge's longstanding associations with the books of the apocalyptic prophecy.

Although Jorge would seem to be the lone "guilty man" because he put poison in the corners of the pages of the forbidden book to safeguard it after he heard the other monks speculating about its existence, the deaths had various causes, and the connections to the apocalypse were accidental as indicated below:

1. Adelmo dies from suicide by jumping from the monastery wall into the snow, and his death is linked to the first trumpet signaled by hail thrown to the earth.
2. Venantius is poisoned by the book, but Berengar, wanting to deflect suspicion from himself, puts his body in the jar of blood—to make it look like drowning—which is interpreted as the second trumpet signaled by the oceans turning into blood.
3. Berengar is poisoned by the book, but he tries to overcome the fever brought on by the poison by going to the baths which is linked to the third trumpet signaled by the poisoning of fresh water.
4. Severinus is killed by Malachi—out of jealousy instigated by Jorge—by being struck on the head with the armillary sphere because it happened to be at hand in the infirmary, and his death is linked to the fourth trumpet signaled by darkness caused by the collision of the celestial spheres.
5. Malachi is also poisoned by the book even though he was warned by Jorge that it would unleash a thousand scorpions which is how the fifth trumpet is signaled.
6. The Abbot dies of suffocation by being locked in the passageway to the library by Jorge which is not associated with a sign of the apocalypse, but Jorge causes the fire in the library which is linked to the sixth trumpet that will bring fire, smoke, and brimstone (sulfer) as God's judgment and vengeance upon the earth.
7. Jorge dies by deliberately swallowing the pages of the book containing the poison which he links to the seventh trumpet: "Seal what the seven thunders have said and to not write it, take and devour it, it will make bitter your belly but to your lips it will be sweet as honey."[49]

William acknowledges being a "fool" for responding to a "remark of Alinardo's" that led him to believe that the deaths followed the seven trumpets of the Apocalypse:

> Hail for Adelmo and his death was a suicide. Blood for Venantius, and there it had been a bizarre notion of Berengar's; water for Berengar himself, and it

had been a random act; the third part of the sky for Severinus, and Malachi had struck him with the armillary sphere because it was the only thing he found handy. And finally scorpions for Malachi...[50]

Consequently the deaths correspond to the signs of the apocalypse, but only by accident, except in two instances: (1) Jorge tells Malachi that the book is plagued by scorpions, knowing that they represent the fifth trumpet, in an attempt to frighten him away from opening the book and being poisoned by it; and (2) Jorge poisons himself with the pages of the book in order to destroy it as a way of deliberately fulfilling the sign of the seventh trumpet. As William concludes after the fire:

> I arrived at Jorge seeking one criminal for all the crimes and we discovered that each crime was committed by a different person, or by no one. I arrived at Jorge pursuing the plan of a perverse and rational mind, and there was no plan, or, rather, Jorge himself was overcome by his own initial design and there began a sequence of causes, and concauses, and causes contradicting one another, which proceeded on their own, creating relations that did not stem from any plan.

Thus, as Eco indicates, "little is discovered and the detective is defeated." William, however, along with a popular readership, can at least feel triumphant about the ingenious discovery that "the plan of the library reproduces the map of the world."[51] But, as William also discovers, the mystery of the labyrinth of the world outside the library, like our contemporary world, has no plan, and thus its order and meaning cannot be ultimately discovered. While a popular readership may have believed that they found out everything that was necessary to know about the circumstances and final causes of the murders, Eco's hint that "very little is discovered and the detective is defeated" refers to the interpretive path followed by the detective, along with the reader, that turns out to be erroneous. Consequently it results in the detective's, and supposedly the reader's, defeat in relation to the normal expectations for a detective story. But in relation to the information provided by the narrative of the novel, the reader effectively discovers everything involved in the mysterious deaths while learning a great deal about the philosophical and religious controversies of the late Middle Ages. A popular readership could thus understandably be puzzled by Eco's reference to the "ingenuous reader " who would not recognize that the conventional expectations for a mystery novel had been deliberately overturned.

In an essay on Eco's intellectual practice for Johns Hopkins University Press, Deborah Parker and Carolyn Veldstra note that: "Eco argues that since mass culture is ubiquitous and inescapable, our efforts ought to focus on ensuring that it mediates positive values, and not the illusory, consolatory, oversimplified, and static values of kitsch."[52] *The Name of the Rose* achieved international recognition for deliberately posing difficult intellectual challenges for a popular readership by not pandering to the desire for "oversimplified" entertainment. But does *The Name of the Rose* effectively overcome the "consolatory" effect of popular culture that provides a temporary diversion while affirming uncritically the prevailing social ideology? While being amused, was a popular readership prodded into learning "something about the world or about language"?[53] Eco's first novel obviously provoked the curiosity of a broad popular readership into seeking a better understanding of its meaning that generated the "Postscript" as well as *The Key to "The Name of the Rose."* The reader's persistent inquiries indicate that the novel motivated them to learn, "something about the world," but was it effective in provoking the "disingenuous" reader into a reflection on "language"? This question can be explored further by considering the origins of the "failed detective" theme in contemporary Italian literature.

LEONARDO SCIASCIA AND THE ANTI-DETECTIVE NOVEL

The defeat of the detective, along with the reader, is what Eco intended as the experience of the intellect confronting the labyrinth of the world which can be seen as an example of what JoAnn Cannon has called the "anti-detective novel"[54] and what Eco has described as "self-voiding fictions" that "demonstrate their own impossibility."[55] As an anti-detective novel, Eco's narrative strategy can be compared to the work of the Sicilian author Leonardo Sciascia (1921–1989) who, according to a study by Joseph Farrell, "was the first Italian writer to make systematic use of the [detective] genre." While the detective novel had become a popular commodity in Italy during the postwar period through translations of foreign authors, no Italian author had adopted it as a deliberate literary strategy prior to the work of Sciascia. But Sciascia's detective stories depart from tradition by subverting the conventional role of the detective. Among his numerous writings, Sciascia wrote four detective novels which were published between 1961 and 1974, and therefore prior to the publication of Eco's first novel in 1980. The distinguishing feature of

Sciascia's detective novels is that the detective's role is either thwarted in solving the crime, the detective falls victim to the perpetrators, or the detective actually becomes a perpetrator. This narrative device allowed Sciascia to call attention to the insidious impact of corruption by the Mafia, and, by extension, with the party politics and ideological struggles that permeated Italy during the seventies and eighties.

As Joseph Farrell points out, Sciascia's detectives, who represent reason, social justice, and civic morality, become the victims rather than the redeemers of Italian society.[56] In the course of their investigations, they threaten rather than restore the social order and, as a result, are doomed to failure. In *Day of the Owl* (1961), set in Sicily, a man is gunned down in a public square. The investigating officer is from northern Italy and thus is ridiculed by the locals as a "mainlander." But the investigator is able to penetrate the local code of silence and extracts confessions from the principal suspects. In doing so, however, he uncovers links between the murderers and influential figures in the Sicilian contracting business who are, in turn, linked to powerful figures in the Italian parliament. As a result, he is suddenly transferred back to the north, the suspects retract their confessions, and "reliable" witnesses come forward to corroborate their "innocence." The investigator, in following the dictates of reason and justice, is defeated by a corrupt social order.

In *Equal Danger* (1971), the situation is even more volatile when the police inspector investigates a murderer who is targeting judges, and discovers a network of government and party officials who are engaged in collusion with the intelligence services to subvert the judicial process. The police inspector concludes that the entire system is corrupt, so he assassinates a corrupt official of the opposition party involved in the conspiracy, and then is murdered by his own police force. In the conventional detective story, the investigator triumphs over a threat to the moral order of society and confirms its values, but, with Sciascia, the situation is inverted such that the investigator finds himself at odds with a society that is corrupt at its core, including the clergy. In addition, in order to provoke a critical reflection on the passive complicity of individuals in maintaining a corrupt society, he called attention to the complicity of the reader who assumes "by custom and convention, a role of inferiority and intellectual passivity."[57] Like Eco, Sciascia was demoralized by the Moro Affair which motivated him to write a scathing denunciation of Italian political leaders of both major parties.[58] Sciascia considered Moro to be the "least implicated" in the events leading to his death,[59] and he accused the Christian

Democrats of refusing to negotiate with the Red Brigades so that Moro would become a "martyr-hero for their party."[60]

ALESSANDRO MANZONI'S *THE BETROTHED*

Besides the influence of the work of Borges and Sciascia, one further literary reference can serve to situate Eco's first narrative work in relation to the Italian literary tradition through a very brief consideration of one of the foundational texts in Italian literature, *The Betrothed* (*I Promessi Sposi*) by Alessandro Manzoni (1785–1873). In both the "Postscript" to *The Name of the Rose* and *Six Walks in the Fictional Woods*, Eco pays homage to Manzoni and the subtle stylistic effects of his classic novel, while acknowledging that his enthusiasm for *The Betrothed* is not generally shared by his fellow Italians because they are required to read it in school. *The Betrothed* was first published in 1827 and became an immediate success both in Italy and abroad where it was hailed as "the great Italian novel."[61] It subsequently engendered the modern emergence of a national Italian literature when it was rewritten in the Tuscan dialect, from the hybrid, literary Italian of the original, for a revised edition in 1840. In the "Postscript," Eco cites Manzoni as an example of the writer who resists the expectations of the reading public in order to construct a model reader: "Manzoni did not write to please the public as it was, but to create a public who could not help liking his novel."[62]

A number of thematic and stylistic similarities can be seen between Eco's first novel and Manzoni's classic of Italian literature. *The Betrothed* is generally considered to be one of the earliest examples of the historical novel which emerged during the late eighteenth and early nineteenth centuries. Manzoni, like Eco, also used numerous references to the reader, the act of reading, and the relation between the simple and the learned. For example, in *The Betrothed*, the mother of the bride notes that: "Poor folk like us see our troubles as more tangled than they really are, because we haven't got the key to them." What the common folk need, she suggests, is "the advice of a man who knows his books..."[63] Through the course of the novel, Manzoni's narrator often addresses the reader concerning the interpretation of the text, for example, by suggesting that "the reader can decide for himself" about aspects of the narrative, "if he feels like it."[64] Eco, in a similar way, includes references to the reader, for example, indirectly when William tells Adso that "you should learn to think with your own head,"[65] and directly when Adso writes that "I must make a confession to my reader," and when he uses the Latin expression "*De te fabula narratur*" (The story is about you).[66]

Foucault's Pendulum

Following the unprecedented popular reception of his first venture in narrative fiction and his resulting international recognition as a public intellectual, Eco's subsequent novels have pursued a similar strategy of provoking a popular readership to reflect on one's understanding of the world of language and culture. Eco's first novel was written to explore the clash of ideologies that was afflicting Italian society and more generally the confrontation of the intellectual with the problem of finding order and meaning in the contemporary world of mass media consumerism. In his second novel, *Foucault's Pendulum*, which was published eight years later in 1988, Eco again employs the detective genre while presenting the reader with a much more provocative confrontation with interpretive ethics.

Like *The Name of the Rose*, *Foucault's Pendulum* exploits the conventions of detective fiction in order to engage a popular readership with the mystery of obscure historical figures and esoteric intellectual and religious traditions that obviously appealed to an untapped desire for intellectual stimulation on the part of a broad, popular audience. *The Name of the Rose* deals with the corrupting effects of conflicting ideologies and the intellectual's confrontation with "the insane passion for the 'truth.'"[67] In a similar way, *Foucault's Pendulum* explores the problem of overinterpretation represented by the search for a secret truth pursued by an occult group of privileged initiates.

Foucault's Pendulum is set in the twentieth century but it also draws on Eco's foundations as a medievalist through a focus on the legacy of the Knights Templar from the early fourteenth century, the same period as *The Name of the Rose*. The mystique associated with the order is due to the legend that, after being disbanded by the French King Phillip IV in 1312 for being too powerful, its survivors held secret knowledge that was passed along to succeeding generations so that at some point in the future they would regain their dominant position of wealth and power. Eco's first two novels also share an organizational structure based on a religious tradition. *The Name of the Rose* is organized around the liturgical hours of worship of the medieval monastery and unfold over seven days corresponding to the seven trumpets of the *Book of Revelation*. *Foucault's Pendulum* is organized according to the ten *sefirot*, the ten forms of emanation from the infinite origin, drawn from the mystical tradition of the Jewish Kaballah. Similar to *The Name of the Rose*, *Foucault's Pendulum* includes cryptic passages in untranslated Latin, as well as Hebrew and other languages.

As in Eco's first novel, *Foucault's Pendulum* involves a mystery associated with books and interpretation. The three protagonists, Casaubon, Belbo, and Diotallevi, are editors for a publishing firm with two outlets. One produces mainstream works for mass publication while the other functions as a vanity press for unmarketable, self-financing authors. The mystery is instigated when the editors are approached by a shadowy figure, Colonel Ardenti, with an obsessive interest in the Knights Templar, who wants to publish a cryptic document he found with the hope of drawing the attention of a select group of messengers bearing a secret plan originating from the Templars who survived the purge in the fourteenth century. The Colonel mysteriously disappears and the editors become increasingly intrigued in deciphering his cryptic document when their enterprising publisher Garamond gives them the task, as part of "Project Hermes," to lure prospective clients from occult groups: "... the Plan first stirred in our minds... as a desire to give shape to shapelessness, to transform into fantasized reality that fantasy that others wanted to be real."[68] This scheme of literary deception, incidentally, is similar to the plot of Leonardo Sciascia's *The Council of Egypt*.

The success of the editors in promoting "the Plan" to lure deluded occultists as prospective clients for the vanity press has the unfortunate consequence of drawing them into the sphere of the "Diabolicals,"[69] the devotees of occult wisdom, who become convinced that the editors possess crucial information that will allow them to finally recover the secret knowledge left by the Templars. Through this encounter, they become trapped in a plot of their own making due to the occult principle that any attempt to deny that they possess secret knowledge will be seen as confirmation of its existence.

Hermetic Thought

As we considered previously, "Project Hermes" takes its name from the Greek god who "knows no spatial limits and may, in different shapes, be in different places at the same time."[70] Due to his ability as a shapeshifter who is not restricted by space and time, Hermes became associated with a long tradition of occult knowledge called "hermetic thought" that was pursued by individuals linked to the Templars, the Masons, the

HERMETIC THOUGHT 259

Rosicrucians, and other secret societies. In the novel, the master occultist Aglie describes the "spiritual knighthood" of the Templars as "a cohort of a few, a very few, elect wise men who journey through human history in order to preserve a core of eternal knowledge."[71] As the editors find out, this eternal knowledge is hidden but accessible, as Casaubon indicates, through "resemblance: the notion that everything might be mysteriously related to everything else."[72] The practitioners of hermetic thought can interpret the secret interconnectedness of things because they are not beholden to the conventional rules of logic and causality. When Belbo informs Aglie that an argument he cites is flawed as an example of "post hoc ergo ante hoc" because it would mean that "What follows causes what came before," Aglie replies that "You must not think linearly," and that "Time is an invention of the West."[73]

In their pursuit of "Project Hermes," the three editors initially begin to engage in a playful game of associations by considering everything as a possibility because "If we admit that in the whole universe there is even a single fact that does not reveal a mystery, then we violate hermetic thought." As a result, they determine that "The Templars have something to do with everything" even "Minnie Mouse."[74] The editors eventually use the random function of a computer in order to generate the interpretive possibilities of the secret document because, as Belbo points out:

> Any fact becomes important when it's connected to another. The connection changes the perspective; it leads you to think that every detail of the world, every voice, every word written or spoken has more than its literal meaning, that it tells of a Secret. The rule is simple: Suspect, only suspect. You can read subtexts even in a traffic sign that says "No littering."[75]

The Name of the Rose was written before the advent of the personal computer, and Eco actually drafted it in longhand and then had it typed by his secretary.[76] For his second novel, however, the new technology of the computer plays a prominent role because of its revolutionary way of instantly processing connections between words and ideas in either a logical or completely random manner. This technical capacity can be seen as a reflection of Peirce's idea of unlimited semiosis in which the meaning of a word is based on its relation to another word and so on indefinitely. But, for Eco, the hermetic mode of interpreting the truth represents unlimited semiosis run amok through links between words or ideas that are secret and elusive because they always point to something other than what they seem to be.

Since Eco's first novel is set in the Middle Ages, its significance for contemporary Italy can only be inferred through historical similarities. *Foucault's Pendulum*, however, is set in contemporary Italy, and there are direct references to particular aspects of Eco's personal history through the character of Belbo's memories of his childhood in a small rural village in northern Italy during the years of Italian fascism and the resistance against the German occupation. Eco has indicated in an interview that the character of Belbo is not autobiographical, but that some of the recollections by Belbo of his childhood are.[77] These stories are shared with the character Casaubon in conversation and through Belbo's computer files. Belbo tells Casaubon, for example, that "In 1943 I was eleven, and at the end of the war, barely 13," and that he "had been evacuated from the city in '43'" during the time of the resistance movement.[78] Eco was born in 1932, so, like Belbo, he was 11 years old in 1943, and 13 at the end of the war. In an interview, Eco recalled that: "To escape the bombings from September 1943 to April 1945—the most traumatic years in our nation's history—my mother, my sister, and I went to live in the countryside, up in Monferrato, a Piedmontese village that was at the epicenter of the resistance."[79] In the novel, Belbo tells Casaubon that during this time "some men on a distant hill were machine-gunning the railroad line in the valley behind me"[80] and having to dodge the bullets. Eco similarly recalled the memory of "shootouts between Fascists and Partisans" and "dodging a bullet myself."[81] Belbo makes reference to the "Salesian parish hall"[82] in the village, another point of intersection with Eco's early childhood at the Salesian oratorium of Don Bosco. In addition, Belbo's experience of the celebration at the end of the war, and his triumphant moment playing the trumpet for the funeral of the partisans is, as Eco has acknowledged, directly autobiographical.[83] In fact, Belbo's description in the novel of the celebration of the end of the war is nearly identical to Eco's personal recollection. The name of the resistance leader is changed in the novel, but otherwise Jacopo Belbo's account, as follows, is essentially the same as Eco's autobiographical account, below it, from his essay "Ur-Fascism" in *Five Moral Pieces:*

> On a balcony of the town hall, Mongo appeared, leaning on his crutch, pale, with one hand he tried to calm the crowd. Jacopo waited for the speech, because his whole childhood, like that of others his age, had been marked by the great historic speeches of Il Duce, whose most significant passages were memorized in school. Actually, the students memorized whole speeches,

HERMETIC THOUGHT 261

because every sentence was a significant declaration. Silence. Mongo spoke in a hoarse voice, barely audible. He said: "Citizens, friends. After so many painful sacrifices... here we are. Glory to those who have fallen for freedom." And that was it. He went back inside. The crowd yelled, and the partisans raised their submachine guns, their Stens, their shotguns, their '91 s, and fired festive volleys.[84]

Eco's personal account from "Ur-Fascism":

He appeared on the balcony of the town hall, pale; with one hand, he tried to calm the crowd. I was waiting for him to begin his speech, given that my entire early childhood had been marked by Mussolini's great historic speeches, the most important parts of which we used to memorize at school. Silence. Mimo's voice was hoarse, you could hardly hear him. He said: "Citizens, friends. After so many painful sacrifices... here we are. Glory to those who fell for freedom." That was it. He went back inside. The crowd gave a shout, the partisans raised their weapons and fired into the air in festive mood.[85]

Other than the circumstances of Eco's childhood during the war, and the fact that Eco also worked as an editor for an Italian publisher, the character of Belbo does not reflect other aspects of the life of Eco, the empirical author. Casaubon, however, as a student of the Middle Ages who spends some time in Brazil as a lecturer, closely reflects Eco's own experience as an academic in Brazil where he attended two cult rituals that he wrote about in the essay "Whose Side Are the Orixa On?" from *Travels in Hyperreality*. In *Foucault's Pendulum*, the occult scholar Aglie takes Casaubon and his girlfriend Amparo to a Brazilian ritual called an "umbanda" where: "The participants will be possessed... by the eguns, spirits of the departed" including "Exu the African Hermes..."[86] At the ritual, Aglie points out "a blonde, a German psychologist who had been participating in the rites for years" but for whom "the trance never came."[87] In the essay from *Travels in Hyperreality*, Eco writes about a cult ritual he attended where his guides "point out a blonde to me: a German psychologist" who participates "in the eager hope of going into a trance." But she becomes "distraught, trying to lose control," and "does not succeed."[88] At the same ritual in the novel, Amparo, who prided herself on being a non-believer, begins to feel nauseous and wants to leave, but she succumbs to a trance state and afterwards suffers an emotional crisis that causes her to sever the relationship with Casaubon.[89] In the essay from *Travels In Hyperreality*, Eco recalls that: "In our party there is a fifteen-year-old European girl with her parents." Like Amparo, she begins "sweating," "feels nausea," and "wants to go outside." The guide advises her parents to let her stay because "the girl clearly has mediumistic qualities," but "the girl wants to leave," and "her parents are frightened."[90]

THE ANTI-HERO

Although Belbo's character is only linked to a particular episode in Eco's childhood during the war, his role in the novel can be seen as a reflection of Eco's conception of the anti-hero which is set out in an essay entitled "Why Are They Laughing in Those Cages?" from 1982 in response to the trial of the assassins of Aldo Moro that appears in *Travels in Hyperreality*:

> Real heroes, those who sacrifice themselves for the collective good, are always people who act *reluctantly*. They die, but they would rather not die; they kill, but they would rather not kill; and in fact afterwards they refuse to boast of having killed in a condition of necessity. Real heroes are always impelled by circumstances; they never choose because, if they could, they would choose not to be heroes..... The real hero is always a hero by mistake; he dreams of being an honest coward like everyone else.... He suffers and keeps his mouth shut; if anything, others then exploit him, making him a myth, while he, the man worthy of esteem, was only a poor creature who reacted with dignity and courage in an event bigger than he was.[91]

In *Foucault's Pendulum*, Belbo is thrust into circumstances by mistake which he afterwards tries to avoid, but he defiantly confronts his death by being hung from the pendulum with dignity and courage in a situation that overwhelms him. Casaubon notes that, after Belbo dies from being hung from the pendulum, the wire from the vault wrapped around Belbo's neck became stationary. As a result, according to Casaubon, "the sphere moved, but only from his body down" while the rest "remained perpendicular": "Thus Belbo had escaped the error of the world and its movements, had now become, himself, the point of suspension, the Fixed Pin, the Place from which the vault of the world is hung..."[92] Belbo as anti-hero had become the axis of his own truth as an individual. Eco's conception of the reluctant anti-hero is consistent with his critique of popular culture heroes such as Superman and James Bond whose superhuman exploits provide a temporary fantasy outlet for overcoming the relative powerlessness of the consumer which, however, confirms those conditions without raising one's awareness of the world.

FICTION AND THEORY INTERTWINED

Foucault's Pendulum includes a number of references to other aspects of Eco's intellectual practice. For example, in relation to Eco's interpretation theory, one of the Diabolicals suggests that "the ideal reader of a collection of this sort would be a Rosicrucian adept,"[93] and Casaubon, while awaiting his death by the Diabolicas at the conclusion of the novel, reflects that "the author has to die in order for the reader to become aware of this truth."[94] Some of Eco's major influences are also mentioned in the novel. For example, one of the characters "spoke in despairing tones reminiscent of Funes, 'el memorioso' of Borges."[95] Quotations are also drawn from James Joyce. In Belbo's computer files a character is quoted as saying "Here Comes Everybody,"[96] and another mentions "An incomprehensible message: 'riverrun, past Eve and Adam's'"[97] which are drawn from *Finnegans Wake*. Eco even quotes loosely from his first novel through the concluding remarks of Adso the narrator of *The Name of the Rose* that "It is cold in the scriptorium, my thumb aches"[98] which is paraphrased in a story from Belbo's computer files as "I am cold in this dungeon, and my thumb hurts."[99] Eco refers as well to the relation between elite and popular culture in a quote from an occult source that "These texts are not addressed to common mortals... Gnostic perception is a path reserved for an elite... For, in the words of the Bible: Do not cast your pearls before swine."[100]

IRRITATING THE READER

Eco has stated that *Foucault's Pendulum* was "conceived to irritate the reader": "I knew it would provoke ambiguous, nonhomogenuous responses because it was a book conceived to point up some contradictions."[101] Like the narrative strategy of *The Name of the Rose*, Eco's second novel uses the genre of the detective novel while frustrating the expectations of a popular readership in a much more confrontational manner. Although Eco's second novel is similar to *The Name of the Rose* as an anti-detective novel, as well as through the thematic focus on obscure religious and philosophical controversies, the narrative strategy of *Foucault's Pendulum* can be seen as the deliberate avoidance of the tendency of writers of bestselling popular fiction to closely replicate the content of their previous success, for example, as in the sequels to *The Da Vinci Code* by Dan Brown. Eco's intention to irritate the reader may also have been motivated by the legacy of the Gruppo 63 that caused intellectuals to reflect more carefully on the difference between "a work for popular consumption and a work for provocation" that he discussed in the "Postscript" to *The Name of the Rose*.[102]

Eco had previously intended *The Name of the Rose* as a "work for provocation" by frustrating the expectations of first-level readers, but it's not clear that the conclusion of the novel would have had the full effect of the anti-detective novel as a self-voiding fiction. *Foucault's Pendulum*, in comparison, functions more closely on the model of Sciascia's anti-detective stories while adhering to Eco's focus on exploring the historical mysteries of religion and philosophy by confronting the reader with an even more daunting journey through a dense forest of obscure historical references. As an indicator of Eco's more provocative approach in his second novel, consider the conclusion of *Foucault's Pendulum* when Casaubon is waiting for the inevitable confrontation with the Diabolicals:

> I have understood. And the certainty that there is nothing to understand should be my peace, my triumph. But I am here, and They are looking for me, thinking I possess the revelation they sordidly desire. It isn't enough to have understood, if others refuse and continue to interrogate.... They know I am here now, They still want the Map. And when I tell Them that there is no Map, They will want it all the more. Belbo was right. Fuck you, fool! You want to kill me? Kill me, then, but I won't tell you there's no Map. If you can't figure it out for yourself, tough shit.

If, instead of referring to the Diabolicals, "They," above, is seen as a reference to a horde of popular readers of detective novels beseeching Eco for the secret meaning of the novel, one can get a sense of how Eco's second novel was intended to "irritate the reader" in a very direct and provocative manner.

The narrative of Eco's second novel also functions, in an even more irritatingly confrontational way, as an anti-detective story to frustrate the expectations of a popular readership because the mystery at the outset of the novel is, in fact, whether the disappearance of the occult figure Ardenti actually involved a murder, a kidnapping or simply a sudden departure. Typical of Eco's use of humor in pointing to the role of the reader, the police inspector suggests a number of hypotheses without a clear idea of how to proceed, which leads him to conclude that: "It all sounds too much like a novel," and that: "Life isn't simple, the way it is in detective stories."[103] Unlike the typical detective story, the police can't confirm that a crime actually occurred, and the police investigation is sidelined when, like Sciascia's failed detectives, inspector De Angelis is thwarted by the protagonists and eventually forced to give up the case after being threatened by the Diabolicals. The "mystery" instead involves an interpretive project by the three editors as literary and historical detectives. Belbo, for example, refers to Casaubon as "the Sam Spade of culture."[104] The focus of their investigation is the interpretation of the document left by Ardenti, even though the editors recognize that the document is a lunatic's obsession.

Instead of inquiring into its meaning as a potentially valid historical document, they use it as a lure to exploit the occult fringe groups who see connections between the Temple of Jerusalem and everything including UFOs, Aryanism, the Kabbala of Jewish mysticism, the pyramids, and Columbus's signature."[105] Rather than serving as agents of interpretive discovery, the editors become perpetrators of an interpretive fraud and inadvertently become victims of their own cleverness when the Diabolicals turn out to be real and are persuaded that the three editors possess the secret they desire.

THE DETECTIVES AS PERPETRATORS AND VICTIMS

The narrative strategy of *Foucault's Pendulum* thus involves a topsy turvy approach to the conventional detective story. To begin with, as indicated above, the initial mystery is whether there is actually a crime to investigate. And, as Linda Hutcheon has noted, the crime in *Foucault's Pendulum* occurs at the end of the novel rather than the beginning.[106] As in Sciascia's crime novels, the police detective, rather than solving the mystery, becomes the victim of the investigation. Furthermore, instead of the suspects selecting their victims, the victims select their suspects by luring them with the cryptic document. The murders occur as the direct outcome of the investigative inquiry by the three editors, instead of the investigation serving as a means of resolving or thwarting the crime. The investigation by the three editors also subverts the conventions of detective fiction because, instead of the detective progressively narrowing the number of suspects, the investigation by the editors causes them instead to continuously proliferate.

In negotiating this convoluted investigative path, the reader is confronted with a seemingly endless succession of references to historical figures that are linked in increasingly obscure ways to the plan of the Templars. The narrative strategy was thus designed to "irritate" the naive reader who is looking for narrative closure while encouraging the reader's participation by the ingenious ways in which the three editors manage to adapt the plan to the occult groups that they encounter. And just when the reader comes to share with the three editors the satisfaction of having finally decoded the mysterious document, Casaubon's wife, Lia, demonstrates, through a much simpler mode of analysis, that their intellectually compelling efforts were a classic case of overinterpretation by revealing that the cryptic document is nothing more than a mundane "laundry list"[107] of a merchant.

Laughing at the Reader

At the end of *Foucault's Pendulum*, Causabon offers some final thoughts about the Plan and the response by the Dabolicals:

> I would have liked to write down everything I thought today. But if They were to read it, They would only derive another dark theory and spend another eternity trying to decipher the secret message hidden behind my words. It's impossible, They would say; he can't only have been making fun of us.[108]

If "They," again, is substituted for a popular readership, "they" will certainly find ample evidence that Eco, in his second novel, is clearly having fun at the reader's expense through his characteristic flare for humor and satire. The use of humor as a critical antidote to "the insane passion for the truth"[109] was a central theme of Eco's first novel, but the playful use of humor is more fully integrated as an essential component of the narrative strategy of *Foucault's Pendulum*. For example, when Casaubon tries to gain access to the files on Belbo's computer, and the computer prompt asks him "Do you have the password?",[110] he tries an exhaustive array of complex formulas including all possible permutations of the tetragrammaton, the four letters of the Hebrew name for God, until finally "drunk" and "in a fit of hate," he types "no" and instantly achieves access.[111] A perfect example of an overinterpretation is thus resolved in the simplest, most logical manner possible.

There are numerous instances of this playfulness throughout the text such as Belbo's explanation of "the four kinds of people in the world: cretins, fools, morons, and lunatics,"[112] and the witty exchange of "Oxymoronics" for Belbo's "School of Comparative Irrelevance" that includes "Urban Planning for Gypsies."[113] Another example would be Eco's use of a quote from Joseph Heller's novel *Catch 22* among the many citations from otherwise obscure and arcane texts beginning each chapter:

"What does the fish remind you of." "Other fish." "And what do other fish remind you of?" "Other fish."[114]

Eco also cites Woody Allen's "Metterling List" from *Getting Even* (the book that Eco and Cathy Berberian translated into Italian in 1962): "6 undershirts, 6 shorts, 6 handkerchiefs...[which] has always puzzled scholars principally because of the total absence of socks."[115] And while discussing the historical contexts of occult organizations such as the Masons and the Rosicrucians, Eco makes frequent reference to pop culture phenomena such as Sam Spade,[116] Minnie Mouse,[117] Superman,[118] the Pink Panther,[119] and Rick's Cafe[120] from the movie *Casablanca* starring Humphrey Bogart (1942). The use of humor and the many references to pop culture icons serve to underscore Eco's practice as a public intellectual who bridges between elite and popular culture. While *The Name of the Rose* is more accessible to first-level readers because of its greater conformity to the conventions of detective fiction, *Foucault's Pendulum* can be seen as more effective as a self-voiding fiction in frustrating the expectations of a popular readership. Perhaps because of this "irritating" narrative strategy, Eco tried to humor a popular readership throughout the novel so that they would endure its annoying intellectual challenges.

THE ISLAND OF THE DAY BEFORE

Eco stated in an interview that his third novel was intended to explore the notion of "desire." Because he imagined an unreachable island, it also became an homage to Robinson Crusoe.[121] In *The Island of the Day Before*, Eco shifts from the genre of detective fiction to that of the adventure story and romance novel by again playing with the expectations of a popular readership while engaging them with his usual synthesis of historical exploration, the relation between elite and popular culture, and a reflection on language and interpretive ethics.

The Island of the Day Before tells the story of Roberto della Griva, a reluctant seventeenth-century adventurer, who finds himself a lone survivor of a shipwreck who, instead of washing ashore, becomes stranded on an abandoned ship, the Daphne, with its provisions intact, between a distant coastline on one side and an island on the other. Unable to swim, he is condemned to an indefinite solitude. Similar to Eco's first two novels, the story focuses on a manuscript, and, like *The Name of the Rose*, it involves an unnamed narrator who recounts the story based on Roberto's recovered letters which shift between the circumstances of his life before and after being shipwrecked. For Roberto, the Daphne thus becomes a "Theater of Memory" in which "every feature recalled to him an episode, remote or recent, in his story."[122]

These tales of adventure, war, romance, espionage, and seafaring, drawn from the memory of Roberto, occupy the first half of the novel. In the second half, he tries to console himself, in his solitude, by deciding to "construct a story" that "would not take place in this world but in a Land of Romances":

> By inventing the story of another world, which existed only in his mind, he would become that world's master, able to ensure that the things that happened there would not exceed his capacity of endurance. On the other hand, as reader of the story whose author he was, he could share in the heartbreak of its characters.

Readers thus find themselves stranded along with Roberto in a narrative that seemed initially to conform to the classic adventure story and romance novel that appeal to the desire for heroic exploits, travel to distant and exotic lands, and the consummation, after many travails, of long deferred passions. But these events occupy only the first half of the novel without resolution, and only as the recollection of Roberto while isolated on an immovable ship within sight of an island that he is unable to reach that, by international convention, is physically located, relative to Roberto, as the day before and thus the historical past. The adventure/romance narrative is thus suspended, and the remainder of the novel is taken up with Roberto's construction of a "romance," while immobilized on the stranded ship, whose "events would unfold parallel" to the world he occupied with "the two sets of adventures never meeting and overlapping."[123] The island of the novel's title thus represents unfulfilled desire, like Roberto's love for the Lady Lilia, and his attempts to recover the past as a "Theater of Memory."

THE ANTI-ROMANCE NOVEL

Eco's third novel, like the previous two, appropriates the narrative structures and stylistic mechanisms of a prominent genre of popular fiction while subverting the conventional expectations of popular readers in order to redirect their attention to their role as collaborators in generating a vision of the world. For this purpose, the novel includes a number of self-reflexive references to these genres of popular fiction in order to provoke a reflection on the way that stories, like language and culture, form our relationship with the world, and our role as either passive or active collaborators in generating its meaning. Early on, for example, the narrator notes about Roberto that his "situation is the stuff of a novel," which is followed by numerous references to storytelling concerning Roberto's manuscript, including that he "ignores the Laws of Genre."[124] The narrator tells us, for example, that, as a young man, "Roberto spent his time...daydreaming of distant lands" and was "inspired" by "romances and chivalric poems."[125] The character Saint-Savin, Roberto's mentor and the model of a romantic hero, acknowledges to Roberto that "I would like to write romances."[126] But, at the same time, he advises Roberto that:

> You have read too many romances...and you try to live one. But the purpose of a story is to teach and please at once, and what it teaches is how to recognize the snares of the world.

Roberto thus recalls Cervantes' *Don Quixote* (1615) who tries to impose on the "real" world the adventures he had encountered in romance novels. As a curative for Roberto's overreliance on romance stories, Saint-Savin advises him that:

> Often men, rather than admit they are the authors of their fate, see this fate as a romance narrated by a fanciful and scoundrel author.

Other allusions to famous scenes from classical romances include the play *Cyrano de Bergerac*, (1897) for example, when Roberto falls in love for the first time, and Saint-Savin dictates a love letter for him because of Roberto's youthful inexperience: "When nature fails, we turn to art." When Roberto questions whether the letter to the lady will be "comprehensible," Saint-Savin responds in a way that reflects Eco's attitude toward a reading public: "The truth is all the more appreciated when it is barbed with difficulties, and a revelation is more respected if it has cost us dearly."[127] And, like Cyrano, when Saint-Savin is challenged to a duel for insulting Monsieur l'Abbe, he responds by giving him, "between a feint and a parry, a lesson in natural philosophy."[128] Even the narrator declares at one point that: "You would think that I was narrating a romance"[129] and elsewhere characterizes his narrative as "our tentative romance,"[130] while making reference to the classic medieval romance, the "Chanson de Roland."[131] The narrator announces at other points his direct intervention in the story, for example, by "freeing [Roberto] from all illness, with authorial arrogance."[132]

Typical of his assertion, from the "Postscript" to *The Name of the Rose* that "books talk among themselves,"[133] Eco has included several intertextual references to his own novels as well. The narrator, for example, includes amusing references to *The Name of the Rose* by noting about Roberto that "he is the sort of author who, to postpone the unmasking of the murderer, gives the reader only the scantiest of clues."[134] Later in the text, the narrator indicates that the captain of the shipwrecked vessel "had read of people who died by wetting a finger with saliva as they leafed through works whose pages had in fact been smeared with a poison,"[135] and that "if from this story I wanted to produce a novel, I would demonstrate once again that it is impossible to write except by making a palimpsest of a rediscovered manuscript."[136] From *Foucault's Pendulum*, Eco includes mention of the "secret" of the "Rosy Cross,"[137] and to an underground passage from Saint-Martin-des-Champs which was the site of the dramatic confrontation with the Diabolicals in *Foucault's Pendulum*.[138] There is a reference as well to "a territory of forked paths"[139] as an allusion to the influence of Jorge Luis Borges. These instances indicate Eco's clever combination of intellectual engagement with a playful attitude toward the reader's interactive participation with the text, for example, when the narrator indicates that "Nor could I elude the childish curiosity of the reader who would want to know if Roberto really wrote the pages in which I have dwelt for so long."[140]

The Multiple Worlds of the Baroque

Whereas *The Name of the Rose* was intended to provoke a reflection on the insane passion for the truth through the antidote of laughter, and *Foucault's Pendulum* with a reflection on the problem of overinterpretation through the example of hermetic thought, *The Island of the Day Before*, with its evocation of parallel worlds, explores the desire for meaning in a world of multiple perspectives through a reflection on the mentality of the Baroque period of seventeenth-century Europe. In *The Open Work*, from 1962, Eco had cited the Baroque as the "first clear manifestation of modern culture and sensitivity" in which "for the first time, man opts out of the canon of authorized responses and finds that he is faced (both in art and in science) by a world in a fluid state which requires corresponding creativity on his part."[141] Roberto's turn to a parallel world of romances, and the island facing him that exists in a parallel time zone are suggestions of the mindset of the Baroque conception of multiple worlds and the role of the spectator which is explored throughout the novel. For example, the narrator discusses the notion of the "theater of the visible arranged in the basin of Space" as a representative idea of "that bizarre century" as well as the conception of an "infinity of worlds."

> What he saw was not just the message the sky was sending him but the result of a friendship among sky, earth, and the position (and the hour, the season, the angle) from which he was observing. Surely, if the ship were anchored along another line crossing the rhombus of the winds, the spectacle would have been different. The sun, the dawn, the sea and land would have been another sun, another dawn, a sea and land twins but distorted. That infinity of worlds of which Saint-Savin spoke to him was to be sought beyond the constellations, in the very center of this bubble of space of which he, pure eye, was now the source of infinite parallaxes.[142]

As Eco indicated in *The Open Work*, the Baroque is the period that ushers in our modern mentality by breaking out of the bonds of a static, predetermined, univocal conception of the universe that is independent of the way we perceive it. The Baroque celebrated multiple perspectives, the dynamic experience of time, and a consciousness of the role of the spectator in creating the world. Eco notes that "Baroque form is dynamic; it tends to an indeterminacy of effect" because it "never allows a privileged, definitive frontal view..."[143] The Baroque signaled a dramatic transition from the fixed, ordered hierarchy that had reflected the earlier imperial and theocratic social order by fostering a sense of infinite perspectives which is reflected in Saint-Savin's reference to Giordano Bruno's vision of infinity in his duel with the Abbe:

> Your holy Roman Church has taught you that this ball of mud of ours is the center of the Universe, which turns around it, acting as its minstrel and strumming the music of the spheres.... But what if, in the great Void, infinite worlds are moving, as a great philosopher said before your similars burned him in Rome, and very many of them are inhabited by creatures like us, and what if all had been created by your God, where does the Redemption then fit?[144]

This fluidity of perception is also indicated by the narrator's comments that Roberto seemed to be

> lost in the remaking of Himself from too many perspectives [in] a world now without any center, made up only of perimeters, here he felt himself truly in the most extreme and most lost of peripheries; because, if there was a center, it lay before him, and he was its immobile satellite.[145]

The narrator notes that: "Roberto practiced a sort of principle of double—indeed, multiple—truths, an idea that in Paris many considered at once foolhardy and prudent."[146] These allusions to the fracturing of perception, parallel and multiple worlds, and irony suggest how the Baroque was the transitional period into the contemporary aesthetics of openness that Eco first theorized about in *The Open Work*.

The novel's focus on the Baroque sense of infinite worlds and multiple perspectives based on the gaze of the spectator is also linked to the focus on laughter from *The Name of The Rose* but now in reference to God: "Could such a God, master of geometry, produce the disorder of Hell, even if, out of justice, and could He laugh at the subverting of every subversion?"[147] If the Baroque period acknowledged a plurality of worlds without a center, where was the place for God as the center of creation other than a God who laughs at the pathetic attempts of humans to impose a single order on the cosmos? The novel includes as well an inquiry concerning the nature of language and being: "For that matter, sir, how can you define being? To define it, it would be necessary to say that it is something. Thus to define being you would first have to say *is* and therefore use in the definition the term being defined."[148] This recalls our consideration in Chapter 3 of the problem of the word "is" that originated in ancient Greek philosophy.

THE PROVOCATEUR OF POPULAR CULTURE

Eco's novels engage in various strategies for provoking the reader into exploring our contemporary problem of finding ourselves in the world through interpretation. *Baudolino* (2001), *The Prague Cemetery* (2011), and *Numero Zero* (2015) for example, all deal in different ways with Eco's conception of semiotics as a "theory of the lie" while exploring narrative strategies for playing with the reader's expectations and easy enjoyment of the novel. *Baudolino* is the story of a peasant who acquires the knowledge and linguistic skills of the elite and creates his own fantastical history. Although its characters, other than the protagonist, are all drawn from history, *The Prague Cemetery* deals with the infamous lie of the document known as *The Protocols of the Elders of Zion*, referred to in *Foucault's Pendulum*, that was appropriated by Hitler as justification for the holocaust. As another example of his provocative narrative strategy, Eco has said about *The Prague Cemetery* that "My intention was to punch the reader in the stomach" by making the main character as unlikable and offensive as possible.[149] In *The Mysterious Flame of Queen Loana* (2005), Eco overturns the expectations generated by his previous novels of arousing the curiosity of a popular readership about the world of elite culture, by exploring the situation of a member of elite culture, an antiquarian bookseller, trying to recover his memory through the products of popular culture from his childhood. Eco's final novel, *Numero Zero*, returns to the focus on the theory of the lie while satirizing the Italian publishing industry through a fabricated account that Mussolini survived after the liberation of Italy and was aided by Church authorities to escape to Argentina to await the revival of a fascist state. Like *Foucault's Pendulum*, *Numero Zero* includes several references to the ideological struggles of postwar Italy through figures such as Aldo Moro and the Red Brigades.

The value of Eco's narrative strategies for the development of a critical consciousness is emphasized in a passage from *The Island of the Day Before*. As indicated previously, Saint-Savin, in counseling Roberto on the drafting of his first letter, asserts that: "The truth is all the more appreciated when it is barbed with difficulties, and a revelation is more respected if it has cost us dearly."[150] Through Eco's exploration of the problem of interpretive ethics in his turn to the novel beginning in 1980, as well as through his journalistic writings since 1960, Eco has developed a distinctive practice as a public intellectual by imposing rigorous demands on a popular readership. He leads them through an unresolved maze of dense historical references and arcane conceptions to arouse an awareness of the fallacy of passively seeking a tidy narrative closure. He plays games with readers' assumptions, and pokes fun at their conformity to convention. He provides just enough narrative thrust to sustain the reader while progressively undermining their facile participation in the course of the narrative's development. These efforts are intended to entertain a popular readership in the broadest sense such that their initial hopes for enjoyment of the text are overturned but their full engagement with the text will bring about a transformative awareness. In *The Island of the Day Before*, the narrator addresses the reader directly at one point concerning the nature of the truth:

> All that the Sacred Scriptures contain *prima facie* shines like silver, but its hidden meaning glows like gold. The inviolable chastity of the word of God, hidden from the eyes of the profane, is as if covered by a veil of modesty and remains in the shadow of mystery. It says that pearls must not be cast before swine. Having the eyes of a dove means not stopping at the literal meaning of words but knowing how to penetrate their mystical sense.[151]

NOTES

1. Bondanella, Peter, *Umberto Eco and the Open Text*, p. 125.
2. Eco, "On Some Functions of Literature," from *On Literature*, translated by Martin McLaughlin (Orlando, Harcourt, Inc., 2004), p. 1.
3. Ginsborg, Paul, *A History of Contemporary Italy*, (London: Penguin Books, 1990), p. 220.
4. Sassoon, Donald, *Contemporary Italy Economy, Society, and Politics since 1945*, (London: Addison Wesley Longman Limited, 1997), p. 262.
5. Clark, Martin, *Modern Italy, 1871–1982*, (London: Longman Publishing Group, 1985), p. 362
6. p. 10.
7. *Writers and Society in Contemporary Italy*, p. 10.
8. Eco, "Postscript" to *The Name of the Rose*, p. 509.

NOTES 275

9. The English translation was published in Eco's *Travels in Hyperreality*, pp. 113–118.
10. Eco, *Travels in Hyperreality*, p. 175.
11. Eco, *Travels in Hyperreality*, p. 123.
12. Lilli, Laura, *Voci Dall'Alfabeto, Interviste con Sciascia, Moravia, Eco nei decenni Settanta e Ottanta*, (Roma: Edizioni minimum fax, 1995), *Voices of the Alphabet, Interviews with Sciascia, Moravia, Eco in the Seventies and Eighties*, p. 85. Translation is my own.
13. Lilli, Laura, *Voci Dall'Alfabeto*, pp. 84–85.
14. Eco, "How and Why I Write," from Bouchard, Norma and Pravadelli, Veronica *Umberto Eco's Alternative, The Politics of Culture and the Ambiguities of Interpretation*, (New York: Peter Lang Publishing, Inc., 1998) p. 281.
15. Eco, "How and Why I Write," from *Umberto Eco's Alternative*, p. 283.
16. Eco, "How and Why I Write," from *Umberto Eco's Alternative*, p. 284.
17. Eco, "Postscript" to *The Name of the Rose*, p. 525.
18. Eco, *Confessions of a Young Novelist*, (Cambridge: Harvard University Press, 2011), p. 6.
19. Eco, "Postscript" to *The Name of the Rose*, pp. 525–526.
20. From the introduction by Lino Pertile to *The New Italian Novel*, edited by Zygmunt Baraski and Lino Pertile, p. 1.
21. Caesar, Michael and Hainsworth, Peter, *Writers and Society in Contemporary Italy*, (New York: St. Martin's Press, 1984), p. 16.
22. Colleen Barry, "Umberto Eco, author of 'The Name of the Rose,' dead at 84," Associated Press, February, 20, 2016.
23. Caesar, Michael and Hainsworth, Peter, *Writers and Society in Contemporary Italy*, pp. 16–19.
24. Eco, "Postscript" to *The Name of the Rose*, p. 518.
25. Eco, *The Name of the Rose*, p. 130.
26. Eco, *The Name of the Rose*, p. 131.
27. Eco, *The Name of the Rose*, p. 132.
28. Eco, *The Name of the Rose*, p. 468.
29. Eco, *The Name of the Rose*, p. 474.
30. Eco, *The Name of the Rose*, p. 478.
31. Eco, *A Theory of Semiotics*, p. 64.
32. Eco, *The Name of the Rose*, p. 49.
33. Eco, *The Name of the Rose*, p. 131.
34. Eco, *The Name of the Rose*, p. 200.
35. Eco, *The Name of the Rose*, p. 152.
36. Eco, *The Name of the Rose*, p. 188.
37. Eco, *The Name of the Rose*, p. 41.
38. Eco, *The Name of the Rose*, p. 61.

39. Eco, *The Name of the Rose*, p. 205.
40. Eco, *The Name of the Rose*, pp. 491–492.
41. Eco, *The Name of the Rose*, pp. 524–526.
42. Eco, The Name of the Rose, p. 535.
43. Eco, *The Name of the Rose*, p. 526.
44. Eco, *The Name of the Rose*, p. 159.
45. Eco, *The Name of the Rose*, p. 94.
46. Eco, *The Name of the Rose*, p. 470.
47. Eco, *The Name of the Rose*, p. 465.
48. Eco, *The Name of the Rose*, p. 470.
49. Eco, *The Name of the Rose*, pp. 480–481.
50. Eco, *The Name of the Rose*, pp. 469–470.
51. Eco, *The Name of the Rose*, p. 314.
52. Deborah Parker and Carolyn Veldstra, *The John Hopkins Guide to Literary Theory and Criticism*, (Baltimore: Johns Hopkins University Press, Second Edition, 2005).
53. Eco, *The Name of the Rose*, p. 526.
54. JoAnn Cannon, *Postmodern Italian Fiction*, p. 9.
55. Eco, *Six Walks in the Fictional Woods*, p. 81.
56. Farrell, Joseph, *Leonardo Sciascia*, (Edinburgh: Edinburgh University Press, 1995)p. 61.
57. Farrell, Joseph, *Leonardo Sciascia*, p. 65.
58. Sciascia, Leonardo, *The Moro Affair*, (New York: Carcanet Press Limited, 1987).
59. Sciascia, *The Moro Affair*, p. 17.
60. Cannon, JoAnn, *Postmodern Italian Fiction, the Crisis of Reason in Calvino, Eco, Sciascia, Malerba*, (Rutherford: Farleigh Dickinson University Press, 1989), p. 27.
61. From the introduction to the English language version of *The Betrothed* by the translator Bruce Penman, (Middlesex, England: Penguin Classics, 1972), p. 11.
62. Eco, "Postscript" to *The Name of the Rose*, p. 524.
63. Manzoni, Alessandro, *The Betrothed*, p. 61.
64. Manzoni, Alessandro, *The Betrothed*, p. 114.
65. Eco, *The Name of the Rose* p. 139.
66. Eco, *The Name of the Rose*, p. 322. The translation of the Latin is from *The Key to "The Name of the Rose,"* p. 155.
67. Eco, *The Name of the Rose*, 491.
68. Eco *Foucault's Pendulum*, pp. 280–281.
69. Eco, *Foucault's Pendulum*, p. 300.
70. Eco, *Interpretation and Overinterpretation*, p. 29.
71. Eco, *Foucault's Pendulum*, p. 174.

72. Eco, *Foucault's Pendulum*, p. 139.
73. Eco, *Foucault's Pendulum*, p. 282.
74. Eco, *Foucault's Pendulum*, p. 312.
75. Eco *Foucault's Pendulum*, p. 314.
76. Lila Azam Zanganeh, "Umberto Eco: The Art of Fiction, No. 197," *The Paris Review*, Summer 2008, No. 185.
77. Lila Azam Zanganeh, "Umberto Eco: The Art of Fiction, No. 197," *The Paris Review*, Summer 2008, No. 185.
78. Eco, *Foucault's Pendulum*, pp. 93–94.
79. Lila Azam Zanganeh, "Umberto Eco: The Art of Fiction, No. 197," *The Paris Review*, Summer 2008, No. 185.
80. Eco, *Foucault's Pendulum*, p. 93.
81. Lila Azam Zanganeh, "Umberto Eco: The Art of Fiction, No. 197," *The Paris Review*, Summer 2008, No. 185.
82. Eco, *Foucault's Pendulum*, p. 270.
83. Lila Azam Zanganeh, "Umberto Eco: The Art of Fiction, No. 197," *The Paris Review*, Summer 2008, No. 185.
84. Eco, *Foucault's Pendulum*, p. 520.
85. Eco, "Ur-Fascism," from *Five Moral Pieces*, p. 66.
86. Eco, *Foucault's Pendulum*, p. 175.
87. Eco, *Foucault's Pendulum*, p. 177.
88. Eco, "Whose Side Are the Orixa On?," from *Travels in Hyperreality*, p. 108.
89. Eco, *Foucault's Pendulum*, p. 179.
90. Eco, "Whose Side Are the Orixa On?," from *Travels in Hyperreality*, p. 109.
91. Eco, "Why Are They Laughing In Those Cages?," from *Travels in Hyperreality*, pp. 122–123.
92. Eco, *Foucault's Pendulum*, p. 495.
93. Eco, *Foucault's Pendulum*, p. 217.
94. Eco, *Foucault's Pendulum*, p. 525.
95. Eco, *Foucault's Pendulum*, p. 152.
96. Eco, *Foucault's Pendulum*, p. 341.
97. Eco, *Foucault's Pendulum*, p. 346.
98. Eco, *The Name of the Rose*, p. 502.
99. Eco, *Foucault's Pendulum*, p. 344.
100. Eco, *Foucault's Pendulum*, p. 431.
101. *Contemporary Authors, New Revision Series, Volume 33*, p. 124, as cited from *Time Magazine*, March 6, 1989.
102. Eco, "Postscript" to *The Name of the Rose*, p. 529.
103. Eco, *Foucault's Pendulum*, pp. 132–133.
104. Eco, *Foucault's Pendulum*, p. 192.
105. Eco, *Foucault's Pendulum*, p. 228.

106. Hutcheon, Linda, "Irony-clad Foucault," from *On Eco, An Anthology*, edited by Capozzi, Rocco (Bloomington: Indiana University Press, 1997).
107. Eco, *Foucault's Pendulum*, p. 438.
108. Eco, *Foucault's Pendulum*, p. 533.
109. Eco, *The Name of the Rose*, p. 491.
110. Eco, *Foucault's Pendulum*, p. 24.
111. Eco, *Foucault's Pendulum*, pp. 36–37.
112. Eco, *Foucault's Pendulum*, p. 54.
113. Eco, *Foucault's Pendulum*, p. 65.
114. Eco, *Foucault's Pendulum*, p. 299.
115. Eco, *Foucault's Pendulum*, p. 436.
116. Eco, *Foucault's Pendulum*, p. 322.
117. Eco, *Foucault's Pendulum*, p. 312.
118. Eco, *Foucault's Pendulum*, p. 252.
119. Eco, *Foucault's Pendulum*, p. 294.
120. Eco, *Foucault's Pendulum*, p. 362.
121. Mel Gussow, "A Word-Bending Wit's Riff on the Unreachable," *New York Times*, November 28, 1995.
122. Eco, *The Island of the Day Before*, (New York: Penguin Books, 1996), p. 106.
123. Eco, *The Island of the Day Before*, p. 367.
124. Eco, *The Island of the Day Before*, p. 462.
125. Eco, *The Island of the Day Before*, p. 21.
126. Eco, *The Island of the Day Before*, p. 79.
127. Eco, *The Island of the Day Before*, pp. 118–119.
128. Eco, *The Island of the Day Before*, p. 137.
129. Eco, *The Island of the Day Before*, p. 244.
130. Eco, *The Island of the Day Before*, p. 260.
131. Eco, *The Island of the Day Before*, p. 267.
132. Eco, *The Island of the Day Before*, p. 280.
133. Eco, "Postscript" to *The Name of the Rose*, p. 535.
134. Eco, *The Island of the Day Before*, p. 20.
135. Eco, *The Island of the Day Before*, p. 248.
136. Eco, *The Island of the Day Before*, p. 512.
137. Eco, *The Island of the Day Before*, p. 405.
138. Eco, *The Island of the Day Before*, p. 4 17.
139. Eco, *The Island of the Day Before*, p. 52.
140. Eco, *The Island of the Day Before*, p. 512.
141. Eco, *The Open Work*, p. 230.
142. Eco, *The Island of the Day Before*, p. 66.
143. Eco, *The Open Work*, p. 7.
144. Eco, *The Island of the Day Before*, p. 139

145. Eco, *The Island of the Day Before*, p. 146.
146. Eco, *The Island of the Day Before*, p. 171.
147. Eco, *The Island of the Day Before*, p. 463.
148. Eco, *The Island of the Day Before*, p. 432.
149. "Complotti: conversazione tra Umberto Eco e il rabbino Di Segni," *L'Espresso* magazine, October 29, 2010.
150. Eco, *The Island of the Day Before*, p. 119.
151. Eco, *The Island of the Day Before*, p. 354.

BIBLIOGRAPHY

Anderson, James, *An Introduction to the Metaphysics of St. Thomas Aquinas*, Washington D.C.: Regnery Publishing Inc, 1997
Aristotle, *Logic, De Interpretatione*, from *A New Aristotle Reader*, edited by J.L. Ackrill, Princeton: Princeton University Press, 1987
Armstrong, Karen, *The Great Transformation, The World in the Time of Buddha, Socrates, Confucius and Jeremiah*, London: Atlantic Books, 2007
Bernstein, William, *Masters of the Word*, New York: Grove Press, 2013
Bickerton, Derek, *Language and Species*, Chicago: The University of Chicago Press, 1990
Boehm, Christopher, *Hierarchy in the Forest: The Evolution of Egalitarian Behavior*, Cambridge, MA: Harvard University Press, 2001
Boggs, Carl, *Intellectuals and the Crisis of Modernity*, Albany: State University of New York, 1993
Bondanella, Peter, *Umberto Eco and the Open Text*, New York: Cambridge University Press, 1997
Bondanella, Peter, editor, *New Essays on Umberto Eco*, Cambridge: Cambridge University Press, 2009
Borges, Jorge Luis, *The Garden of Forking Paths*, from *Collected Fictions*, translated by Andrew Hurley, New York: Penguin Books, 1998
Bouchard, Norman, Eco and Popular Culture, from *New Essays on Umberto Eco*, edited by Peter Bondanella, New York: Cambridge University Press, 2009
Brent, Joseph, *Charles Sanders Peirce, a Life*, Bloomington: Indiana University Press, 1993
Burwick, Frederick, *The Damnation of Newton: Goethe's Color Theory and Romantic Perception*, New York: Walter de Gruyter Inc., 1986

Caesar, Michael and Hainsworth, Peter, editors, *Writers and Society in Contemporary Italy*, New York: St. Martin's Press, 1984
Calvino, Italo, *Six Memos for the Next Millennium*, New York: Vintage Books, 1993
Cannon, JoAnn, *Postmodern Italian Fiction*, London: Associated University Presses, 1989
Carravetta, Peter, Form, Person, and Inexhaustible Interpretation: Luigi Pareyson, from *Existence, Interpretation, Freedom, Selected Writings*, translated by Paolo Diego Bubbio, Aurora: Davies Group Publishers, 2009, from *Parrhesia*, Number 12, 2010
Clark, Martin, *Modern Italy 1871–1982*, London: Longman Group Limited, 1984
Coletti, Theresa, *Naming the Rose: Eco, Medieval Signs, and Modern Theory*, Ithaca: Cornell University Press, 1988
Contemporary Authors, *New Revision Series*, Volume 12, Detroit: Gale Research Co., 1981
Coser, Lewis A., *Men of Ideas, a Sociologist's View*, New York: The Free Press, 1970
Culler, Jonathan, *Ferdinand de Saussure*, Ithaca: Cornell University Press, 1988
Darnton, Robert, *The Great Cat Massacre and Other Episodes from French Cultural History*, New York: Basic Books, 1984
Devlin, Keith, *The Math Gene*, Great Britain: Basic Books, 2000
Dickie, John, *Mafia Republic*, London: Hodder and Stoughton Ltd., 2013
Dunbar, Robin, *Grooming, Gossip, and the Evolution of Language*, London: Faber and Faber, 1996
Eco, *A Theory of Semiotics*, Bloomington: Indiana University Press, 1979
Eco, *The Role of the Reader*, Bloomington: Indiana University Press, 1984
Eco, *Travels in Hyperreality*, New York: Harcourt, Brace, Jovanovich, 1986
Eco, *The Aesthetics of Thomas Aquinas*, Cambridge: Harvard University Press, 1988
Eco, *The Aesthetics of Chaosmos, The Middle Ages of James Joyce*, translated by Ellen Esrock, Cambridge: Harvard University Press, 1989
Eco, *The Limits of Interpretation*, Bloomington: Indiana University Press, 1990a
Eco, *Foucault's Pendulum*, translated by William Weaver, New York: Ballantine Books, 1990b
Eco, *Interpretation and Overinterpretation*, Cambridge: Cambridge University Press, 1992
Eco, *Misreadings*, translated by William Weaver, Orlando: Harcourt Brace and Company, 1993
Eco, *The Name of the Rose*, New York: Harcourt Brace and Company, 1994a
Eco, *Apocalypse Postponed*, Bloomington: Indiana University Press, 1994b (This is a substantially modified English version of *Apocalittici e Integrati*, edited by Robert Lumley.)

Eco, *Apocalittici e Integrati, Communicazione di massa e teorie della cultura di massa*, Milan: Gruppo Editoriale Fabbri, Bompiani, Sonzogno, Etas S.p.A., 1994c

Eco, *Six Walks in the Fictional Woods*, Harvard University Press, 1995

Eco, *The Island of the Day Before*, New York: Penguin Books, 1996

Eco, *The Open Work*, Milan: Bompiani, 1997a

Eco, *Opera Aperta*, Milan: RCS Libri S.p.a., 1997b

Eco, How and Why I Write, from *Umberto Eco's Alternative, The Politics of Culture and the Ambiguities of Interpretation*, edited by Norma Bouchard and Veronica Pravadelli, New York: Peter Lang Publishing, Inc., 1998

Eco, *Five Moral Pieces*, translated by Alistair McEwen, New York: Harcourt, Inc., 2001

Eco, *Confessions of a Young Novelist*, Cambridge: Harvard University Press, 2011

Eco, *Struttura Assente, La Ricerca Semioticca e il Metodo Strutturale*, Milan: Bompiani, 19682015

Ellmann, Richard, *James Joyce*, Oxford: Oxford University Press, 1982

Erdal, D. and Whiten, A., On human Egalitarianism: An Evolutionary Product of Machiavellian Status Escalation, *Current Anthropology* 35(2): 175–18, 1994

Erdal, D. and Whiten, A., Egalitarianism and Machiavellian intelligence in human evolution, from *Modelling the Early Human Mind*, edited by P. Mellars and K. Gibson, Cambridge: McDonald Institute Monograph, 1996

Farrell, Joseph, *Leonardo Sciascia*, Edinburgh: Edinburgh University Press, 1995a

Farrell, Joseph, *Leonardo Sciascia*, Edinburgh: Edinburgh University Press, 1995b

Forgacs, David, *Italian Culture in the Industrial Era, 1880–1890: Cultural Industries, Politics, and the Public*, Manchester: Manchester University Press, 1990

Forgacs, David and Lumley, Robert, editors, Cultural Consumption, 1940's to 1990's, from *Italian Cultural Studies, An Introduction*, Oxford: Oxford University Press, 1996

Foucault, Michel, *The Order of Things*, New York, Vintage Books, 1973

Ginsborg, Paul, *A History of Contemporary Italy*, London: Penguin Books, 1990

Ginzburg, Carlo, *The Cheese and the Worms*, Baltimore: The Johns Hopkins University Press, 1980

Gould, Stephen Jay, *The Mismeasure of Man*, New York: W.W. Norton and Company, 1996

Gouldner, Alvin W., *The Future of Intellectuals and the Rise of the New Class*, New York: The Seabury Press, 1979

Gramsci, Antonio, The Intellectuals, from *Selections from the Prison Notebooks*, edited and translated by Quinton Hoare and Geoffrey Nowell Smith, New York: International Publishers, 1971

Griffin, Jasper, Greek Myth and Hesiod, from *The Oxford History of Greece and the Hellenistic World*, edited by John Boardman, Jasper Griffin, and Oswyn Murray, Oxford: Oxford University Press, 1991

Guerzoni, Giuseppe, *Garibaldi: con documenti editi e inediti*, Volume 11, Florence: Barbera, 1882

Haft, Adele J., White, Jane G. and Robert, J., *The Key to 'The Name of the Rose' Including Translations of All Non-English Passages*, Ann Arbor: The University of Michigan Press, 1999

Hookway Christopher, *Peirce*, New York: Routledge, 1992

Hutcheon, Linda, Irony-clad Foucault, from *On Eco*, edited by Capozzi, Rocco, Bloomington: Indiana University Press, 1997

Inge, Thomas, editor, *Naming the Rose*, Jackson: University Press of Mississippi, 1988

Joyce, James, *Finnegans Wake*, New York: Penguin Books, 1999

Kant, Immanuel, *Critique of Judgment*, translated by J.H. Bernard, Minneola: Dover Publications, Inc., 2005

Kolakowski, Nick, *How to Become an Intellectual: 100 Mandatory Maxims to Metamorphose into the Most Learned of Thinkers*, Avon, MA: F&W Media Inc., 2012

Leakey, Richard, *Origins Reconsidered*, New York: Anchor Books, 1992

Lilli, Laura, *Voci Dall'Alfabeto, Interviste con Sciascia, Moravia, Eco nei decenni Settanta e Ottanta*, Roma: Edizioni minimum fax, 1995, *Voices of the Alphabet, Interviews with Sciascia, Moravia, Eco in the Seventies and Eighties*

Lodge, David, from the introduction to the 2006 edition of *The Name of the Rose*, New York: Everyman's Library, 2006

Manzoni, Alessandro, *The Betrothed*, Middlesex, England: Penguin Classics, 1972

Mays, J.C.C., Foreword: Italian-Irish Celebrations, from *Talking of Joyce*, edited by Liberato Santoro-Brienza, Dublin: University College Dublin Press, 1998

Menand, Louis, *The Metaphysical Club*, New York: Farrar, Strauss and Giroux, 2001

Nussbaum, Martha, *Cultivating Humanity*, Cambridge: Harvard University Press, 1997

Pansa, Francesca, and Vinci, Anna, *Effeto Eco*, Rome: Nuova Edizioni dei Gallo, 1990

Pareyson, Luigi, *Estetica: Teoria della Formativita*, Milan: Bompiani, 2005

Penman, Bruce, Introduction, from *The Betrothed*, Middlesex, London: Penguin Classics, 1972

Peirce, Charles Sanders, *Collected Papers of Charles Sanders Peirce*, edited by C. Hartshorne and P. Weiss, Cambridge: Harvard University Press, 1931

Peirce, Charles Sanders, On a New List of Categories, from *Peirce on Signs*, edited by James Hoopes, Chapel Hill: The University of North Carolina Press, 1991

Peirce, Charles Sanders, A New List of Categories, from *The Essential Peirce Volume 1 (1867–1893)*, edited by Nathan Houser and Christian Kloesel, Bloomington: Indiana University Press, 1992
Pertile, Lino, Introduction, from *The New Italian Novel*, edited by Zygmunt Baraski and Lino Pertile, Edinburgh: Edinburgh University Press, 1993
Plato, Cratylus, translated by B. Jowett, from *The Collected Dialogues of Plato*, edited by Edith Hamilton and Huntington Cairns, Princeton: Princeton University Press, 1989
Plato, *Republic*, translated by G.M.A. Grube and revised by C.D.C. Reeve, Hackett Publishing Company, Inc., 1992
Poggioli, Renato, *The Theory of the Avant-Garde*, Cambridge: Harvard University Press, 1968
Richter, David H., The Mirrored World: Form and Ideology in Umberto Eco's *The Name of the Rose*, from *Reading Eco, An Anthology*, edited by Rocco Capozzi, Bloomington: Indiana University Press, 1997
Rieff, Phillip, editor, *On Intellectuals*, New York: Doubleday and Co., 1969
Sadri, Ahmed, *Max Weber's Sociology of Intellectuals*, New York: Oxford University Press, 1992
Sassoon, Donald, *Contemporary Italy, Economy, Society and Politics since 1945*, London: Addison Wesley Longman Limited, 1997
Saussure, Ferdinand de, *Course in General Linguistics*, edited by Charles Bally and Albert Sechehaye, La Salle: Open Court Publishing Company, 1991
Sciascia, Leonardo, *Equal Danger*, translated by Adrienne Foulke, New York: New York Review Books, 1973
Sciascia, Leonardo, *The Moro Affair*, New York: Carcanet Press Limited, 1987
Sciascia, Leonardo, *The Council of Egypt*, translated by Adrienne Foulke, New York: Carcanet Press Limited, 1988
Sciascia, Leonardo, *To Each His Own*, translated by Adrienne Foulke, New York: New York Review Books, 2000
Sciascia, Leonardo, *The Day of the Owl*, translated by Anthony Oliver, New York: New York Review Books, 2003
Shils, Edward, *The Intellectuals and the Powers*, Chicago: University of Chicago Press, 1972
Thomson, Garrett and Missner, Marshall, *On Aristotle*, Belmont: Wadsworth, 2000
Weber, Max, *From Max Weber*, edited by H.H. Gerth and C. Wright Mills, New York: Oxford University Press, 1958
Williams, Raymond, *Keywords*, Oxford: Oxford University Press, 1976

INDEX

A
Adventures of Sherlock Holmes, The, 3
Aesthetics
  Aesthetica of Alexander
    Baumgarten, 70
  aesthetic idiolect, 194–195
  aesthetic species, 30
  and beauty, 21, 31, 34, 52, 69–76,
    90–92, 109, 112–118, 133,
    140, 150, 195, 201–202, 206
  definition by Raymond Williams, 69
  Eco's works with "aesthetic
    value", 119
  E.R. Curtius conception of medieval
    versus modern aesthetics, 70
  Immanuel Kant's "puposiveness
    without purpose", 67
  of James Joyce, 104–105, 119–120,
    225
  of Luigi Pareyson, 69, 75, 76, 115,
    119, 201, 223
  of Thomas Aquinas, 14, 52, 53, 59,
    69–71, 80, 89, 92, 93, 105,
    119, 240
  of Umberto Eco, 14
Agricultural Revolution, 32, 40
Allais, Alphonse, *A Most Parisian
  Episode*, 206, 210–213, 215,
  222, 251

Allen, Woody, 20, 103
Anti-detective novel, 254, 264
Apocalittici e Integrati (Apocalyptics
  and Integrationists, Mass
  Communication and, Theories of
  Mass Culture), 137, 149–151,
  153, 158, 164
Apocalypse, 150, 243, 245, 246, 248,
  251–253
Apocalyptics, 149, 151, 245–248
Aquinas
  Aesthetics of Thomas Aquinas, The,
    Eco, 14, 52–53, 59, 69–70, 80,
    89, 92, 93, 105, 119, 150, 240
  Albertus Magnus, 73
  the beautiful, 68, 71, 73, 74,
    90, 113
  existentialism of, 33–34, 75–76,
    114, 115
  formativity, 74–76, 115–116,
    118–119, 121
  transcendentals, 73
Aristotle
  Analytics, 65
  categories, 66–67, 73, 180–181,
    184
  and *Cratylus* of Plato, 65
  four causes, 68–69, 73
  On Interpretation, 67

© The Author(s) 2017
D. Merrell, *Umberto Eco, The Da Vinci Code, and the Intellectual
in the Age of Popular Culture*, DOI 10.1007/978-3-319-54789-3

Aristotle (*cont.*)
  Lyceum, 58
  the one and the many, 66
  Physics, 66, 68, 112, 212
  and Plato's Academy, 61, 62, 65, 66, 170, 181
  structuralist approach of, 185–186
Art and Beauty in the Middle Ages, Eco, 52, 69
Augustine, St, 61, 64, 203
  Confessions, 64
  and Neoplatonism, 64
Avant-garde
  and folk culture, 134–135, 138
  Futurist movement, 133
  historical origins of, 17, 98, 121, 132–133, 135, 145, 201
  Marcel Duchamp and Dadaist movement, 133
  and Romanticism as precursor, 122, 132–133

B
Bacon, Roger, 248
Baroque, 122–123, 271–273
  Eco's *The Island of the Day Before*
Barthes, Roland, 143, 178
Baudolino, Eco, 189, 273
Baumgarten, Alexander, 70
Beautiful, the
  and "the good" and "the true", 73
  as "harmonious design", 73
  medieval conception as God's creativity through harmonious design, 71, 75, 107, 117, 201–202
  and popular culture, 21, 31, 34, 36, 52, 71, 72, 92, 115, 134, 150, 195
  as transcendental for Aquinas, 73, 76

Belief or Nonbelief, Eco, 108, 182, 183, 196, 230, 247
Berberian, Cathy, 103–105, 158, 267
Berio Luciano, 103–105, 121, 158
Bernard of Clairvaux, St., 150
Bernstein, William, *Masters of the Word*, 41
Bickerton, Derek
  Language and Species, 26–27
  offline thinking, 27
Boggs, Carl, 45
Bompiani, Valentino, Eco publisher, 98, 151, 241
Bonaventure, St., 73, 248
Bondanella, Peter, *Umberto Eco and the Open Text*, 59, 86, 92–93
Bond, James, 20, 120, 224–226, 228, 263
Bongiorno, Mike, television host, 94, 160–163
Borges, Jorge Luis, 215, 241, 243, 256, 263, 270
Bosco, Giovanni, St, 54–55
Bouchard, Norma, "Eco and Popular Culture", 226
Boulez, Pierre, 121–122
Brent, Joseph, biograp-hy of Peirce, 179
Brown, Dan, *The Da Vinci Code*, 4–5, 8, 9–14, 19, 141, 145–146, 224, 229, 264

C
Calvino, Italo
  If On A Winter's Night a Traveler, 104
  reader-response theory, 202, 205, 206, 212, 215
Cannon, JoAnn, *Postmodern Italian Fiction*, 98, 254
Capozzi, Rocco, 218

Carmi, Eugenio, illustrator of Eco's
  books for children, 20
Categories
  of Aristotle, 66, 67, 72–73, 181,
    184
  of Charles Sanders Peirce, 67
  of Immanuel Kant, 67, 180–181
Charlie Brown comics, 151, 159
Christian Democrats, 81, 85, 95, 236,
  237
Christie, Agatha, 3, 5, 155
Clark, Martin, 81, 96–97
Coletti, Theresa, *Naming the Rose*, 5,
  7, 20
Communist Party, Italian, 35, 81, 85,
  86, 88, 89, 236, 237, 245
Compromesso storico, 236
Correto, Carlo, 85, 86
Coser, Lewis, 41, 45
Council of Egypt, The, Leonardo
  Sciascia, 258
Cratylus of Plato, 65, 77n25
Croce, Benedetto, 106
Curtius, E.R., 70

D

Darnton, Robert, *The Great Cat
  Massacre*, 146n7
Da Vinci Code, The, 4–13, 18–19, 51,
  137, 141–145, 224–226, 229,
  264
Day of the Owl, The, Leonardo
  Sciascia, 255
Diabolicals in *Foucault's
  Pendulum*, 258, 263–265, 270
Dialectic, 64, 106, 110, 197, 217
Disputation of the Sacrament, The, 60
Dolcinians, in *The Name of the Rose*,
  246–247
Duchamp, Marcel and Dadaism, 133

E

To Each His Own, Leonardo
  Sciascia, 254, 258
Economic miracle, Italian, 93, 97,
  152, 236, 242
Eco's Chaosmos, Cristina Farronato, 7
Eco, Umberto
  aesthetics of, 14, 20, 34, 52–53, 59,
    68–76, 80, 89, 90, 92–93, 98,
    104–106, 108, 109, 110–114,
    115, 117, 119–120, 121–123,
    137, 139, 144, 149–152, 185,
    188–189, 192–193, 194, 201,
    222, 226–227, 240, 272
  Aesthetics of Chaosmos, The, 105,
    110
  *Aesthetics of Thomas Aquinas,
    The*, 14, 52–53, 59, 69–70, 80,
    92–93, 105, 119, 150, 240
  on "aesthetic value", 72, 119, 143,
    155, 159, 202, 222, 223, 227
  Apocalittici e Integrati
    (Apocalyptics and
    Integrationists, Mass
    Communication and Theories
    of Mass Culture), 149; Bernard
    of Clairvaux, St, 150;
    Bompiani, Valentino,
    publisher, on title, 151; *fumetti*
    (comics), 153; Suger,
    Abbot, 150–151
  Apocalypse Postponed, 166n2
  *Art and Beauty in the Middle
    Ages*, 52, 69
  Baudolino, 189, 273
  Beauty; Medieval conception
    of, 109, 150
  Belief or Nonbelief, 108, 182, 183,
    196, 230, 247
  on Charlie Brown, 149, 151,
    159–160, 165

Eco, Umberto (*cont.*)
Confessions of a Young Novelist, 77n19, 275n18
and Fascism, 56, 260, 261
Five Moral Pieces, 260
Foucault's Pendulum; antihero, 262; Eco's childhood under fascism and WWII, 261–262; failed detective, 265; and Gruppo, 63, 236; hermetic thought, 204, 259, 271; irritating the reader, 263; overinterpretation, 219, 257, 266, 271; Red Brigades, 273; student protests of 1968, 237; Templars, 9, 257–258, 266
Gruppo, 63, 104–106, 131, 133, 142, 162, 223, 236, 264
Interpretation and Overinterpretation, 215, 219, 221, 233n41
interpretive ethics, 202, 205–206, 216, 217, 220–222, 257, 268, 274
interrelational formativity of, 123
and Italian Youth for Catholic Action, 83–84; as anti-romance novel, 269; Baroque, multiple perspectives of, 271–272; on desire, 267, 271; infinite worlds, 272; laughing God, 190, 262, 272; theater of memory, 269
Island of the Day Before, The, 169, 267, 271, 273
Mysterious Flame of Queen Loana, The, 273
Name of the Rose, The, 5–7, 10, 16, 19, 21, 29, 44, 51, 52, 60, 91, 93, 104, 123, 125, 141–143, 145, 163, 163, 169–171,
190–191, 215, 218–219, 235, 238, 241, 243, 247–250, 254, 256, 257–259, 263–264, 267, 270, 272; and Alessandro Manzoni's *The Betrothed*, 256; as anti-detective novel, 254, 264; and Aristotle's book on comedy, 244; and experience of the labyrinth, 240; and heresy, 79, 89, 243, 244, 247; and influence of Leonardo Sciascia, 254, 258; and Moro Affair, 236, 238–240, 244, 249, 255; and poverty of Christ, 243; and Red Brigades, 238
Numero Zero, 273
Open Work, The, 14, 21, 103–104, 105, 110, 111, 112, 121–126, 144, 149, 151, 178, 196–197, 201, 202, 271–272; ambiguity of, 126, 196, 201; collaborative role of the audience, 122–123, 125–126, 201; defamiliarization of, 124, 144, 201; indeterminacy of, 124, 271; interrelational formativity of, 123
"Postscript" to *The Name of the Rose*, 6–7, 51–52, 93, 104, 123, 125, 142, 143, 218, 238, 249, 250, 254, 256, 264, 270
Prague Cemetery, The, 8, 189, 273
reader response theory, 202, 205, 206, 211, 215
Role of the Reader, The, 120, 146, 154, 197, 205, 206, 213, 265
Salesian Order, 54–55, 59
structuralist approach of, 154, 178, 185–186
on Superman comics, 152, 154, 155, 161, 225

INDEX 291

Theory of Semiotics, A, 120, 178, 179, 182, 184, 188, 197, 201, 217
Travels in Hyperreality, 14, 16, 19, 21, 51, 139, 261–262
and WWII, 17, 18, 20, 54, 55, 57, 80, 81, 84, 93, 96, 133, 153, 156, 160, 170, 236
Educational species, 34
Empirical author and empirical reader, 216–222, 261
Encyclopedia, Eco's concept of, 228
Enlightenment Philosophers, 46
Equal Danger, Leonardo Sciascia, 255
Eriugena, John Scotus, 73
Escapist entertainment, 142, 146, 156, 226–227
Existentialism
of Aquinas, 33–34, 75–76
of Eco's interrelational formativity, 75–76
of human species, 33, 75–76
of Luigi Pareyson, 75

F
Farrell, Joseph, 254–255
Farronato, Cristina, *Eco's Chaosmos*, 7
Feiffer, Jules, *Passionella*, 103, 158–159, 226
Ferrante, Elena, 217
Fictional world and real world, 43, 229–231, 269
Finnegans Wake
accessibility for a popular readership, 144–146, 225, 263
art of adventure, 106–111, 114, 122, 124, 126–127
as epistemological metaphor, 126
exemplary open work, 145
Giambattista Vico, influence of, 107, 109

Giordano Bruno, influence of, 107, 109
multi-layered puns, 114
as synthesis of cosmos and chaos, 110
and unlimited semiosis of Peirce, 204
First and second level reader, 216, 222
Fleming, Ian, 224
Forgacs, David, 95–96, 153
Formal Cause
of Aristotle, 68, 74
Foucault, Michel and resemblance, 72, 259
Foucault's Pendulum, Eco, 7–9, 12, 57, 189, 204, 219, 237, 257–258, 260–267, 270, 273
Four Causes of Aristotle, 68–69, 73
Franciscan Spirituals, 245, 247
Francis de Sales, St, 54–55
Fry, Stephen, 12
fumetti,(comics), 153
Futurist Movement, 84, 133

G
Garibaldi, Giuseppe, 82–83
Giallo (Italian mass market detective novel), 242
Ginsborg, Paul, 96, 236
Giovane Italia, 82
Gioventu Italiani di Azione Cattolica (GIAC), 53, 58, 80, 82, 84–90, 92
Gouldner, Alvin, 46, 47
humanistic intellectuals and intelligentsia, 46–47
theoreticity, 46
Gramsci, Antonio
hegemony, 86
permanent persuader, 37, 98
traditional and organic intellectuals, 36

Greek Dark Ages, 113
Greenberg, Clement, 137–138, 156
 and highcult, midcult, and masscult, 140
 and Kitsch, 137, 138, 156
Guglielmi, Angelo, 131

H
Hegemony, 86
Hermetic thought, 203, 258–262, 271
Foucault's Pendulum
High brow culture, 225
Historical whodunit, 5, 7, 11, 20, 51, 155, 224, 242
Homo Faber, 26, 29, 32, 118
Homo Ludens, 28
Homo Sapiens, 27, 29, 30, 32, 118
Huizinga, Johan, 28
Hunter-gatherer societies, 38, 39, 43

I
Inferential Walks, 214–215, 216, 220, 228, 241
Inge, Thomas, *Naming the Rose*, 7
Intellectuals
 humanistic intellectuals and technical intelligentsia, 41
 intellectual species, 25–47
 public intellectuals, 14, 15, 19, 25, 31, 47, 52, 71, 95, 98, 109, 115, 119–120, 121, 152, 165, 170, 238, 240, 244, 247, 257, 267, 274
 traditional and organic intellectuals of Antonio Gramsci, 36
On Interpretation, Aristotle, 67
Interpretation and Overinterpretation, Eco, 215, 219, 221
Interpretive ethics of Eco, 202, 205, 206, 216–222, 257, 268, 274
Interrelational Formativity, 123
intertextual frames, 270
Island of the Day Before, The, Eco, 169, 267, 271, 273
Italian Communist Party (PCI), 35, 81, 85, 86, 88, 89, 237, 245
Italian humanist-historicist tradition, 32–33, 91, 109, 120, 185–186, 217

J
John Scotus Eriugena, 73
Joyce, James
 Finnegans Wake, 106, 107–108, 110, 111, 114, 122, 124, 126, 127, 144, 145, 193, 204, 221, 225, 263; critique by H.G. Wells, 144; as "grandiose epistemological metaphor", 126
 Portrait of the Artist as a Young Man, 108
 Ulysses, 106, 111, 114, 225

K
Kant, Immanuel
 categories of, 67
Key to The Name of the Rose, The, 5–7, 10, 16, 19, 21, 29, 44, 51, 52, 60, 91, 93, 104, 123, 125, 141–143, 145, 163, 169–171, 190, 191, 215, 218, 219, 235, 238, 241, 243, 247, 248, 249, 250, 254, 256–259, 263, 264, 267, 270, 272
King, Stephen, 12
Kitsch, 137–142, 56, 195, 225, 227, 254

INDEX   293

L
Labyrinth, experience of, 192, 239–241, 243, 249–251, 253, 254
Last Supper, The, 7, 8, 16–19, 139
Leakey, Richard, 30, 31, 34, 38–40
Levi-Strauss, Claude, 178, 185
Liceo Classico, 57–58, 59
Literacy, 43–44, 95, 97, 136, 153
Lodge, David, 6
Lumley, Robert, 96, 153
Luther, Martin, 44, 171
Lycophron, 62, 66

M
Macdonald, Dwight, *Against the American Grain: Essays on the Effects of Mass culture*, 140
Magnus, Albertus, 73
Mallarme, Stephane, 121, 122
Manzoni, Alessandro, *The Betrothed*, 256–257
Marinetti, Fillipo Tommaso and Futurism, 133
Maritain, Jacques, 86, 87
Maslin, Janet, 13
Mazzini, Giuseppe, 82
McCarthy, Joseph, 89
Medieval Scholasticism, 42, 44, 58, 61, 203
Menand, Louis, *The Metaphysical Club*, 179
Metatextual demonstration, of Allais' *A Most Parisian Episode*, 211
Michelangelo, 60, 139, 241
Midcult, 140, 141, 142, 225
Middle Ages, 6, 14, 21, 44, 51–53, 59, 68, 69, 71, 73, 91–93, 104–106, 109, 110, 112, 113, 120, 123, 136, 150, 170, 171, 239, 240, 246, 250, 253, 260, 261

conception of beauty, 71, 91–92, 109, 112, 113, 150
Miller, Laura, 8
Model author and model reader, 216, 223
Moro Affair, *The* Leonardo Sciascia, 255
Moro, Aldo, Moro Affair, 236, 249, 262, 273
Most Parisian Episode, A of Alphonse Allais, 206, 210–212, 215, 222, 251
   as metatextual demonstration, 211
Mussolini, Benito, 14, 35, 55–57, 80, 81, 84–86, 273
Mysteres de Paris, Les, Eugene Sue, 224, 225
Mysterious Flame of Queen Loana, The, Eco, 273

N
Name of the Rose, The, Eco, 5–7, 10, 16, 19, 21, 29, 44, 51, 52, 60, 91, 93, 104, 123, 125, 141–143, 145, 163, 169–171, 190, 191, 215, 218, 219, 235, 238, 241, 243, 247–250, 254, 256–259, 263, 264, 267, 270, 272
Narrative text, 215, 222
Neo-avant-garde, Italian, 17, 104, 110, 112, 119, 120, 121, 122, 131, 137, 142, 149, 151, 223
Neoplatonism, 64
Numero Zero, Eco, 273

O
One and the Many, The, of Plato and Aristotle, 66
Open and closed texts, 223–224
Open Work, The, Eco, 103–127, 149

P

Pansa and Vinci (Francesca Pansa and Anna Vinci, Eco chroniclers), 87
Papal States, 82
Pareyson, Luigi
   aesthetics of, 117
   and Aristotle's formal cause, 68
   existentialism of, 76
   form and formativity of, 75–76
Parsons, Talcott, 41
Peirce, Charles Sanders
   categories of firstness, secondness, thirdness, 185–186
   interpretant, 183, 186–188
   unlimited semiosis, 184, 186, 188, 204, 241, 259
Pertile, Leno, "The New Italian Novel", 241
Phillip Neri, St., 54
Philosophical rationalism, 42, 62
Pius IX, 82
Pius X, 83, 93
Pius XII, 80, 81, 86, 88
Plato
   the cave, 64
   Cratylus, 65
   dialectic, 64
   the forms, 122
   the good, 61, 73
   historicist perspective of, 33, 80
   knowledge vs. opinion, 65
   the one and the many, 66
   and Pythagoras, 60
   Republic, 62–64, 77n22, 77n24
   and Socrates, 42
Popular Culture
   Apocalittici e Integrati, Eco, 153, 158
   Apocalypse Postponed, Eco, 150
   Charlie Brown, 151, 159, 160, 165
   Clement Greenberg, 156
   Dwight MacDonald, *Against the American Grain: Essays on the Effects of Mass, Culture*, 140
   Enlightenment, 45, 46, 71, 136
   high cult, midcult, and masscult, 140, 225
   Jules Feiffer's *Passionella*, 103, 158
   Kitsch, 141, 142, 156, 195, 225, 227, 254
   Kitsch as "bad taste", 140
   Mike Bongiorno, television host, 94, 161
   Ray Bradbury on Picasso, 140–141
   seven liberal arts, 136
   Superman comics, 152, 154, 161, 225
Portrait of the Artist as a Young Man, Joyce, 108
"Postscript" to *The Name of the Rose*, Eco, 6, 52, 123, 125, 142, 143, 218, 238, 249, 256, 264, 270
Pousseur, Henri, 121–122
Public Intellectual, 14, 15, 19–20, 25, 31, 47, 52, 71, 95, 98, 109, 115, 119, 120, 121, 152, 165, 170, 238, 240, 244, 247, 257, 267, 274
Pullum, Geoffrey, 12–13
Putnam, Hilary, 43, 230
Pythagoras, 60

R

RAI (Radiotelevisione Italiana), 93–95, 98, 103, 161
Raphael, 60–61, 64, 241
Red Brigades, 237–238, 245, 246, 256, 273
Renaissance
   and education, 136
   and interpretation, 113

and popular culture, 19, 141
Republic, The, 61–64
Revelation, Book of, 150, 171, 246, 257
Rhizome, 241
Richter, David H., 6
Rights of the text in interpretation theory, 205–206
Risorgimento, 58, 82
Romanticism
  and Avant-garde, 122, 132–133
  heart over the head, 132
  William Blake, 132
Room of the Segnatura, Vatican Museum, 60
Rossi, Mario, 85–86, 88
Rushdie, Salman, 12
Russell, Bertrand, 172, 180

S
Salesian Order
  Francis de Sales, 54–55
  Giovanni Bosco, 54–55
  Phillip Neri, 54
Sassoon, Donald, 96, 97
Saussure, Ferdinand de
  linguistics of, 172, 173–174, 175, 176, 182
  signifier/signified, 176, 186
  structuralism of, 178, 186
Scholasticism, 42, 44, 58, 61, 136, 203
School of Athens, The, 60, 61, 64
Schulz, Charles M., 158, 159–160
Sciascia, Leonardo, 254–256, 258, 264, 265
Scotti, Enzo, 86–88
Semantic vs. semiotic or ideal reader, 144, 222, 263
Semiotics

of Umberto Eco, 60; aesthetic text as key semiotic concept, 195; as general theory of culture, 30, 174, 184–186; sign production as aesthetics, 192–194; theory of codes and sign production, 188–189, 191; as theory of laughing, 190–191; Aristophanes' *The Clouds*, 190; *The Name of the Rose* on comedy, 190; as theory of lying, 189–190
of Charles Sanders Peirce, 67, 171, 172, 179; and American pragmatism, 182; categories of firstness, secondness, thirdness, 186; and categories of Immanuel Kant, 67, 171, 180, 181; interpretant, 183, 186–188; typology of signs, icons, indexes, and symbols, 186; unlimited semiosis, 184, 186, 188, 204, 241, 259; and William James, 179
historical causes, 20, 143, 172, 185, 187, 188, 189, 191, 195, 201
origin of term "semiotics", 174
Saussure, Ferdinand de, 172–180, 182–186, 205, 212; and Claude Levi-Strauss, anthropologist, 178, 185; *Course in General Linguistics*, 173; paradigmatic and syntagmatic relations, 177; and Roland Barthes, 143, 178; signifier/signified, 176, 177, 186; signs as arbitrary, 176–177; structuralist approach of, 178, 185, 186

Shaman, 39, 40, 41, 43
Sheldon, Sidney, 10–11
Sherlock Holmes, 3, 5, 20
Shils, Edward, 41, 46
Simple, the, in *The Name of the Rose*, 247
Six Walks in the Fictional Woods, Eco, 256
Societa della Gioventu Cattolica Italiana, 58, 83, 84
Socrates, 42, 190
Strategia della tensione, 237
Structuralism, 178, 186
Sue, Eugene, *Les Mysteres de Paris*, 224
Suger, Abbot, 150–151
Superman comics, 152, 154, 155, 161, 225
Suspension of disbelief, 230

T
Templars, 258, 259, 266
Terroni, 236
Textual strategy, 220, 222, 223, 226
Theoreticity, of Alvin Gouldner, 46
Tractatus Logico-Philosophicus, Wittgenstein, 235
Trivium, 136

U
Ulysses, James Joyce, 106, 111, 114, 225
Unlimited Semiosis, 184, 186, 188, 204, 241, 259

V
Vico, Giambattista, 32, 91, 107, 109, 117

W
Warhol, Andy, 17, 195, 229
Weber, Max, 45–46
Wells, H.G., critique of *Finnegans Wake*, 144
Williams, Raymond, 69
Wittgenstein, Ludwig, 235

Y
Years of *contestazione*, 237
Young Italians for Catholic Action (GIAC), 53

GPSR Compliance
The European Union's (EU) General Product Safety Regulation (GPSR) is a set of rules that requires consumer products to be safe and our obligations to ensure this.

If you have any concerns about our products, you can contact us on

ProductSafety@springernature.com

In case Publisher is established outside the EU, the EU authorized representative is:

Springer Nature Customer Service Center GmbH
Europaplatz 3
69115 Heidelberg, Germany

www.ingramcontent.com/pod-product-compliance
Lightning Source LLC
LaVergne TN
LVHW012034070526
838202LV00056B/5495